THE DIGITAL RIGHTS DELUSION

This book examines the ever-increasing impact of technology on our lives and explores a range of legal and constitutional questions that this raises. It considers the extent to which concepts such as 'cyberspace' and 'digital rights' advance or undermine our understanding of this development and proposes a number of novel approaches to the effective protection of our rights in this rapidly evolving environment. Finally, it shows how the abuse of the adjective digital has demoted legal rights into subjective and individual claims.

The work will be of particular interest to scholars of privacy, artificial intelligence and free speech, as well as policymakers and the general reader.

Andrea Monti is an Italian lawyer, journalist, and academic, whose expertise ranges from biotechnology to privacy and high-tech law. He previously taught Public Order and Security at the Gabriele d'Annunzio, University of Chieti, Italy, where he is now an Adjunct Professor of Digital Law. He is also an Adjunct Professor of Cybersecurity Contracts at the da Vinci online University in Italy. Over the last few years, he has delivered lectures as part of the Italian State Police training programmes. He has published several papers on bio-information, computer forensics, technology, and public order, as well as books on computer hacking. His most recent publications are *Protecting Personal Information: The Right to Privacy Reconsidered* (2019), *COVID-19 and Public Policy in the Digital Age* (2021), *National Security in the New World Order* (2022) with Raymond Wacks, and, in Italian, *Cybercrime e responsabilità da reato degli enti* (2022).

THE DIGITAL RIGHTS DELUSION

Humans, Machines
and the Technology of Information

Andrea Monti

Routledge
Taylor & Francis Group

LONDON AND NEW YORK

Designed cover image: Courtesy of the Author

First published 2023
by Routledge
4 Park Square, Milton Park, Abingdon, Oxon OX14 4RN

and by Routledge
605 Third Avenue, New York, NY 10158

Routledge is an imprint of the Taylor & Francis Group, an informa business

© 2023 Andrea Monti

The right of Andrea Monti to be identified as author of this work has been asserted in accordance with sections 77 and 78 of the Copyright, Designs and Patents Act 1988.

British Library Cataloguing-in-Publication Data
A catalogue record for this book is available from the British Library

ISBN: 978-1-032-15459-6 (hbk)
ISBN: 978-1-032-44730-8 (pbk)
ISBN: 978-1-003-37363-6 (ebk)

DOI: 10.4324/9781003373636

Typeset in Sabon
by Deanta Global Publishing Services, Chennai, India

CONTENTS

PREFACE

My commitment to civil rights dates back to almost 30 years ago, when Giancarlo Livraghi, a giant of international advertising, had just decided to leave that world to devote himself to the cultural impact of the nascent Internet.

Before many others, Giancarlo understood how strong the impact of information technologies could be on civil rights. This is why he gave birth to ALCEI, whose name is the acronym for *Associazione per la libertà nella comunicazione elettronica interattiva*—Association for freedom in interactive electronic communication. Outside the USA, ALCEI was the first NGO in the world exclusively devoted to this critical topic.

At the time, it was unclear to me why Giancarlo had chosen the wording 'interactive electronic communication' instead of 'digital rights'. The latter was much more concise, compelling, and it would have been easier to understand.

Over the years, however, I have realised the reasons for this choice, which can be summed up in one sentence: there is no such thing as digital rights.

Working as an activist in ALCEI and in court as a litigator defending hackers and people accused of computer crimes, I had to face concrete problems whose solution could affect the freedom of society and individuals. Gradually, I became uncomfortable using concepts such as 'virtual', 'cyberspace', 'digital', and all the rhetorical arsenal of the Internet narrative. Inevitably, I ended up concentrating on facts and 'traditional' rights instead of science fiction.

With this mindset, I realised there was no need to create new legal entities such as 'digital rights'. If a right is born when there is a new fact to regulate, well, in the case of the Internet, there are no 'new rights' to be recognised, but only old rights to be protected from new and more aggressive threats. This is why, as Giancarlo Livraghi had guessed and I finally realised, it made more sense to study how information technologies affect for better or worse the freedom of communication, instead of trying to make sense out of marketing buzzwords and ideological, delusional claims.

Another fundamental step that led me to write this book was meeting Raymond Wacks, Emeritus Professor of Law and Legal Theory at the University of Hong Kong, and leading international authority on free speech and privacy. Over the years, our scientific collaboration produced three books (on protecting personal information, the relationship between pandemics, technology and public policy, technology and national security). His long and deep experience has made my approach much more rigorous. He led me through the intricate maze of law and politics while I was focused mainly on technology, missing crucial links. He reminded me of the importance of keeping law and rights at the centre of the analysis of technological phenomena.

This is, in short, what led to putting 'there is no such thing as digital rights' at the core of this book. Its tenet is that favouring a vague concept over well-established legal categories makes it challenging to understand how the technology of information reshaped the role of rights in contemporary society.

One might think this thesis is just as fanciful as the objects it analyses. In the end, net of the public narrative of journalists, intellectuals, and politicians, 'cyberspace', 'digital rights', 'virtual', 'metaverse', and all the other buzzwords belonging to the technology of information business have not had a real legislative and jurisprudential impact.

In reality, this is not the case. For years—as witnessed by the international literature of the concerned disciplines—these concepts have formed the basis of theoretical constructions on individual responsibility and rights, civil and criminal jurisdiction, and relations between Countries. Over time, the concrete effects of these theories have manifested themselves in an increasingly overbearing way. They are based upon a rebranding of natural law theories, that are instrumental to the creation of a global rights system more and more alienated from the relationship with people. This is not to say that a global conspiracy is deploying. More simply, the complexity generated by the uncontrolled diffusion of information technologies is not accompanied by an adequate awareness of their impact. As a consequence, it has elicited irrational reactions.

For years the EU peruses the word 'digital' in all conceivable ways to label its technology-related proposal. Last but not least, by claiming, in its support of the EU Digital Service Act, that 'what is illegal offline should be illegal online', the Council of the EU affirmed the existence of a dichotomy that must be eliminated. However, that dichotomy should not have even been considered at all, as it does not exist. Nonetheless, it has become a key component of the EU public policy strategies.

A similar trend surfaces in about every other country.

The evanescent nature of these concepts allowed a severe curtailing of the people/State dialectics. In the name of privacy, a French legislation issued in 2022 banned AI-powered judge profiling meant to prevent a public scrutiny of biases in judicial rulings. The US hack back strikes on foreign soil by the police authorities (as in the ReVIL case, analysed in Chapter 4) are gaining international support. If performed without proper arrangements, they are, plain and simple, a violation of national sovereignty. That would have been out of the question if they had been physically performed instead of being done by computer. Indeed, it would be at least challenging to find a legal basis for a SWAT team of Country A crossing the border with Country B to arrest a criminal without resorting to mutual legal assistance treaties. China and Russia have, more overtly, weaponised 'digital rights' imposing strict controls over information flows and data localisation.

Based on technologically questionable assumptions and argumentative fallacies, we are stubbornly questioning nonsense issues such as the regulation of artificial life or AI responsibility.

These are just a few examples supporting the thesis of this book, and many others could be easily found. However, they are sufficient to say that the negative impact of the loss of rigour in the technical use of the legal instrument in favour of literary or sociological categories is real, proven, and, probably, beyond remediation.

From a methodological point of view, this book's assumption is that law does not exist in a vacuum or in an ideal, Platonic world. Consequently, it first starts from an outlook of the cultural, industrial, and political assumptions on which the building of digital rights rested and then proceeds with matching them with the legal and regulatory issues.

As per the structure, the book is organised into two parts and five chapters, plus a conclusion.

Part one lays down the theoretical framework. It analyses the relationship between cyberspace and digital rights, and questions whether they individually exist and if one can exist without the other.

The first chapter explores the legal validity of the idea that cyberspace exists objectively or whether it is appropriate and valuable to consider it as a legal metaphor or legal fiction.

The second chapter is dedicated to digital rights. Following the same approach, it explores the genesis of the idea. It links them to human rights and highlights that they represent a reboot of the concept of natural law, in contrast to the theories of law as an instrument for regulating social relations, according to criteria defined by the associates themselves.

The chapter also highlights how the narrative on digital rights presupposes the obliteration of the cultural differences at the core of individual legal systems.

This sociocultural homologation has proved essential to maximise the diffusion of technologies and services that, with the promise of freedom, have locked people in gilded cages.

The alliance de facto, if not de jure, between Big Tech and governments of any latitude, has put the former at the latter's level. The consequence is that now, more than in the past, large private entities define people's rights and to what extent they can exercise them.

Another side of the problem is the fascination of lawmakers and the media with the science fiction promises of the Big Tech industry. Machine learning, AI, and other buzzwords of technological marketing have been taken at their face value to ground political and legislative choices of highly questionable content.

Part two proposes an empirical verification of these ideas. In particular, it explores the impact of three essential technologies of the information society: social networking (Chapter 3), cryptography (Chapter 4), and robotics/AI (Chapter 5).

The *fil rouge* of the three chapters is the delusion surrounding the call for digital rights.

The social network-enhanced loneliness capitalism breaks the social bond. It creates the delusion of being part of a 'community', even if the reality is that the user—not a person anymore—is alone in his room, with a computer and an Internet connection. It makes it easier to demote the value of individual rights down to a negotiable thing. Loneliness becomes hyperindividualism, and rights are what the king of his one-man kingdom demands they have to be. However, this is an illusory power because Big Tech is exercising its own. It decides what the right to privacy is and to what extent it must be protected, how the rights of those who buy online must be exercised, how far one can go in expressing an opinion, and whether or not to collaborate with police investigations. These are just a few examples of the real power that Big Tech has seized in the course of time.

The cryptography debate, which has been going on for at least 30 years, is the best example of this state of affairs. The online shift of both private and civil services-related activities requires security and, in particular, extremely robust encryption. At the same time, governments do not tolerate the widespread diffusion of this technology among citizens but are aware that they cannot weaken it. The everlasting excuse of child protection has made it possible to celebrate a marriage of convenience between Big Tech and governments to impose the bypass of cryptographic security without weakening it—client-side scanning. At the same time, however, Big Tech opposes the requests for cooperation from the police forces in the name of digital rights.

If social networking and cryptography are two existing and widespread technologies whose legal impact can be observed, robotics and AI are still at an embryonic stage. Nonetheless, there is a frenzied rush to regulate a phenomenon without understanding its nature and effects. The fear that machines can rebel against their creators and that artificial intelligence can enslave the human being has produced, on the one hand, a plethora of regulatory proposals and, on the other, the invocation of ethical principles to regulate the phenomenon. Once again, using the word 'digital' in conjunction with another term—ethics in this case—reappears. Claiming the need for ethical regulation because the law would not be sufficient or suitable is dangerous and misleading. Ethics is a serious discipline, exceptionally challenging to handle, and not to be confused with personal beliefs or—worse—with political goals. However, in the political arena, invoking ethics translates into attributing the power to influence people's lives to a small number of experts' beliefs. In this scenario, there is no longer much difference between a democracy and an autocracy based on a phantom 'state ethics'.

Social networks, cryptography, and AI are just three examples, perhaps the most macroscopic, of how information technologies have significantly changed the perception and function of law. In this context, digital rights have proved to be instrumental in achieving the purpose. However, for years, good faith activists and concerned citizens have dedicated—and still do—an important part of their lives to chasing a dream they continue to believe in, no matter what: the digital rights delusion.

Andrea Monti

ACKNOWLEDGEMENTS

This book is dedicated to the memory of my mentor, the late Giancarlo Livraghi.

As always happens with books, the author is but the material maker. Indeed, it would have been impossible to write it without the help and support of my family, friends, and colleagues around the world. Above all, I am forever indebted to Raymond Wacks for his continuous support and infinite patience, as well as for having encouraged me to accept the challenge of dealing with a complex topic such as digital rights.

I also thank, for their support, Laura Bonanni of Chieti-Pescara University, Giorgio Colombo of Nagoya University, Takashi Ikegami of Tokyo University, Enrico Maestri of Ferrara University, Masahiro Matsumura of St. Andrews University, Hiroshi Miyashita of Chuo University, Pierluigi Perri of Milan-Statale University, Mariarosaria Taddeo of the Oxford Internet Institute at the University of Oxford, and counsellor Ikuo Takahashi, cybersecurity law expert.

I hope I did not miss anyone—and, if so, I apologise in advance.

Finally, never as in this case, I am grateful to Brinda Sen and Aakash Chakrabarty of Routledge for their encouragement, assistance, and patience.

AM

1

AIN'T NO SUCH THING AS 'CYBERSPACE'

Digital rights are born in cyberspace.

Like the fictional dimension of the Hollywood franchise, *The Matrix*, cyberspace is everywhere. It is a centre without borders. It allows us to live on another plane, where we experience alternate realities. In cyberspace, we shape our gender, appearance, and self the way we want. In cyberspace, we can even choose to be a ghost in the shell, an identity-less stream of data appearing like a sound, an image, or a flow of consciousness. On the other hand, cyberspace is where Big Techs steal our data to mould our perception of reality and manufacture our consent. They want to turn us into brainless automatons whose only duty is to purchase their products. Finally, cyberspace is the ultimate battlefield for political struggles, whether in national elections or armed conflicts between countries. Cyberspace is where the ultimate place where the battle for digital rights is fought by a growing number of individuals who oppose the overwhelming surveillance society in which we have been lured to live.

Online privacy and digital free speech, access to the Internet as a fundamental right, personal information 'as the new oil', Artificial Intelligence (AI) as deserving the legal status of a natural person and the power to (verbatim) rule our life in daily activities, health matters, court, and war … These are but a few of the allegedly 'unprecedented' challenges that we suppose to face because of cyberspace.

We do need digital rights to protect our digital selves in 'cyberspace'.

If this summary of the narrative commonly associated with digital rights and cyberspace reminds us of the plot of a dystopic science fiction novel, it is exactly because it is a tale of fiction. Cyberspace does not exist; therefore, there is no such thing as 'digital rights' either.

To understand the meaning of this bold statement, it is essential to travel back in time towards the Big Bang that in the late 1980s made the general public aware of the existence of an 'information society' and, contrary to the law of physics, way earlier.

DOI: 10.4324/9781003373636-1

The birth of cybernetics

In 1948, Norbert Wiener, a brilliant American-born mathematician of German and Polish parenthood, published *Cybernetics: Or Control and Communication in the Animal and the Machine*. Together with Alan Turing, Claude Shannon, William Shockley, and John von Neumann, Wiener is credited as a ground-breaking contributor to various information-connected disciplines. He was the first to use the word 'cyber' in connection to a theory of information and fostered the (r)evolution of research in AI.

> It tells you something about Norbert Wiener's qualifications as a prophet that Cybernetics has been republished twice since it first appeared in 1948, and that on each of those occasions his thoughts and predictions about the technologies he helped create have seemed more ingenious, more prescient, and, in some respects, more troubling.[1]

Wiener coined the word *cybernetics* because no other existing definition matched his field of research.

> After much consideration, we have come to the conclusion that all the existing terminology has too heavy a bias to one side or another to serve the future development of the field as well as it should; and as happens so often to scientists, we have been forced to coin at least one artificial neo-Greek expression to fill the gap. We have decided to call the entire field of control and communication theory, whether in the machine or in the animal, by the name Cybernetics, which we form from the Greek χυβερνήτης or steersman.[2]

The difference between the meaning Wiener gave to the cyber- prefix and the one media, business, politicians, and legal scholars attribute to the word is apparent and revealing. Wiener used the term in its original Greek meaning: 'governor'. In that, he was right, as the outcome of 'cybernetics' would have been a way to exert a *command* of the physical world. It was rooted in reality. It was not meant to create a 'virtual elsewhere'.

From cybernetics to cyberspace

In the early 1980s, the prefix 'cyber-' experienced a semantic shift. In 1980, American novelist Bruce Bethke wrote a short story, published later in 1983 and titled *Cyberpunk*.[3]

> The invention of the c-word was a conscious and deliberate act of creation on my part. I wrote the story in the early spring of 1980,

and from the very first draft, it was titled 'Cyberpunk'. In calling it that, I was actively trying to invent a new term that grokked the juxtaposition of punk attitudes and high technology. ... How did I actually create the word? The way any new word comes into being, I guess: through synthesis. I took a handful of roots—cyber, techno, et al—mixed them up with a bunch of terms for socially misdirected youth, and tried out the various combinations until one just plain sounded right.[4]

Bethke's use of the cyber- prefix was still somehow connected with its original meaning. It defined clever youngsters with an anarchic attitude, using computers to *command* and *control* their environment—and affect people's lives.

More or less in the same years, the prefix joined the word 'space' and changed its meaning. It became related to a somehow mystical plane where 'cyberselves', disembodied ghosts, lived in a 'world' made of digitised information. However, this new word and the meaning it wanted to convey were just meaningless, as its creator plainly acknowledged from the start.

In his 1984 novel, *Neuromancer*, science fiction author and (at the time, self-professed) computer non-expert William Gibson made extensive use of cyberspace to describe the relationship between individuals and computer networks. In his words, cyberspace is

A consensual hallucination experienced daily by billions of legitimate operators, in every nation, by children being taught mathematical concepts... A graphic representation of data abstracted from the banks of every computer in the human system. Unthinkable complexity. Lines of light ranged in the nonspace of the mind, clusters and constellations of data. Like city lights, receding[5]

It was a visionary suggestion, as powerful for the imagination as meaningless in its relationship with reality. The vagueness of cyberspace was evident to its creator, who, in a 2000 interview, recalled:

All I knew about the word 'cyberspace' when I coined it was that it seemed like an effective buzzword. It seemed evocative and essentially meaningless. It was suggestive of something, but had no real semantic meaning, even for me, as I saw it emerge on the page.

Lately, in 2013, he came back to the topic with an adamantine statement:

As I stared at it in red sharpie on a yellow legal pad my whole delight was that I knew it meant absolutely nothing.[6]

3

Notwithstanding, since the publication of *Neuromancer*, cyberspace has become a ubiquitous presence in media and intellectual circles. It soon left the niche of science fiction readers. It became an idea that united computer programmers and network administrators—*geeks* as they are disrespectfully referred to still today—under a flag. It found its way into the fast-growing software and telecommunication marketing strategies. Between 1982 and 1992, Hollywood ignited the cyber-frenziness with three motion pictures that attained a 'cult' status: *Tron* (1982), *Wargames* (1983), and *Sneakers* (1992). Strictly speaking, none of them used the term 'cyberspace'. However, all made wide use of the narrative elements found in the cyberpunk literary genre.

Everything went 'cyber'.

In some cases, the media exposed the cavalier attitude towards the abuse of the prefix. The following quote is more than a decade old but could have been written today, and nobody would have noticed:

> How can you tell the difference between a real report about online vulnerabilities and someone who is trying to scare you about the security of the Internet because they have an agenda, such as landing lucrative, secret contracts from the government?
>
> Here's a simple test: Count the number of times they use the adjective 'cyber.' Nobody uses the word 'cyber' anymore, except people trying to scare you and trying to make the Internet seem scary or foreign. (Think, for instance, of the term 'cyberbullying,' which is somehow much more crazy and new and in need of legislation than 'online bullying.')[7]

Such warnings, however, remained largely ignored, and the *vulgata* mainly fostered by the (not yet that) Big Tech industry and media went on telling a different story.

The at-large availability of electronic communication tools once reserved for the academic, corporate, and civil service sectors challenged politicians and members of the legal community. They were (and mostly still are) not at ease with the complexity of science and technology.

The need for a shortcut to describe 'this computer thing' led to a broad acritical acceptance of cyberspace as a substitute for a thorough analysis of the technical issues underlying the just-born 'information society'. It negatively affected the role of law and rights as an instrument to regulate social interactions. To the detriment of a proper taxonomy, metaphors superseded legal definitions.

Cyberspace cleared the way for other fascinating albeit vague metaphors. 'Electronic frontier', 'virtual', 'digital'—hence, digital rights—and other science fiction (and later, Big Tech's marketing) driven ideas soon emerged. However, none have been as society-disruptive as cyberspace did.

4

To understand it, it is crucial to comprehend the 'hacker culture' contribution to building this evanescent—and, therefore, powerful—suggestive idea.

Hacking culture, technoanarchism, and the 'new' rights

Since its early outcomes, in the 1970s, members of the (not yet defined) hacker movement advocated for themselves the right to satisfy their intellectual hunger no matter what. They wanted to *command* a technology nobody—even its creators—fully understood. They were ready to do—and did it, eventually—whatever it took to fulfil their craving for knowledge.

The following quote is revealing. It comes from John 'Captain Crunch' Draper. He was the 'father' of phone phreaking—the 'art' of exploiting the deficiency of a telephone network to use it at will.

> I do phreaking for one reason and one reason only... I'm learning about a system. The phone company is a System. A computer is a System. Do you understand? If I do what I do, it is only to explore a System. Computers. Systems. ... The phone company is nothing but a computer.[8]

The transition from a 'pure' telephone network to computerised systems enhanced the early quest for unrestricted access to information.

> This was when, for the first time, information relating to individuals was generated natively in a digitised form by these individuals and by way of a machine-to-machine data exchange. And this was also the moment when a (relatively) small number of people began to ask themselves questions about the impact of this technology on fundamental rights. A rich bibliography flourished in this period, accounting for the birth of the hacking movement in the United States and Europe, the criminal and the digital underground, and the early development of the core concepts of the pro-privacy and anti-techno-surveillance culture as well as of the free-software and open source movements. It is not our purpose to provide a comprehensive history of the role of hacking in shaping the World as we know and experience it today. Suffice it to say, in contrast to received wisdom, that hacking culture played a fundamental role in developing the digital industry and setting the legal and political agenda in many countries.[9]

Like jazz and the apple pie, hacking is generally considered as being born and fostered in the USA to gain a universal status lately and everywhere.

> Yet, two aspects complicate the claim of universality. In a technical sense, hacking defies clear demarcation; a more helpful definition of

hacking is to look at the motives of computer users who 'hacked.' Hacking is defined by users' unconventional, playful mastery and unique, outsider expertise. That very definition undermines the claim of technological universality. In geographical terms, the global influence of computers beyond the US borders has been wide and deep; in Europe, the rapid appropriation of personal computers on both sides of the Iron Curtain was impressive indeed. Yet, by examining how such a technological culture became embedded in other cultural and political contexts, we can appreciate the severe limits to the computers' claim of universality. The appeal of personal computers was neither inherent in the technology nor a foregone conclusion.[10]

Despite the similarities, hacking in Europe grew differently, developing unique traits. Indeed, it would be reductive to think of the European way of hacking as limited to the eager desire to 'master' a new technology.

Given the American dominance in computing, we need to consider the prominent position of the United States as a geopolitical power in its ability to set global standards and position itself as a seductive symbol of market capitalism in postwar Europe. ... in the context of the US postwar global power, the ability of American social actors to shape industry standards better explains why computers were adopted relatively quickly than their intrinsic appeal. US-based products and technologies often came with elaborate global public-relations campaigns; moreover, many consumer goods ... came to be associated with America's youth culture, acquiring a status of superiority and sensuality. ... Europeans struggled with the sense of their outsider position in relation to the US global power. ... Were the hacking Europeans outsiders to an American corporate culture, who nevertheless mastered the artifacts and knowledge of the system? Or were they outsiders to their local community, who showed their mastery by flaunting their ability to access exquisite, global products and who participated in a global, transnational community defying national boundaries? These questions point to a crucial juncture at which European histories of hacker culture diverge from the US narratives. Hacker communities played an active role in appropriating the technology. ... On the one hand, users were trying to make sense of microcomputers and networks in their own way. On the other hand, European users explored how much room they had to create their own codes within the context of US cultural, political, and technological dominance.[11]

Since the late 1980s, throughout Europe, the hacking communities have been well aware of the political and legal issues connected with the upcoming computer revolution. The French underground community was deeply influenced by the USA. *Noway*—the electronic magazine published between 1994 and 1997—translated the 'hacker manifesto' known as *The Conscience of a Hacker* written under the *nom de plume* of *The Mentor*. However, probably not a European black swan, the French government 'hacked the hackers' by infiltrating them from the beginning of their career.[12] In 1989, the *Direction de la Surveillance du territoire*, with the help of Jean-Bernard Condat, set up a hacker group named *Chaos Computer Club France* as a front. It was entirely unrelated, but for the name, to the German 'original' *Chaos Computer Club* established in 1981. However, it fulfilled the goal for which it was created. It exposed French hackers and affected for years to come the French hacking scene.[13]

In the meantime, the German *Chaos Computer Club* built its reputation also outside the boundaries of the hacking scenes by performing hacking stunts to expose the weakness of the civil services. CCC—as it is colloquially known—was not alien to controversies, such as the one raised by the mystery surrounding the death of one of its members, Karl Koch[14] and, previously, by the alleged involvement of the man in Russian KGB-sponsored activities against US targets.[15]

In the Netherlands, Hack-tic, a hacker club, created one of the largest Internet Service Providers in the Country (XS4All) that championed free speech. In Italy, a multitude of groups gave voice to the composite hacking community built around collectives with a technopolitical agenda—such as Metro Olografix and Strano Network—and publishers such as Shake Edizioni that spread the Cyberpunk and hacking culture. [16]

Diversity, indeed, was another essential brick in the building of the hacker's cultural identity. The *phreak* prefix used to identify the act of exploiting a telephone network (*phreaking*), and those who performed it (*phreaker*) comes from the word *freak*. It is not just a pun. It overtly suggests the importance of being apart from the packs.

However, at least for a legal scholar, the quest for absolute freedom is more relevant. It was based upon the contrast between values and norms, hence between (individual) ethics and law—nowadays a highly controversial topic in the attempts to regulate AI. *Cognoscenti*—and *cognoscenti* only—should have the right to access every system and information.

At the core of the hacker culture lies the ubiquitous mantra *information wants to be free*. It became the war cry of a revolution. It generated a tide that submerged the world and changed it forever, not always for good.

The call for free access to information was not meant—as a cursory reading of the word would imply—to be read as gratis. Supporters of the hacking culture venerate the idea that people should have unrestricted, unscrutinised, and uncensored access to knowledge. Richard Stallman, the MIT computer scientist who pioneered the idea of free software, explained the concept with an iconic line: 'free as in free speech, not as in free beer.'

Rebellion was (and remains) a core component of the hacking culture. In parallel with Stallman's call for action to free the right to access and modify computer programmes' source code, this technological rebellion assumed other forms.[17]

Hacker culture is a mosaic made of many tesseracts that do not always fit perfectly. It was an extraordinarily complex and interesting cultural *milieu* that influenced the idea of cyberspace. The melting pot in which the hacking culture blended with science, literature, philosophy, politics, economics, and—last but not least—crime and disorder has been essential to determine the semantic shift of the cyber- prefix towards the idea of 'cyberlaw' and, lately, 'digital rights'.

The conceptualisation of cyberspace

Cyberspace became a core concept of almost every legal analysis and found its conceptual basis in the *Declaration of Independence of cyberspace*,[18] drafted in 1996 by American rock band *Grateful Dead*'s songwriter and Electronic Frontier Foundation co-founder John Perry Barlow.

Barlow's *Declaration*, however, did not come from a vacuum. It was the outcome of a complex cultural evolution that mixed various components of the US society, on the verge of upcoming massive changes. A vision based on the idea of *New Communalism* gained momentum.

[It] turned away from political action and toward technology and the transformation of consciousness as the primary sources of social change. If mainstream America had become a culture of conflict, with riots at home and war abroad, the commune world would be one of harmony. If the American state deployed massive weapons systems in order to destroy faraway peoples, the New Communalists would deploy small-scale technologies—ranging from axes and hoes to amplifiers, strobe lights, slide projectors, and LSD—to bring people together and allow them to experience their common humanity. Finally, if the bureaucracies of industry and government demanded that men and women become psychologically fragmented specialists, the technology-induced experience of togetherness would allow them to become both self-sufficient and whole once again. For this wing of the counterculture, the technological and intellectual output of American research culture held enormous appeal. Although they rejected the military-industrial complex as a whole, as well as the political process that brought it into being, hippies from Manhattan to Haight-Ashbury read

Norbert Wiener, Buckminster Fuller, and Marshall McLuhan. Through their writings, young Americans encountered a cybernetic vision of the world, one in which material reality could be imagined as an information system. To a generation that had grown up in a world beset by massive armies and by the threat of nuclear holocaust, the cybernetic notion of the globe as a single, interlinked pattern of information was deeply comforting: in the invisible play of information, many thought they could see the possibility of global harmony.[19]

Other intellectuals, writers, and businessmen contributed to the delivery. *Whole Earth Lectronic Link* (WELL)'s Stuart Brand, *Wired*'s Kevin Kelly, Howard Rheingold and his focus on virtual communities, *1.0*'s Ester Dyson, and *Cyberdelic*'s Timoty Leary are probably the best-known parents of the upcoming baby. However, there have been many more who supported the idea. Barlow was hardly the only one in the delivery room when cyberspace was born.

Is cyberspace a space?

Since the publication of Barlow's *Declaration*, the idea that cyberspace was not just a work of fiction became *res judicata*. Even those (legal) analyses that looked critically at the matter providing more reality-based solutions, one way or another, used the cyberspace concept as a shortcut or—see *infra*—a metaphor.

Barlow's text is visionary and romantic, as every utopia should be. However engaging as it may sound, it contains factual mistakes and misunderstandings of the involved technologies of information.

The core of Barlow's argument is that cyberspace is a place where (a certain kind of) people gather, regardless of their individual status.

This assumption is entirely correct from a *sociological* perspective. Every community is made of interconnected individuals; otherwise, it could not be considered as such. Hence, there is no problem in acknowledging that a connection does not require physical proximity to exist. Nor *networked* communities were peculiar to 'cyberspace'. Whoever is old enough to remember the pre-Internet *pen pal* networks knows that for a fact. Nor the distance-based interaction makes the cultural and social exchange less real. Hence, there is nothing 'virtual' in a correspondence network—be that operated by letters, email, chat, or instant messaging.

A now-forgotten Internet sibling supports this conclusion: FidoNet.

Created in 1983—the same year of the split between Arpanet and other TCP/IP-based networks for civilian use—FidoNet was a piece of software that allowed building a network with low-tech resources. Communication systems were installed on small computers, and data were exchanged via modem calls over the landline. Born as a ham-radio computer-based alternative, it spread all over the world as a way to correspond. In the words of FidoNet creator Tom Jennings,

> FidoNet is no longer just a piece of software; it has become a complex organism. There are about 160 Fidos in FidoNet right now; this does not include Fidos being run as Bulletin Board only systems, just ones that you can converse with over the net. ... Its purpose: to see if it could be done, merely for the fun of it, like ham radio. It quickly became useful; instead of trying to call each others' boards up to leave messages, or expensive voice phone calls, FidoNet messages became more or less routine.[20]

Eventually, the spreading data transfer services based on Internet protocols took over FidoNet. Nonetheless, its history shows that Jennings and other clever people who built and managed the Internet 'little brother' only wanted to *communicate*. They were not interested in experiencing alter(n)ate realities or pursuing an ideological message of anarchy and freedom.

By contrast, the emphasis on personal experience and the lack of consideration for the technical nature of the remote interaction among people allowed Barlow to move a step further. He claimed no governmental sovereignty over the 'place', lack of borders, refusal to acknowledge the power of 'ordinary' rulers, and the irrelevance of 'material' legal categories. These conclusions are coherent; however, the argument as a whole is flawed by an *ex falso, quodlibet* fallacy.

The debate about the existence of cyberspace will have a (not so) fresh start with the announcement of the upcoming 'metaverse'—another literary invention created in 1992 by American writer Neal Stephenson in his novel *Snow Crash*.

High-tech companies such as Meta (formerly Facebook) and Microsoft have announced the creation of a 'place' where people command their avatars. They can 'own' real estate, 'access' workplaces, malls, or cinemas, and 'stay' secluded from the prying eyes of the curious. At the same time, 'inhabitants' of the metaverse can feel experiences not allowed to their human clones (the inversion of the roles is not a coincidence).

The metaverse as a computer-mediated experience is no news. The attempt to mimic the environment we live in through a standalone computer and, later, a network is as old as the videogames. Early computerised versions or role-playing games known as 'adventures' projected the player into an environment with which he had to interact. *Sherlock*, one of the most sophisticated adventure games written in 1984 for Sir Clive Sinclair's ZX Spectrum, even included a forerunner of natural language processing to let the player solve the riddle. Getting through the maze of the investigation required speaking *Inglish*—a simplified language that the game engine could parse to let the game go ahead. It was not even remotely similar to technologies such as the (still raw) ChatGPT. It neither was, actually, a natural language processing system. However, it created—the limitation of hardware being complemented by the player's imagination—the illusion of being 'there'. In 1984, *Hacker*, another game written for the ZX Spectrum, crossed the line between fantasy and reality. The player was confronted with a 'system' to gain 'access' and explore illegally. Going ahead with the game, the suspension of disbelief suddenly kicked in. Whether the player was hacking his own microcomputer or an existing remote system was not relevant anymore.

In the 1990s, first-person games took advantage of increased computing power. How close the gameplay was to reality became a differentiating factor in determining the success or failure of a game. Often, games such as *Wolfenstein 3D* and the iterations of the *Doom* franchise were of a violent and pulp nature. However, simulators of every kind were the most eager to offer a faithful reproduction of reality. Over time, games developed an 'intelligent' engine to give characters a 'will'. Initially, games were deterministic. There were only one (or a few) ways to win. The player ought to discover the right one. Any other course of action would achieve nothing but failure. In some *shoot-em-up* games, the goal was not 'to survive' but 'staying alive' as much as possible, while the software increased the game's difficulty. Electronic Arts' *The Sims*, released in 2000, raised the bar. It allowed characters to take 'autonomous' decisions if not directed by the God-like player. Props and items are on sale (in exchange for real currencies) to be used in the game. In 2016, Russian horror video game *Hello Neighbour* featured an AI-powered villain capable of learning how the player behaves and react accordingly.

Car chases, flying trips, sports competitions, 'real'-life... they all started by giving a mere 'look-alike' graphical appearance of an environment.

Moreover, games (and gamified real entertainment) incorporated complex physics models to have objects (inter)act according to the laws of nature. They cloned the 'signature moves' and biometric data of athletes and artists to create avatars that look and *behave* like their real counterparts.

eSports blurred the line between a 'pure' gaming experience and the watching of an actual event on the screen. Combining all the advancements in various fields of science and technology, an eSports platform can offer the perception of a highly realistic match where athletes and anchors are almost indistinguishable from what is usually broadcasted on screen.

If eSports have blurred the line between games and real events, the American basketball team Brooklyn Nets crossed it. In 2022, they experimented with Canon's *Free Viewpoint Video System* to record a game, turn it into an interactive piece of software, and let the audience interact with it:

it uses 110 data-capturing cameras placed around the court to carefully track player movement. Then it combines that data in real-time with 3D models that have been built of each player, and renders it, very similar to how things would work while you're playing NBA 2K. That creates the ability for virtual camera operators to show off the action from any angle they want to, as virtual cameras swoop around the floor like drones.[21]

The exploitation of these technologies is not limited to sports, as they found their way into entertainment and news.

'Virtual duets', such as the one performed in 2016 by Natalie Cole with her defunct father, Nat King Cole, are nothing special anymore. However, in 2022 Swedish pop band *Abba* put the most ambitious and astonishing project in the music business on stage. While recording their last album, *Voyage*, they tracked themselves while performing the songs using sophisticated motion capture technologies. Acquired data allowed the creation of digitised clones to appear on stage together with real musicians. Fans attending the show will see Abba as they were in their youth, performing with the same energy and feeling. They have been made (digitally) immortal.

In 2018 Chinese Xinhua agency introduced its AI-powered news anchor[22] automating a technology now commonly used in deep-fakes to make parodies of VIPs or spread disinformation and propaganda[23]

These examples partially account for the multiple ways digital technologies can offer a reality-based experience. However, they are enough to demonstrate how the *psychological* perception of interacting with software and people is exploited for profit and affects the legal approach.

At the user level, the *appearance* of an artificially created environment— be the metaverse or a videogame—naturally leads to thinking in terms of 'things'. It seems, therefore, natural to 'buy' a 'manor' on a 'secluded island'. Hence, the flourishing of agencies selling 'exclusive estates' on the metaverse.

> After being crowned by Neymar as one of the best midfielders he has ever played with, Marco Verratti has reached another big milestone, but this time off the pitch. The PSG midfielder is the first footballer in the world to invest in digital real estate in the Metaverse, a few days ago Verratti bought just one of 25 different islands put up for sale on The Sandbox by Exclusible, a marketplace specialising in luxury NFTs.[24]

Once having got a proper hut, dressing comes next.

> Digital fashion has the most obvious application in the gaming world, where players look to express themselves and their personalities through purchasing digital outfits that their avatars can wear. ... They also typically have a younger consumer base—digital

natives who are growing up finding it entirely normal to spend real money to purchase items that only exist in the digital realm. This intersection of fashion and gaming is nothing new. In 2019, Louis Vuitton collaborated with Riot Games' League of Legends. Gucci created a virtual space in Roblox in 2021.[25]

Wearing proper attire eases participation in social events in 'metaverse venues', hence—once again—the multiplication of 'space' and 'facility' lenders.

A metaverse platform is not just a way to furtherly gamify an individual's life to give him an escape from the dumbness of his daily routine. It allows designing interactive catalogues of goods located in various places without wasting time and money on travels, at least for the first contact. It can offer a way to rehearse a show and check the effectiveness of the stage settings.

As much as immersive the metaverse experience can be, that should not deflect or confuse the legal analysis into believing that the *perception* of a physical reality needs to be subjected in the same way. In other words, the question is whether we aim at regulating a *psychological experience* or what makes it possible.

'Purchasing' lands, dresses, cars, or whatever else does not mean acquiring, *per se*, ownership rights over something. The object of the purchase is a piece of software that can be used only within a specific computer platform. In other words, the contract to 'purchase' our 'Roman villa' and organise a 'live event' is actually made of a service agreement to access a physical server, a license to use the installed platform, another licence to expand usage rights to whatever props we are ready to buy, a contract to regulate the use of one-to-one, one-to-many, or many-to-many interactive communication services, booking and Customer Relationship Management (CRM) included.

Defined as such, the metaverse loses its *charme*. It reveals its true nature: a complex electronic communication service made possible by combining multiple individual achievements in technology and business models: image capturing and processing, visual devices, high-speed network computing, and mathematics.

Telecommunication infrastructure is not a 'space'

Be an old *FidoNet* bulletin board system, a centralised online service provider as was *America online* or a multinationally available Internet-based platform, roughly speaking, they are all made of the same things: personal computers, servers, network devices, telecommunication lines, protocols, operating systems and application software, power grids.

Big Tech, telecommunication carriers, and Internet service providers at an access-transport layer own an autonomous power to decide who, how, and when can access online services. That has been true since the beginning of the telecommunication industry, as the history of the phreaking/hacking movements elucidates.

In more recent times, the Coronavirus pandemic has shown how robust Big Tech's grip is on the lives of states and individuals. Moreover, the 2019 Hong Kong protests and the sanctions imposed against Russia for the 2022 military attack on Ukraine provide further evidence of how critical private companies' role is in supporting (or affecting) the political agenda of a sovereign State.

As a metaphor—on that, later—one may affirm that this power translates into *preventing* somebody from *entering* a *space*. As a matter of fact, though, what happens is *impeding* the *use* of a *service*.

Rather than resorting to the vague notion of cyberspace, it would have made more sense to focus on protecting fundamental rights related to electronic communication services.

Contrary to the approach of the American and almost all other civil rights groups around the world, that was the intuition of a group of Italian intellectuals that, in 1994, gave birth to ALCEI, the World's oldest civil society group outside the USA[26] and later founding member of the *European Digital Rights Initiative*.

Focusing back on human behaviour (*interactive communication*) was less fascinating, although a more realistic approach from a legal perspective. However, it went largely unnoticed in the legal and political debate around the impact on society at large of the technology of information.

Infrastructures and standards are heavily regulated

Another essential part of Barlow's *Declaration* accompanying the 'borderless' nature of cyberspace is its resilience to every attempt of (local) State-issued regulation. A similar claim backs the (perceived) value of technologies such as blockchain and its applications, from cryptocurrencies to NFTs.

The independence of cyberspace from the national powers attained almost mythical status. It was—and still is—at the core of 'digital rights' activism and Big Tech profiting from the possibility of delocalising its operations, maximising incomes, and playing a direct political role in the international scenario.

However, a reality check shows that 'national security' and economic interest of many countries, including China, Russia, the USA, and some EU members, led the Parliaments to reaffirm their primacy on the telecommunication infrastructures. They put a 'network kill switch' in the hands of the executives. In case of need, there would be no doubt about the capability of a government to prevent people from accessing networks and platforms. The reactions of powers-that-be to civil protest in North Africa and the Middle East and, once again, the Ukrainian invasion speak for themselves.

The idea that cyberspace is a space is also inconsistent at a more abstract level with that of the current Internet governance framework.

Indeed, the physical part of the Internet is the propriety of those private entities that own hardware and cables. At the more abstract layer made of technical protocols, IP numbers, and domain names, the power is in the hands of an at-large, non-State ruled community collectively known as *Internet governance*.

The *Internet Corporation for Assigning Name and Numbers* (ICANN) that manages the domain name system, the five IP number registries[27], the *Internet Assigned Numbers Authority* (IANA) ensure the global coordination of the DNS Root, IP addressing, and other Internet protocol resources. They all can decide on their own authority that can be part of the Big Internet, who cannot and who should not.

Primarily considered a mere possibility, the involvement of the Big Internet governance in a diplomatic crisis has become a reality. For the third time in a few paragraphs, referring to the Ukrainian crisis is necessary.

On 3 March 2022, the deputy prime minister of Ukraine, Mykhailo Fedorov, asked RIPE NCC to revoke the right to use IPv4 and IPv6 addresses from all Russian members. If accepted, the Ukrainian demands would have resulted in the immediate exclusion of Russian entities from interconnection with the other networks that make up the global Internet without requiring special measures or state intervention.

Contrary to the trend set by commercial Internet-based companies, RIPE NCC did not follow the Ukrainian requests for two reasons. The first is the limited effectiveness of the Russian ban, weighted against the global disruption of Internet operations. The second is the refusal to involve Internet governance in political struggles and avoiding the settlement of a principle that, in the next future, might lead to a less open Internet.

On one hand, the RIPE NCC/Ukraine debate shows that

> The libertarian principles on which the global Internet was built are not just a utopia but have actual effectiveness in the lives of individuals and nations. These principles constitute a form of technological diplomacy that could even contribute to solving the Ukrainian crisis by leaving a (weak) channel of communication open between all parties involved.[28]

On the other hand, though, it is inevitable to ask what would have happened if an independent body had granted the Russian ban without any governmental oversight or a broader diplomatic assessment of the consequences of its decisions. Internet governance can hardly be called 'virtual' or 'cyber'.

Goods are sold, and services are provided from a seller to a buyer

Distance sales existed way before the e-commerce giants took over this market. As international payment systems do, vending machine and ATM agreements are also in place for decades. Services provided worldwide or cross-nationally—such as insurance or medical assistance—existed before the Internet.

Conceptually, selling products and services online is nothing different than before. The legal challenges were the same: confirming the parties' identity, avoiding the aliud pro alio, acknowledging the receipt of the goods and the money, and challenging the defaulting counterpart. As far as the agreement is concerned, it does not matter where a storage facility is located or from or which entity fulfils the order. That is also true for online services. As soon as a customer enters into an agreement with the provider, the mutual duties and liabilities are on each side. It does not matter if there are middlemen behind the front. A company can be easily incorporated into a remote part of the World or simply in a friendly jurisdiction. The organisation can be built by renting everything, from janitors to senior managers, from IT platforms to logistics and depots. A physical place is not even a must, as a facility-less model— smart working, as they call it—allows to spread the 'smart' workers in various jurisdictions.

On the one hand, this decentralised model still does not suffer from a lack of legislation. On the other hand, transactions' *scale* and interactions with many jurisdictions create new challenges for the legal community.

A carefully drafted agreement is at the core of a negotiation. If well designed, it prevents quarrels, and if they happen, it handles the litigation to minimise its adverse consequences. However, playing by the book does not work when confronted with the reality of millions of per-day transactions or complex claims involving the whole supply chain in the four corners of the Planet. Online transactions happen fast. Users do not read agreements. Even if they ticked all the checkboxes of the online form, they could challenge the seller nonetheless; (international) class actions are more frequent. The cost of handling the relationship with customers in such a manner would deadly affect the profitability of any business. Of course, it is impossible to avoid litigations at all. However, it is unsurprising that companies operating online are developing alternative strategies. The golden standard in the online business is Amazon. Overall, Amazon designed its processes to avoid, in principle, the possibility of being taken to court by a customer. It is impossible to purchase something by mistake; by contrast, returning goods is possible beyond the mandatory terms set forth by 'ordinary' consumer protection legislation. Other suppliers may not be as efficient or fair, especially in the cloud market. The point, however, remains: there is nothing 'virtual' about how online services are provided. Sellers and customers act through telecommunication systems, commerce and digital platforms, payment gateways, and logistics services. Every component of the supply chain possibly raises problems that do not happen in 'cyberspace'.

Crime hits real victims

Criminal law and armed conflict are two fields where many scholars advocate the existence of cyberspace as an autonomous domain. A few reasons in both cases suggest that it is not necessarily so.

Since the early beginning of the at-large use of network-based services and its exploitation to commit criminal offences, warnings have been raised about the difficulty of determining the proper jurisdiction to put the defendant on trial because 'the crime happened in cyberspace'.

The previous (cursory) description of how users interact with telecommunication and computer networks and these latter work helps to clarify the issue.

A computer crime is performed by using a device located in a specific place. Firstly, the perpetrator connects his device to an access service located, broadly speaking, in the same place. Using various anonymisation and obfuscation techniques (if known), the perpetrator connects to other networks located abroad and hits the target physically located in a different place. He then commits the criminal offence directly, launching an army of computer zombies through a botnet, or unleashing viruses and malware. The criminal offence may cause harm in the same jurisdiction where the perpetrator has initiated it, in the jurisdiction where the target is located, and in all the jurisdictions involved in the intermediate parts of the actions. That makes it utterly challenging to run a criminal investigation in terms of practical activities.

Whoever—be a defence counsel, a prosecutor, or a judge—has ever been involved in such investigations knows at heart how difficult it would be. However, challenges come from operational issues, not from a lack of legal principles to find the correct jurisdictions.

Be under a common or continental law system, deciding which jurisdiction should investigate and put the defendant on trial is a matter of factual assessment, not of (lack of) law.

Since 1911, the US Supreme Court affirmed the principle according to which

> [a]cts done outside a jurisdiction, but intended to produce and producing detrimental effects within it, justify a state in punishing the cause of the harm as if he had been present at the effect, if the state should succeed in getting him within its power.[29]

Article 6 of the Italian Penal Code, dating back to 1930, states that

> Whoever commits an offence in the territory of the State shall be punished according to Italian law.
>
> The offence shall be deemed to have been committed in the territory of the State when the act or omission constituting the offence has been committed wholly or partly in the territory of the State, or when the event which is the consequence of the act or omission has occurred in the territory of the State.

Also the Japanese Penal Code adopts a similar approach.

> In Japan, the ubiquity doctrine is the most common. According to this doctrine, if the perpetrator carries even a part of *iter criminis* on Japanese soil, it is enough to affirm Japanese courts' jurisdiction. It allows the application of national criminal law against infringements of the national legal interests of the Country, regardless of the place of the offence and the nationality of the offender.[30]

Moreover, according to the Japanese Supreme Court, in some instances, it is possible to enforce abroad a locally issued warrant without resorting to legal assistance treaties.

> Where a recording medium on which electronic or magnetic records are stored is located in a State party to the Convention on Cybercrime and a person who has the lawful authority to disclose the same records gives the lawful and voluntary consent to the disclosure thereof, it is permitted to remotely access the recording medium and copy the same records without depending on international assistance in the investigation.[31]

The British Crown Prosecution Services provides several criteria to solve the riddle.

> There are several factors that can affect the final decision, and this will depend on the circumstances of each case. Prosecutors should balance all of these factors carefully and fairly, as this will weigh heavily on whether there is enough evidence to prosecute and whether it would be in the public interest to do so. ... There are several ways by which a state can exercise jurisdiction: Statute and Criminal Codes (i.e. explicit reference in statute to the jurisdictional reach of the offences created in the statute); Territory;

Active personality (i.e. the accused may be prosecuted in the country of the nationality of the offender); Passive personality (i.e. the
accused may be prosecuted in the country of the nationality of the
victim); and Universal jurisdiction (i.e. the state will be able to pros-
ecute regardless of the nationality of the offender, the victim, and
where the offence was committed, e.g. torture).[32]

EU and Chinese data protection regulations also assert national jurisdiction for processing performed abroad. Russia imposed a duty to localise
Russian citizens' personal data and Russian personal data-processing foreign companies.

Different national legislation might have nuances in the criteria allowing
a defendant to be put on trial when the criminal action starts abroad and
spreads its effect within a given State (or vice versa). However, they all share
the idea that finding the proper jurisdiction is a matter of practical analysis
of the law to solve the riddle on a per-case basis.

Both case law and (in many states) statutory authority provide a
legal basis for states to rely upon in prosecuting out-of-state defendants who victimise their populations using the Internet technology.
In common law jurisdictions like Michigan, the state's burden is
to show detrimental effects within the forum state and intent to
cause such effects. In states with extraterritorial jurisdictional statutes, the specific terms of the law must be examined to determine
whether the conduct is covered.[33]

A prosecutor investigating a cross-national computer-related criminal
offence must interact with his foreign equivalent under mutual legal assistance treaties (if in place) or seek other ways to obtain relevant and court-
actionable evidence. He is hanged to the operational capabilities of another
legal system on which he exerts neither authority nor control. He may also
face a country that is unwilling to cooperate.

Two cases with opposite ends elucidate the matter.

On 11 May 2020, the Court of Rome (IT) blocked access from Italy
to various copyright-infringing Telegram channels and the website of the
public domain online library *Project Gutenberg*.[34] There are many reasons
to believe that *Project Gutenberg* has been included in the blocking order
by mistake (echoes of the *Steve Jackson Games, Inc. v. United States Secret
Service*[35] case resound loudly). However, the point is that it will never be
possible to know it for sure because the court order has not been officially
notified following the proper procedures for mutual investigation assistance. The online library has been deprived of its right to defence. Affirming
the jurisdiction of an Italian criminal court for an (alleged) crime only in

part taking place in Italy was not difficult. By contrast, the *enforcement* of the order has proven to be challenging.

On 8 November 2021, Europol[36] and the US Department of Justice[37] jointly announced the results of an international operation that led to the arrest of members of a Ukrainian crew. They were accused of spreading ransomware (a virus that encrypts the contents of a mass storage device) for extortion purposes. They demanded payments in cryptocurrency to give the victim the decryption key and prevent the data from being (publicly) released.

The details of this operation are largely unknown, so we do not have complete information about what happened. However, what is certain is that the involvement of the American military and national security authorities creates a legal—and therefore political—problem that is not easy to solve: the legitimacy of retaliation following an attack during a criminal investigation.

> Every Western jurisdiction sets a clear distinction between ... judicial investigations, which are subject to the control of the judiciary and do not permit the committing of crimes at home or abroad, those relative to national security which, within certain (extensive) margins, are the competence of the executive, and those military activities – which Parliament must authorise. In the first case, there is the possibility of carrying out undercover activities without participating in crimes. In the second, members of the secret services can also commit crimes ... In the third, there are rules of engagement allowing preemptive defence, if not outright attack.
>
> The freedom of different operational areas matches the objectives pursued. Bringing someone to justice implies following the fair trial rules, while protecting national interests through the services and the military apparatus implies having fewer legal constraints ... Protecting national security can justify offensive actions even committed within the borders of another country. ... However, this approach cannot be applied to criminal investigations because it gathers evidence in substantial violation of the right of defence.[38]

Only the records of the trials—when and if made public—shall provide an answer to several open questions. A court should likely rule on the extension and the limits of the international mutual assistance treaties, the involvement of the military, companies, and 'other actors' in a sort of coalition of goodwill, the relationship between the due process and the US hack back that allowed to identify, track, and arrest the suspects.

In the meantime, it is a fair assumption that the problem of this case, and— broadly speaking—those involving multiple countries, lies in investigative rules designed for crimes committed in a single jurisdiction and in a time-frame that measures actions in terms of hours, days, months, and years rather than in a split second. A split second only is enough for ransomware to start stealing data or an exploit to give access to a system.

Once again, the matter to solve is *how* it would be possible to perform an effective investigation, not (no)*where*.

Both cases show that a solution is essential and urgent. Boundaries are a matter of democracy. They provide a barrier against arbitrary enforcement of public powers beyond their jurisdiction. Even if cyberspace existed—as it does not—it could not have been a borderless and uncontrollable place.

A similar argument applies to 'cyberwarfare'.

War targets tangible things, not abstractions

Fighting through computer networks is more convenient than putting boots on the ground. It allows easier deniable operations, it does not require a for-mal declaration of a parliament to wage war, it does not force a prime min-ister to take the blame for the national flag-covered coffins coming home. However, this kind of warfare is no less lethal than a conflict fought with bullets, bombs, and missiles.

Governments increased their dependence on privately owned technolo-gies in the military domain. The business practices of the digital technolo-gies sector weakened the robustness of the basic infrastructures of which a modern country is made. Our daily life is plagued by flawed 'interconnected' appliances, including essential things such as cars and medical devices. They always wait for the next patch to fix 'a known issue'.

The building of this Colossus of Rhodes made it easier for an attacker—be it a criminal or a State-sponsored entity—to exploit the vulnerabilities of digital technologies for fighting purposes. We still have not reached the peak of the consequences caused by a coordinated attack against the critical infra-structures and the 'ordinary' systems that govern our activities. However, we may get a (not so rough) idea by looking at what happens if the tube or the electricity supplies stops for a few hours. The 2019 service disruption of the London Tube Jubilee Line and Docklands Light Railway caused by climate change protesters[39] or the power outage that in 2012 affected about 620 million of people in India[40] are but two of the many possible exam-ples of what could happen if the disruption results from a planned hostile strategy.

A similar exercise can be performed with the systems that make the Big Internet work. A domain name is registered through a 'registrar'—a private company credited by ICANN to maintain the association between an IP number and an alphanumeric sequence, the domain. The registrar owns the key to the operational status of its client. If something happens to his domain records, even the most powerful country becomes unreachable.

Worse, if the registrar is a rogue—or is the victim of an illegal trespass—it is possible to reconfigure the domain name to point at a different resource on the network. All emails directed to president@bigcountry.com would find a different route, ending in the mailbox of the attacker. Customers of a bank find their accounts disabled and are asked to re-insert their passwords and confirmation PINS. VoIP (Voice-over-IP) calls are redirected through foreign switches, causing huge bills in favour of complacent companies located in lost (or too dangerous) parts of the world.

There is no need to articulate further the seriousness of the consequences caused just by a single human being in the right place at the right moment, behind a keyboard. However, it is crucial to understand that these scenarios—not fictional, by the way—are much smaller than the tip of the iceberg. It can hardly be sustained that these 'virtual' disasters happen in 'cyberspace', as well known to drivers locked out (or in) their Tesla because of a server outage that occurred in 2021.[41]

Moreover, there is nothing virtual in modern weapon systems once reserved for the Air Force, the Navy, and the Army's armoured divisions. Soldiers handle shoulder-fired weapons, assault carbines, and sniper rifles powered by augmented reality systems that make them more lethal.

ARCAS stands for *AI-Powered, Computerised Solution for Assault Rifles*. It makes it easier for a soldier to analyse a scenario and make decisions about engaging opponents. It is a system built around the concept of the assault rifle that allows soldiers to identify threats in advance, optimise firing trajectories, engage targets and have visual information on the weapon, and interact with the environment. In addition, the system allows the operator to receive information from the control room and other team members equipped with the same tool. Everything is visually communicated through a visor in the helmet. Like in video games, images on the helmet's visor may look like a shapeless multicoloured humanoid. However, they are nothing short of real. Deadly real. They fight back with lead bullets, if not with worse ordnances. Even the civil market has a similar videogame-like—although lethal—gadget. The Russian Kalashnikov MP-155 is online-ready. It allows real-time shooting session stream in a first-person field of view. When the hit blows, it does not happen in cyberspace.

The military made a looser use of the cyber- prefix. 'cyberspace' is routinely used with 'cybernetics', making it more complicated to make sense of this semantic overlapping. Be that as it may, it did not happen just because of the need to collectively name a battlefield. It was instrumental in creating a different area of public policy to be governed separately.

Stripped of these public policy implications, the 'cyberdomain' where 'cyberwarfare' is waged is but a metaphor to identify collectively a set of targets to attack or defend and who is supposed to do it. 'Critical infrastructures' is a more apt legal category recently introduced in the EU and national pieces of legislation. It identifies those physical components of a country's 'nervous system' whose security must be protected at all costs. Hardly a separate 'space'.

cyberspace as a metaphor

One may wonder why it is so important to have a clear definition of the words in the military and other domains. At the end of the day, 'cyberwhatever' is just the usual shortcut to describe 'this computer thing'. Let us be content with that and move over. Unfortunately, it is not possible.

Those branches of human knowledge that do not need to define clearly the object of their investigation can afford the luxury of being loose. Others—such as mathematics, medicine, and law—cannot. In the case of quantitative sciences, definitions are essential to demonstrate hypotheses. In law, the precise meaning of a word is a matter of freedom and, in some jurisdictions, life and death.

It has been established that when a user interacts through electronic communication service, he is not 'entering a space'. He is corresponding with somebody else.

Each participant in the communication flow stays where he is and, without moving, exchanges messages with his counterpart. Regardless of the underlying technicalities, be they an old-fashioned *FidoNet* relay system or an Internet-based instant messaging platform, the interaction between individuals is consistent with the legal protection granted in all Western jurisdictions for decades. Often at the Constitutional level, correspondence (the message itself) and communication (the exchange of message) are protected by a right to secrecy and confidentiality that only a court warrant can break. Once again, a network infrastructure, as a whole, is a *communication* tool, not a *space*.

> cyberspace is not an actual physical space available for high-tech exploration, like outer space, but rather more like the space between our ears, a conceptual arena in which we 'move' around and accomplish things by 'visiting' or 'going to' sites, among other things, without physically leaving our living rooms, offices, or command centres. The fact that we tend to think of cyberspace as a space we can move through or inhabit reflects the extent to which we 'place' ourselves within it, the extent to which we perceive ourselves as located within the system rather than as looking on at its operation from a distance. The equation of 'virtual worlds' and 'virtual meeting spaces' with physical space is so natural to many of us that it is perhaps harder to remember the metaphoric nature of this 'space' than it is to accept it as a literal description.[42]

According to the doctrine that advocates for cyberspace as a legal metaphor, though, its existence depends on the *interaction* between a human being and the huge apparatus of wires, chips, and electricity of which a network is made, as well as the interaction among human beings *through* a networked communication system. Therefore—so the theory goes—people live in a *psychological* or *social space*: that space is the cyberspace.

These two claims have already been proven factually incorrect. However, at least at first sight, cyberspace could be considered useful as a metaphor in the legal context.

The academic debate about the legal meaning of this literary metaphor witnesses how challenging the attempt is.

> The appropriate role of metaphor in cyberlaw, and particularly of place- and space-based metaphors for the Internet and its constituent nodes and networks, is hotly contested. The 'cyberspace' metaphor, which originated in science fiction, first migrated into legal discourse via the work of academic commentators who advanced unabashedly exceptionalist arguments about the nature and appropriate legal treatment of Internet-based activities. Although these arguments did not go unchallenged, the claim that cyberspace is deeply and essentially different from 'real space' was a compelling one for many scholars. Even though conventional wisdom now rejects the initial exceptionalist claim that cyberspace is inherently more free than 'real space,' the belief that it is nonetheless inherently different has persisted.[43]

The resort to a spatial metaphor, it is said, comes from the practical necessity of describing in layman's terms the technicalities involved in computer and telecommunication services. Once again, few changed from the publication, dating back to 2003, of the paper from which the following quote is extracted.

> The CYBERSPACE AS PLACE metaphor is also clearly evident in legal material. There are now numerous cases that have decided issues relating to the Internet and the Web. In keeping with the observation of the use of spatial terms in lay speech ... This process of mapping the physical onto the virtual is pervasive in legal academic discourse, judicial pronouncements, and legislative enactments.[44]

Metaphors in legal interpretation operate as a Trojan Horse—a metaphor!—through which affect the legal thinking and, finally, the 'real' world.

If metaphors are so dangerous—or challenging to handle with proper care—should we ban them from legal thinking and the law drafting process?

Of course, the answer is negative. However, that does not imply that all metaphors should be accepted at face value without carefully assessing their usefulness.

A purely positivistic approach to legal theory and interpretation would challenge the use of metaphors.

Like in a computer programme—where each variable has its definition— legal definitions should have only one meaning, directly connected with the fact that they ought to regulate.

> The myth-prejudice of literal interpretation is perhaps one of the most ideologically resistant metaphors to critical scrutiny: with its call for simplification, with its aiming at a good and uncontaminated source of meaning in a remote act performed by someone else, the call for neutralising the deciding subjectivity satisfies the desire to escape from freedom that broods in every jurist. Now, from a hermeneutical point of view, it is evident that literal interpretation literally does not exist. The sequence of l-e-t-t-e-r-s does not produce meaning, nor does it evoke it. Normative language is not a mosaic, but an organism. To examine individual trees by refusing to see the forest is to deny that the choice made is evaluative, ideological or strategic. [45]

However, the approach inspired by the Illuministic utopia—and reinforced by issues implied by AI-based ruling—has proven ineffective. Indeed, metaphors are by long time an essential component of legal interpretation. They are part of the legal thinking in all its epiphanies.

A closing argument must convey meaning to the jury. A ruling must tell the appellate court that the first judge did not make a mistake, and the appeal must be rejected. A contract must elucidate the actual will of the parties. Resorting to the verbatim meaning of the words might not suffice, particularly when the matter involves knowledge outside the legal field. They influence how we—at first—and our counterparts, secondly, understand a fact. Metaphors are also instrumental in filling the knowledge gap when confronting a situation never before faced or never analysed from a specific perspective. Metaphors are a gateway between the mind and reality. This is what makes them useful in psychotherapy methods such as Milton Erikson's hypnosis. However, when it comes to law and rights, it does not matter if a legal metaphor is but a weapon of the rhetorical arsenal of a prosecutor or an essential component of our cognitive processes. What matters is whether or not there is an alternative to their use.

Wielding Occam's Razor, rather than arguing about cyberspace's metaphorical existence in terms of a separate space or an autonomous legal entity, it makes more sense to reframe the initial question as follows: if cyberspace is a metaphor, is it useful to solve a problem that the current legal theory cannot address?

Before answering the question, however, it is necessary to address the last possibility: that cyberspace is *fictional* as in *legal fiction*.

cyberspace as a legal fiction

It is not always easy to tell a metaphor from legal fiction. In terms of definition, the goal seems attainable. When made operational, though, it becomes challenging.

A metaphor is about understanding through similarity and continuity. It explains the unknown through what it is (supposedly) known. A legal fiction—*fictio juris*—has nothing to do with reality. It is an exposed lie—a true false—publicly known as such but valuable to attain a regulatory result.

A legal fiction is instrumental—like in the case of euthanasia—in managing issues affecting the core values of a social group when the Parliament does not legislate on the matter.

> Famous, but just 'exceptional', is the legal 'fiction' used by the Court of Appeal of Milan to acquit the husband who had deliberately disconnected the machines that kept his wife alive, albeit in a desperate and irreversible condition. The judge, with a probably hazardous motivation—beyond what may be the moral reasons of the case and of the decision—did not consider ascertained the vital state of the woman 'in the period of time between the last monitoring and the moment of extubation'; in substance, as has been effectively pointed out, he chose 'to presume that the woman would have (already) ceased to live'.[46]

In other cases, the *fictio* is necessary to adapt the law *adelante, con juicio*— fast, but cautiously.

> Legal fiction is capable of performing a dual function: one heuristic, the other performative ... The fictio iuris is, in fact, brought into play by constitutional law when, on the one hand, there is a need to adopt concepts that respond to new situations, but on the other hand there remains a need to refer to those that already exist. Fiction gives the law a way of setting in motion a complex manoeuvre of 'conservative change'.[47]

Would a similar interpretative process work for cyberspace? Should we make it legally 'real' even if it is not?

Thinking of cyberspace as a legal fiction might have a few advantages. It tells apart literature from the law. It makes it easier to create specific rules without the need to be coherent with other doctrines. For instance, 'metaverse purchases' could be subjected to a '*sui generis*' ownership that is in between the real propriety and usage licence rights.

Like metaphors, also legal fictions should be handled with care as they can disrupt a legal system. A way to ascertain the fitness of a legal fiction is a three-step process in which it should be investigated

> Whether or not the fiction (1) is labelled explicitly as a fiction; (2) rests on complete factual falsity instead of reduction of evidentiary proof; or (3) allows the court to reach a result consistent with well-established legal or other social values.[48]

According to this test, as far as cyberspace is concerned, the second option is the most relevant.

> Some legal fictions rest upon complete factual falsity, such that everyone knows that it is false and no one is deceived by its falsity. ... The legal fiction of corporation as a person is another example. In that case, everyone knows corporations are not human beings. ... The complete factual falsity serves as a reminder of the doctrine's fictional nature because everyone knows it to be false. The risk that anyone would be deceived by the fiction is small because of how humans think.[49]

Among the many fictions belonging to law, the one associated with 'legal person', the *persona ficta*, plays an essential role in the analysis of the relationship between cyberspace and digital rights.

Notwithstanding its core importance for business and commercial law, it has faced harsh criticism. Over time, important Anglo-Saxon scholars of law and theory of the State, such as Coke, Hobbes, and Locke, were uncomfortable with the idea that there could be a *person* that is not *human*. In the course of time, the importance of the legal person has become paramount. It would be utterly challenging to think of a legal system that would not use it.

> It is unreasonable to attempt to erase from the legal lexicon concepts such as the legal person, the incorporation of a right in a title of credit, or the qualification of intellectual works, industrial inventions and distinctive signs as immaterial goods. We would deprive ourselves of practical verbal syntheses and would have to replace them with long and complicated speeches. However, it is just as unreasonable to take the metaphor seriously and proclaim that legal persons are always and for all intents and purposes persons, securities are things, and intangible assets are material goods.[50]

However, implying that also *non*-humans (such as companies and other entities alike) could inhabit the legal world opens the border to other kinds of person, namely, the artificial ones. The advocated inclusion of AI into the category of 'person' aims at shaping reality rather than setting it straight.

The apparent falsity of the legal person allows for its effective use in legal practice. As said, nobody thinks of a corporation as a 'natural person', therefore making the fiction works as a tool to shape specific interests of the society. However, when, like in the case of AI, the falsity of the legal fiction is purposely made disappear, it becomes useless. The very same conclusion can be extended to cyberspace.

Is cyberspace useful in law?

As it has already been elucidated, the technology of information sector is subjected to various pieces of legislation: patents, copyright, license and service agreements, consumer protection, communication, market and data protection regulations, rule of evidence, and national security legislation. Also, providing online services and selling the tools to use them is a highly regulated sector.

The same is valid from the point of view of the individual. A consumer is entitled to file a complaint against an e-commerce giant, and a subscriber has the right to challenge the demonetisation of his content unilaterally enforced by a content-sharing platform. An individual can claim the infringement of his right to privacy when monitored in the search for sensitive content or free speech because of the 'censorship' of an alleged hate-igniting post on a publicly available instant messaging platform. One may argue on the merit of specific legislative choices such as the latitude of investigative powers or the validity of online service terms and conditions. On the other hand, a complaint might target the lack of *enforceable* remedies for the weaker party. Indeed, when it is necessary to start an arbitration, file a legal complaint, or initiate a criminal investigation, the effectiveness of available legal instruments decreases.

Would a customer invest substantial money to start a legal battle in a foreign jurisdiction to recover a few hundred Euros? Would a national public prosecutor invest time and human resources to investigate an alien outside its reach because of petty computer hacking? Is a specific legal community learned enough to handle such kinds of claims? Sometimes—mostly in high-profile cases—it happens; more often, when the claims are small or of a little general interest, it does not. Be that as it may, it is apparent that the lack of legal remedies is not an obstacle to law enforcement in private and State-related affairs. cyberspace—be it a metaphor or a legal fiction—does not offer a substantial advantage in regulating how the technology of information should be used. The same conclusion is valid in the grey area of national security and international affairs, where law and politics blend in a way that makes it impossible to tell one from the other.

cyberspace and digital rights

Another question waiting for an answer is whether cyberspace and digital rights are so intertwined that by removing the first part of the equation, the second disappears.

This question will be addressed in the following chapter that also tries to ascertain what is the nature of digital rights and, before that, if they actually exist in the legal domain.

Notes

1 Hill 2019:7.
2 Wiener 1961: 54–54.
3 Bethke, Bruce, 'Cyberpunk', in *Amazing Science Fiction Stories*, Volume 57, Number 4, November 1983.
4 Bethke, Bruce, *Cyberpunk, a short story*, December 1997 http://www.infinityplus .co.uk/stories/cpunk.htm (visited 12 March 2022).
5 Gibson 1984:69.
6 Gibson, William, *LIVE from the NYPL*, 16 July 2013, https://youtu.be/ae3z7O-e3XF4 (visited 4 January 2022).
7 Singel, Ryan, 'Check the Hype -- There's No Such Thing As 'Cyber'', *Wired* online edition 26 March 2010, https://www.wired.com/2010/03/cyber-hype/ (visited 4 January 2022).
8 Levy 1984:245.
9 Monti-Wacks 2020:89.
10 Alberts, Oldenziel 2014:4.
11 Alberts, Oldenziel 2014: *ibidem*.
12 Nossiter, A., Sanger, D., *Hackers Came, but the French Were Prepared*, The New York Times, 9 May 2017, https://www.nytimes.com/2017/05/09/world/europe/ hackers-came-but-the-french-were-prepared.html, visited 17 March 2022.
13 Various, *International scenes*, Phrack #64 file 15, 27 May 2007 http://phrack.org /issues/64/17.html visited 15 March 2022.
14 Schmid, Gutmann 1999.
15 Stoll 1989.
16 Chiccarelli-Monti 2011.
17 Monti-Wacks 2021:105.
18 Barlow, John Perry, *A Declaration of the Independence of cyberspace*, 8 February 1996 https://www.eff.org/cyberspace-independence (visited 5 January 2022).
19 Turner 2008: 4.
20 Jennings, Tom et al., *FidoNet History and Operation*, 8 February 1985 http:// www.olografix.org/gubi/estate/archivio/fido/fido.htm visited 17 March 2022.
21 Lawler, Richard. 'The first NBA broadcast rendered with volumetric video puts basketball in the uncanny valley'. *The Verge* 16 March 2022 https://www .theverge.com/2022/3/16/22982243/nets-mavericks-espn-nba-volumetric-video -canon visited 20 March 2022.
22 Baraniuk, Chris 'China's Xinhua agency unveils AI news presenter'. *BBC News Tech* 8 November 2018 https://www.bbc.com/news/technology-46136504 visited 20 March 2022.
23 Smith, Hannah, Mansted, Katherine, 'Weaponised deep fakes: National security and democracy'. *Australian Strategic Policy Institute Policy Brief* Report 28/2020 https://www.jstor.org/stable/resrep25129.1?seq=1 visited 20 March 2022.

24 D'Angelo, Emanuele. *Marco Verratti has bought an island in the metaverse* 17 February 2022 https://www.nssmag.com/en/sports/28996/marco-verratti -island-metaverse visited 25 March 2022.

25 Erdly Catherine, 'Fashion Embraces The Metaverse: Will 15% Of Our Wardrobe Become Digital?' *Forbes* 6 March 2022 https://www.forbes.com/sites/cath- erineerdly/2022/03/06/fashion-embraces-the-metaversewill-15-of-our-wardrobe -become-digital/?sh=34abc18f5921 visited 20 March 2022.

26 Ludlow 1996:507.

27 RIPE NCC in Europe, APNIC in the Asia-Pacific, LACNIC in Latin America, LACNIC, AFRINIC in Africa, ARIN in North America, Canada and the Caribbean.

28 Monti, Andrea, 'Salvare Internet dai venti di guerra', *Wired.it* 14 march 2022 https://www.wired.it/article/Internet-venti-guerra-russia-ucraina/ (visited 14 march 2022).

29 US Supreme Court, *Strassheim v. Daily*, 221 U.S. 280 (1911).

30 Personal interview with Japanese High-Tech Law expert Takahashi Ikuo, 15 March 2022.

31 最高裁判所Case 2018 (A) 1381, verdict issued on 01 February 2021, https:// www.courts.go.jp/app/hanrei_en/detail?id=1811 (visited 15 March 2022).

32 UK Crown Prosecutor Service – Legal Guidance – Jurisdiction https://www.cps .gov.uk/legal-guidance/jurisdiction (visited 10 March 2022).

33 Berg, Terrence 'State Criminal Jurisdiction in cyberspace: Is There a Sheriff on the Electronic Frontier?' in *Michigan Bar Journal* vol. 79 n. 6 June 2000 https:// www.michbar.org/journal/Details/State-Criminal-Jurisdiction-in-cyberspace-Is -There-a-Sheriff-on-the-Electronic-Frontier?ArticleID=94 (visited 10 March 2022).

34 Angius, Raffaele, 'Perché il Progetto Gutenberg sarà sotto sequestro per sempre', *Wired.it* 30 June 2020 https://www.wired.it/Internet/web/2020/06/30/progetto -gutenberg-sequestro/ visited 15 March 2022.

35 US Court of Appeals for the Fifth Circuit - 36 F.3d 457 (5th Cir. 1994) *Steve Jackson Games, Incorporated, et al., Plaintiffs-appellants, v. United States Secret Service, et al., Defendants, United States Secret Service and United States of America, defendants-appellees.*

36 Europol, 'Five affiliates to Sodinokibi/REvil unplugged', 8 November 2021 https:// www.europol.europa.eu/media-press/newsroom/news/five-affiliates-to-sodinok- ibi/revil-unplugged

37 The United States Department of Justice – Office of Public Affairs, 'Ukrainian Arrested and Charged with Ransomware Attack on Kaseya', 8 November 2021 https://www.justice.gov/opa/pr/ukrainian-arrested-and-charged-ransom- ware-attack-kaseya visited 15 March 2022.

38 Monti, Andrea, 'Il contrasto ai ransomware è ancora una questione di diritto', in *Formiche.net* 10 November 2021 https://formiche.net/2021/11/ransomware -diritto-operazioni-militari-sicurezza/ visited 16 March 2022. English translation by Andrea Monti.

39 BBC, 'Extinction Rebellion protesters dragged from Tube train roof', *BBC News* 17 October 2019, https://www.bbc.com/news/uk-england-london-50079716 visited 18 March 2022.

40 Pidd, Helen, 'India blackouts leave 700 million without power', *The Guardian* 31 July 2012, https://www.theguardian.com/world/2012/jul/31/india-blackout -electricity-power-cuts visited 18 March 2022.

41 Lambert, Fred, 'Tesla suffers worldwide app server outage, owners can't con-
    nect to their cars (update: back)' Electrek 19 November 2021 https://electrek
    .co/2021/11/19/tesla-suffers-nationwide-app-server-outage-owners-cant-connect
    -cars/ visited 19 March 2022.
42 Lapointe, Adriane, 'When good metaphors go bad: The Metaphoric 'Branding'
    of cyberspace', 9 September 2011 https://www.csis.org/analysis/when-good-met-
    aphors-go-bad-metaphoric-branding-cyberspace (visited 12 March 2022).
43 Cohen 2007:210–211.
44 Hunter 2003:474.
45 Vespaziani 2009:3.
46 D'Aloia, Antonio. 2012, Eutanasia (Dir. Cost), in Enciclopedia del *Diritto*,
    Milan-IT, Giuffrè.
47 Olivito, Elisa 2013: 273–275.
48 Leonhard 2017:388.
49 Leonhard 2017:403–404.
50 Galgano 2010:22.

2

THE QUEST FOR DIGITAL RIGHTS

This chapter attempts to show how the legal and conceptual limitations of the notion of 'cyberspace' affected the so-called 'digital rights'. Next, it shows how the business model of Big Tech, the rise of supra-national entities and the cultish attitude towards 'globalised rights' are progressively disbanding the traditional role of law. Moreover, it questions the conceptual autonomy of digital rights. It concludes that—at the very best—digital rights can work as an 'umbrella word' instead of a legal category.

It is a well-established fact that Big Tech's obsession with collecting data led to business models based on the *gratis* ruse and, later, on the massive scraping of publicly available information for business, political, social, and market intelligence as well as AI training. The dimension of this phenomenon is so paramount that it originated the definition of 'data economy' and, consequently, data-oriented pieces of legislation. Many countries—including China—set limits to the use of data about individuals. The EU went so far as to acknowledge personal data protection as a fundamental right.

Data-oriented pieces of legislation impose companies challenging duties and heavy fines in case of infringement of the relevant provisions. Data transfers towards 'unsafe' countries— such as the USA, from an EU perspective—are forbidden. Data subjects have the right to be informed about the data lifecycle and even to object to the processing. Data controllers must operate in strict compliance with data-subject consent and invest significant money to protect personal information. Courts and independent authorities exert strict control over the misuse of data.

The reality, though, tells a different story.

A new set of social rites defined and affected by business practice reduces the effectiveness of legal formalities. Data transfers, even those of critical nature, continues unhindered. 'Isolation capitalism' turned social rites and individual creeds into a faster and more efficient substitute for law as a tool for social behaviour regulation. Therefore, those who dictate social rites rule the society.

DOI: 10.4324/9781003373636-2

Instant social justice—sometimes in the form of public outrage tides known as 'shitstorms'—is done at a speed that sometimes achieves in a short timeframe more than a legal action does in years.

It has been known for decades that *free* does not always mean *gratis*. Data subjects are submerged by endless 'privacy policies', kindergarten-grade 'icons' and banners. These legal forms are routinely skipped to quickly satisfy the feverish need to check if a new 'like' is added to a post or a picture. One can enjoy the power of 'being in control' by filling his home with remotely controlled furniture—IoT's domotic—and voice-operated 'personal assistants', being careless about 'who' is actually controlling 'who'. The same is true for cars and transportation. Small businesses, big companies, and civil services are 'going in the Cloud', thus putting a significant part of their operational capabilities in the hand of Big Tech—and at miscreants' reach.

Ill-conceived and poorly implemented statutes on 'digital rights' induced in individuals a sort of auto-immune reaction against their own rights. The former have become a bureaucratic encumbrance of which getting rid to satisfy as fast as possible is the (induced) need of the moment or 'moving to the next level'.

It is still too early to tell what is going to happen with the metaverse and other fast-growing gimmicks such as cryptocurrencies and NFTs. However, there are signs of a general loss of interest in reclaiming individual rights. People are ready to expose their private life, personal beliefs, and business activity or accept substantial limitations with a click of a mouse—or a gesture on a smartphone. If withdrawing a right becomes easy, a right is easily withdrawn. When it happens, rights become currencies that can be traded in exchange for whatever the market has to offer. The marketplace where 'digital rights' are traded is in 'cyberspace' where 'ordinary' rules do not apply. Each individual is a king, and life can be lived 'differently'. This is why cyberspace is essential to digital rights. They are almost inescapably associated, so it becomes challenging to think of the former without the latter.

Chapter 1 has demonstrated that cyberspace does not exist; it is neither a fiction nor a legally valuable metaphor to regulate the technology of information. Nonetheless, it does not cease to affect the legal debate about rights and technologies negatively. This is true, in particular, when digital rights come on stage.

What are digital rights made of?

In this regard, two are the questions on the floor: is there such thing as 'digital rights'? If so, would digital rights continue to stand even half-legged when disconnected from cyberspace?

The starting point is to distil the essence of digital rights—hence, what these words stand for and in which relationship they are, or might be, with 'cyberspace'.

> Cyber-rights recognise the right of individuals to access, use, create and publish digital media, and the right of access to the computers, electronic devices and telecommunications networks necessary to exercise them. ... In 1996, in an article entitled *A Declaration of the Independence of Cyberspace*, Barlow highlighted the discrepancy between the fundamental rights enshrined in the US Constitution and the violation of citizens' rights on the Internet. [1]

The following citation, coming like the former from the website of a multinational energy sector company, is an example of the confusion affecting the commonly accepted narrative about digital rights.

> In the era of digitalisation, law needs to be adapted to protect and safeguard fundamental rights. Digital rights, closely linked to freedom of expression and privacy, are those that allow people to access, use, create and publish digital media, as well as access and use computers, other electronic devices and communications networks. Digital technologies are transforming the way basic rights such as freedom of expression and access to information are exercised, protected and violated, and are also leading to the recognition of new rights. The law is therefore adapting to this new era with the development of digital rights and digital citizenship, allowing and regulating access to online information in a secure and transparent manner.[2]

The webpage goes on to acknowledge the lack of consensus at the international level on a shared definition of digital rights. Broadly speaking, though, it says it is possible to draw a safelist. The list should include universal and equal access, freedom of expression, information and communication, privacy and data protection, right to anonymity, right to be forgotten, protection of minors, intellectual property, 'digital will', and right to disconnection.

That would not have been a significant issue if this loose definition of digital rights were limited to a customer engagement-oriented media strategy. Unfortunately, it is not the case. Adopting fideistic categories in the law-making process affected public policy design and its implementation in statutes. Moreover, big companies are shaping the content of 'digital' rights in pursuing their strategies.

In the last 30 years, several Internet-related 'declarations', 'charters', or 'frameworks' flourished, addressing issues such as gender equality, sustainable development, cultural diversity, science, education, and accountability.[3] Last but not least, in January 2022, the European Commission endorsed a similar view concerning digital rights based on similar assumptions.[4] To the usual narrative (access, privacy, etc.), the EC adds rights such as 'interaction with algorithms and artificial intelligence systems', 'online empowering', and 'digital identity'.

Such a list exposes the main problem affecting the idea of digital rights: confusion.

Some of its elements already exist as a legal right or can be derived from existing statutes. Others are essentially a rose by another name or a mere statement about what should be acknowledged as a legal right without an actual public debate. That exacerbates the disconnection of rights from society. They are less and less defined by a grassroots domestic public debate and more and more determined at a political, supra-national level by various political organisations or transnational groups worshipping ideologies or creeds.

Because of their direct interconnection with the technologies of information and the 'borderless nature of the Internet' mantra, digital rights are an obvious candidate to become the flag of these movements. As much as they lay on opposing fronts, supra-national organisations and movements of various allegiance claim a vested interest in 'digital rights' to achieve their goals.

As in the case of cyberspace, such confusion comes from conceptual mistakes exacerbated by the peruse of the 'digital' adjective.

> While human rights have been more clearly defined through the UN Declaration of Human Rights (UDHR) ... the same cannot be said for the terms 'digital', 'technology', or the 'internet'. In unpacking these terms, we'll find the interpretations vary much more widely. For example, the term digital is often conflated with online or the Internet. But not everything digital is always connected to the Internet. Biometric data, such as facial recognition and fingerprint checking at border crossings, is one example of how the digital may not be online or connected to the Internet. ... Another pair of terms that often get mixed up is 'real' and 'virtual', which imply that physical interactions are more 'real' than digital, 'virtual' interactions. But if we're making that assumption, are we saying that all digital interactions are not real? And what is the implication of this assumption? Does it imply that 'virtual' spaces and online harassment are not 'real'? And, consequently, are all physical interactions always real? Is the boundary between online and offline always clearly defined, or do they influence and implicate each other?[5]

As much as this latter position rightly points out some consequences of a superficial resort to *cliché* in dealing with digital rights, it is still flawed by the assumption that 'offline' and 'online' are two different, equally real domains.

Over three decades are gone, and cyberspace still haunts (digital) rights like an evil spirit.

From society to law or vice versa?

Digital rights are commonly associated with 'human rights', 'civil rights', 'individual rights', or 'fundamental rights' in a 'cyber' attire. Indeed, in a colloquial dimension, these latter definitions are interchangeable. Unfortunately, equal liberty is not available in a legal context, where it is necessary to avoid as many synonyms or words as possible with partially superimposable meanings. That would be essential, particularly in a continental legal system where rights are only those formally acknowledged by the law or indirectly through judicial interpretation.

However, challenging digital rights and digital law concepts requires taking a stand in the endless debate about a fundamental question: what is law?

> In very broad terms, two principal answers have been given to this deceptively simple question. On the one hand, is the view that law consists of a set of universal moral principles in accordance with nature. ... For so-called legal positivists, on the other hand, law is nothing more than a collection of valid rules, commands or norms that may lack any moral content. ... Other perceives the las as fundamentally a vehicle for the protection of individual rights ... Few believe that law can be divorced from its social content.[6]

As the late Piero Angela, a very well-known Italian scientific journalist said,[7] a raise of hands does not decide the speed of light. By contrast, telling what substantiate laws and rights requires, to say the least, undoing a tangled net of intertwined social creeds, political allegiances and market dynamics. Moreover, the question must admit more than one and only answer; otherwise, the law would become a matter of faith, not logic or, more precisely, anthropology. Still, for this book, rather than taking a side in this millennial-enduring argument, it is more pragmatic to acknowledge what law and rights are for.

> It is easy, especially for lawyers, to exaggerate the significance of the law. Yet history teaches that the law is an essential force in facilitating human progress. This is no small achievement. ... If we are to survive the calamities that await us, if civilized values and justice are to prevail and endure, the law is surely indispensable.[8]

Regardless of their source—a truth revealed by divine powers or imposition by secular authorities—law and rights are instrumental in handling different views of the world held by various components of a society. They act as a proxy to mitigate—or suppress—the social conflict that would inevitably arise from a confrontation among multiple creeds. They are necessary *ne cives ad arma ruant*—to avoid citizens taking the law into their own hands. Also, they are a necessary tool to smooth the rough edges of individuals' social bearing: as Macrobius used to say, *leges bonae ex malis moribus procreantur*—good laws come from bad behaviours. Law and rights are also instrumental to the self-preservation of power—be it that of a king, a government, a country, or a company.

In synthesis, they 'freeze' the political mediation among different ethical, social, and economic *zeitgeists* in a binding agreement and keep the social order steady. Depending on the ideological allegiance of a country at a given time, the pendulum swings continuously between the two extremes. External factors might force authoritarian regimes to release their stranglehold and pass (quasi)democratic reforms. In the name of the 'greater good' or parochial interests, democratic countries could step back from the altar of freedom and crack down on citizens' rights.

Regardless of ethics being an explicit or hidden attribute of the ruling, what tells a democracy is precisely the absence of a 'superior', State-imposed moral. All morals compete against each other, and the law seals mediation.

Looking at law and rights as social tools bypasses the (post) Kelsenian, valueless approach. A democratic system accounts for a different set of moral values as soon as those who support them are strong enough to be heard from the parliament or get a seat. Regardless of individual opinions on a given issue, divorce, abortion—and now the environment—single beliefs count nothing until they become shared by a significant number of people or a well-organised and equipped minority, strong enough to force the ruling group(s) into a political negotiation.

This approach challenges the notion that the State is an 'absolute idea' because, if so, that would imply the existence of but one set of moral values (usually that of the rulers) grounding the law. In other words, rules are (or should be) morally grounded. However, the notion that only a single set of abstract moral values is embodied in the laws should be rejected.

A disturbing sign of what might happens if, by contrast, State-defined ethics takes over is the EU's decision to set rules for AI.[9] Anticipating what will be told in the concerned chapter, a 'between the lines' reading of this proposal exposes the Trojan Horse role played by a vague definition of 'digital rights' in disrupting the function of law and the rule of law itself.

The rule of law fosters social evolution and integration because it makes it happen the ethical mediation between ruling parties and those who are not (yet) in power. It is based on the shared assumption that statutes must also be abided by the State. It separates democracy from theocracy or—that is the same—tyranny. In a (religious or secular) theocracy, only one set of moral tenets is embodied in laws. No matter how gentle and human-centric its principles are, a theocratic system is not democratic. Differences are tolerated, not accepted and just up to a threshold after which they are obliterated.

However, the rule of law is not a magical spell whose enchantment prevents authoritarian regimes—or privileged actors of the international community—from cracking down on citizens 'in the name of law'.

> The metamorphosis of an idea into a ritualistic incantation is a sign of trouble. Nor is the rhetorical exploitation of the rule of law the monopoly of politicians; it pervades international declarations and pious expressions of support for freedom and anxiety about injustice. And it affords rebarbative regimes a convenient means by which to camouflage authoritarian control as they simultaneously flaunt and flout the values of this democratic ideal.[10]

Should the rule of law be considered only from a formal legality point of view? Would it be more efficient to protect the people's rights to give the rule of law ethical flesh and bones? The debate is longstanding and still open.

The main flaw of a purely formal idea of the rule of law is that it can quickly become rule by law. One example, among many, is the transparency statutes enacted in China. They are instrumental in strengthening the grip of the Communist Party on its internal structure rather than being a way to let citizens cross the doors of the palace of power:

> by adopting a law-based administrative process, the Chinese government appears to have sought closer control of the activities of civil servants rather than granting its citizens an instrument to facilitate democratic participation in the administrative life of the country.[11]

Western democracies, however, are not immune from this temptation. They try to bury it under thick layers of norms and regulations. They use rhetoric, nudging, and other consent manufacturing techniques to preserve the exteriority of compliance with the rule of law. In the reality of the political arena, they sacrifice this principle on the altar of political struggles.

The law itself becomes an exception.

Law and/as an exception

The rule of law reaches its limits when the dialogue is no more possible (or allowed) and politics continues in the form of riots and, as von Clausewitz said, armed conflicts. As counterintuitive as it might seem, however, even in times of war, whether formally declared or not, the rule of law still acts as a regulator.

38

Like all law, the international law relating to armed conflicts and the use of force has always been somewhat vague and ambiguous; and, to a degree, this can be seen as a virtue rather than a vice in a system that lacks a judiciary and a reliable enforcement mechanism. Up to a point, legal vagueness and ambiguity give states face-saving ways to avoid direct conflict, enabling them to 'look the other way' if a particular state occasionally engages in challenging but not manifestly illegal behavior. Vagueness and ambiguity can also sometimes offer an efficient way for consensus-based changes in the law: for instance, amending the language of international treaties might be cumbersome or impossible, but some degree of vagueness and ambiguity in treaty language can permit shared interpretations to be modified over time, thus providing the community of states with a relatively simple 'backdoor' means of changing the effect of a treaty.

Beyond a certain point, however, vagueness and ambiguity are crippling. When key international law concepts and categories lose all fixed meaning, consensus breaks down about how to evaluate state behavior; and although legal rules may continue to exist on paper, they no longer do much to ensure that states will behave in a predictable, nonarbitrary fashion.[12]

When an emergency happens, be it real or not, it is often claimed that the rule of law should concede to the 'state of exception'. In a state of exception, powers-that-be rule arbitrarily according to their needs. Extra-legal rulesets override the lawful exercise of power. Any connection with the social contract, the delegation of power through representation, and other signs of a democratic regime are lost.

As Agamben points out,[13] this is what happened during the Nazi rise in pre-WWII Germany and in different times and jurisdictions in the decades to come.

However, choices affecting the existence itself of a country in dire moments—such as a war declaration or temporary limitation of fundamental freedoms because of pandemics—can (and should) be taken only through a transparent process, in strict compliance with laws and parliamentary procedures. Rules must be abided by, and if they are not fit for the job, they should be amended to make them work. Every democratic constitution contains safety mechanisms to ensure that parliaments and executives can issue emergency regulations in case of need. Until a State exists, by definition, no emergency can be handled by infringing (rule of) law. Therefore, it is neither possible nor correct to equate a state of emergency and a state of exception. A *fortiori*, it should not be possible to derive the latter from the former. Indeed, a state of emergency presupposes the permanence of the rule of law, while a state of exception is 'a suspension of the juridical order itself, it defines law's threshold or limit concept'.[14] A state of exception is intrinsically connected with a regime change, whether or not temporary and/or achieved by force.

There is, however, another option to consider.

During an emergency, so goes the *vulgata*, there is no time to think, no time to debate and—neither—to defer the decision to proper authorities following the 'ordinary' procedures. Due to this (non-demonstrated) assumption, the law is no longer the outcome of a constitutional process. It is made by those who can exert power in a given moment. There is no time to indulge in legal hairsplitting. It is necessary to do 'whatever it takes'.

That would be a blatant infringement of the rule of law. However, the expedient of calling for a moral duty, national security, or evanescent 'national interests' made look the disregard for the forms like necessary collateral damage. Using laws outside their scope and (formal) limits is not an irrelevant particular, though. Forms and procedures are as essential as the rights that a provision should protect or regulate. The disregard for the process demotes the rule of law to nothing more than a rhetorical figure of speech. The rule of law in itself—pun intended—becomes an exception.

Out of a Pavlovian reflex, every time a statute interferes with or blocks a particular desired course of action, it reveals the uneasiness of politics and politicians to consider rules and principles. However, the rule of law is neither a fetish nor a totem to worship as an epiphenomenon of a religious creed (and to be disregarded according to the moment's convenience). It has an efficient function and should be respected because it works and is necessary to survive a democratic rule. The fact that politicians try to circumvent it in all ways is a testament to its effectiveness.

Empirical evidence: pandemic and Ukrainian crisis

The 2020 Coronavirus pandemic and the 2022 Ukrainian crisis bring empirical confirmation of the idea that law itself can become an exception.

Nudging methods have been widely enforced to contain the circulation of the Coronavirus with mixed results. They made come true the longstanding concerns about nudging being a possible way to circumvent the parliamentary oversight over the executive.

> In particular, one needs to ask how much 'smart thinking' may be delegated to the executive power and what legal instruments should ensure the appropriate 'checks and balances' on the exercise of this newly formed governmental power. While it is not contended that behaviorally informed tools appear to be less coercive than conventional regulatory intervention, this does not make less cogent the need to ensure that these tools are subject to appropriate control

of public power while regulating citizens' behavior through persuasive, soft, and smart instruments.[15]

However, protests and unrests erupted in many countries were fuelled by the perception that vaccination rules—or the lack of them—were *unjust*. By contrast, 'vaccine believers' labelled those who did not want to take the sting as *morally despicable*, regardless of the motivation. A confrontation about facts became a matter of *faith* in a *creed*.

In places like Italy that did not impose (a general) mandatory vaccination, the public debate sat from the beginning on a 'moral ground'. It was aggravated by social networks' pervasiveness that radicalised confrontation and let 'crusaders' of one creed wage war against 'infidels' worshipping the blasphemy cult. Roles, of course, were exchanged according to the camp. At least in part, professional media too contributed to igniting confrontations. Having to be always on air, they lacked the resources to search and analyse an overwhelming quantity of events. They opened the dams and let a flood of opinions submerge hard facts.[16] In this confusing scenario, judicial rulings warned the presidency of the ministries' council to reconsider the de facto latitude self-given to its powers, nugated the role of ministries' FAQs as a binding source for the interpretation of COVID-19 provisions. Notwithstanding, nobody cared about what the courts said. There was an *emergency* to handle. With a similar approach, a poorly conceived 'right to privacy' fuelled by the delusional 'digital rights' narrative that sees a State as an 'enemy by default' heavily reduced the effectiveness of contact-tracing and collection of personal data to limit the contagion and support the search for a cure.

During the pandemic, the negative impact of digital rights was produced by the protests of a noisy, even if not majority, part of civil society. By contrast, in the Ukrainian crisis, it was the EU that played fast and loose by creatively imposing what can be called *reverse censorship*. Instead of banning somebody from *talk*ing, the EU prevented people from *listening* regardless of their capability to *understand* the message.

On 1 March 2022, the Council of the European Union adopted Regulation 350/2022 and Decision 351/2022 prohibiting broadcasters, Internet providers, and platforms from carrying contents delivered by *Russia Today* and *Sputnik*. The regulation was also meant to enforce web filtering through Internet and Access Service Providers. The two Russian media agencies were identified as critical elements of what the Council describes as a

systematic, international campaign of media manipulation and distortion of facts in order to enhance its strategy of destabilisation of its neighbouring countries and of the Union and its Member States.[17]

The rationale is explicit: it claims that Russian actors are committing hostile acts against the EU (a treaty, not a State, it is worth remembering) and its members. In less euphemistic words, the Council states that since Russia is attacking EU Members, it is necessary to stop it by imposing measures on *European* broadcast and Internet service providers and—finally—on the citizen.

It is not the subject of this book to analyse the legitimacy of decisions taken by the Council of EU on defence and national security and the compatibility of these decisions with the European treaties.[18] What matters is that censorship was enforced by expanding the web blocking method, initially imposed by domestic courts to counter the online circulation of illegal content. For some time, this choice of public policy has been considered questionable because instead of hitting the perpetrators (those who circulate and those who use illegal content), it attributes duties and liabilities to neutral entities—Internet Service Providers—that they should not have. Well before these latter statutes, web filtering had become *jus receptum*.

A Council Regulation might not be the right legislative instrument to address the matter. If needed, it can be challenged in the EU Court of Justice. In the meantime, though, the law must be abided even if it is formally wrong. Russian media spread hostile propaganda and misinformation from within the EU Member States. They have to be stopped. Therefore, here comes the twist, citizens of the Member States must be forbidden from accessing and being reached by *news* coming from the *enemy*. Their right to be informed must be curtailed.

As a matter of fact, the EU declares that journalists neither charged nor condemned for crimes against sovereign countries are forbidden from releasing their information. It also orders that EU Members State citizens must not access these contents because the EU *knows* what is in the *best* interest of individuals. Its decisions, seemingly, are *morally* grounded.

The *non sequitur* between the regulatory need and its verbatim translation into a provision is apparent. The *excusatio non-petita* of Decision 351/22's Whereas 11 can hardly be read differently:

> Consistent with the fundamental rights and freedoms recognised in the Charter of Fundamental Rights, in particular with the right to freedom of expression and information, the freedom to conduct a business and the right to property as recognised in Articles 11, 16 and 17 thereof, these measures do not prevent those media outlets and their staff from carrying out other activities in the Union than broadcasting, such as research and interviews. In particular, these measures do not modify the obligation to respect the rights, freedoms and principles referred to in Article 6 of the Treaty on European Union, including in the Charter of Fundamental Rights,

and in Member States' constitutions, within their respective fields of application.

If such a decision had directly restricted freedom of expression, it would have been much more difficult to accept unless in a formally declared state of war. On the other hand, the ban on offering Internet services and the obligation to filter content are a much more convenient way of achieving the goal. Ultimately, these rules only work in cyberspace. Do not they?

In other words, the acceptance of this regulation is favoured by the disconnection of the norm from the perception of its effects. The subjugation of constitutional rights to contingent political needs by disregarding formal legality shortens the distance between the rule *of* law and the rule *by* law. It weaponises 'universal rights', of which digital rights have become synonymous. It questions the truly universal nature of the latter.

The universality of 'universal rights'

'Universal rights', 'natural law', 'human rights', and similar denominations are like English gardens: they pretend to be 'natural' while being an artificial way to relate to nature. The countryside is made of forests, unkempt bushes, unpaved sheep tracks, and animals living in the wild. Animals kill to eat. Plants reclaim their space. Parasites infect their hosts. That has nothing to do with neatly trimmed grass, flowers, and imitations of Gothic ruins.

Turning the artificial notion of human rights into binding statutes has been a long, controversial, and still unaccomplished endeavour. Its journey from society to parliaments and, eventually, to courts has been eventful. Their ambiguous exploitation in the political domain affected the general acknowledgement of such a legal category. Instead of being discussed in the proper place—civil society, parliament, and courts—they became the flag in the name of which to wage war and let conflicts erupt among nations and between citizens and State.

> The global ambition of human rights discourse has been long disputed on the grounds of sociological illegitimacy. ... The most illustrative moment of such critique remains the protest by anthropologists during the drafting of the most quintessential human rights document, the Universal Declaration of Human Rights. The American Anthropological Association challenged the emerging Declaration on both epistemological and representative grounds. If human beings do not 'function outside the societies of which they form a part,' then it is highly likely that any 'human right in one society may be regarded as antisocial by another people'.[19]

In particular, critics of human rights focused on their non-universal,[20] colonialist,[21] individualistic ethic-based nature.[22] Counter-criticism pointed out that the relativist argument encompasses a debilitating self-contradiction; by postulating that the only sources of moral validity are individual cultures themselves, one is precluded from making any consistent moral judgements ... In a practical sense, the cultural relativist position is foundationally incompatible with human rights, as human rights themselves could not exist if they were stripped of common moral judgement.[23]

The difference between the two positions is irresolvable because there is no common ground on which to build a mediation. The claim for a *common moral* as a basis for *universal rights* precludes any logical analysis. Like in the case of divine powers, also in the case of human rights, it is not possible to demonstrate that syllogism's major premise (their common moral foundation) is true. As a consequence, the claim for universal rights becomes a political expedient.

The formal notion of human rights dates back to the United Nations' *Universal Declaration of Human Rights* proclaimed in 1948. Counterintuitively to many, however, the *Declaration* does not acknowledge them as a legal right. Unlike a treaty or a convention, it is a mere political statement, a non-legally binding text.

Unlike the *Declaration*—which profoundly inspired it—the 1953 *European Convention on Human Rights* is enforceable through judicial redress. However, like the *Declaration*, the *Convention* is not backed by a sovereign power. Its authority comes from a contract. Its rulings are binding, but if a State does not comply, there is no way to coerce it. Consequently, the court would not be entitled to perform one of the most crucial functions of judicial power: keeping laws alive by adapting them to the change in society. The court did it notwithstanding and raised a not ungrounded criticism.

> For some, this criticism is based on the argument that the ECtHR has applied particular provisions of the Convention in ways that would not have been foreseen by those who originally drafted it ... It has also been argued that some of the Court's decisions do not take sufficient account of the historical, cultural and other differences between the 47 Council of Europe states ... Jonathan Sumption QC (2011: 14) has argued that there is a lack of legitimacy for this perceived extension of the ECHR's remit.[24]

The growing discomfort with the expansion of the ECHR left the academic criticism domain. On 14 December 2021, the British Ministry of Justice announced a plan to reform the Human Rights Act so that ECHR rulings lose their automatic enforceability in the national legal system. Formally, this is not a repeal of the 1953 Convention; although de facto, it can hardly be understood differently.

> The UK will remain party to the ECHR and continue to meet its obligations under the Convention and all other international human rights treaties. However, Ministers will ensure the UK Supreme Court has the final say on UK rights by making clear that they should not blindly follow the Strasbourg Court. It will mean that rights are interpreted in a UK context, with respect for the Country's case law, traditions, and the intention of its elected law makers.[25]

This twist of the British attitude is revealing, considering that the United Kingdom has been among the founding father of the Convention that, in the words of then Prime Minister Sir Winston Churchill, has at its centre 'the idea of a Charter of Human Rights, guarded by freedom and sustained by law'.[26]

The wording changed with the *International Covenants on Civil and Political Rights and Economic, Social and Cultural Rights* (ICERS) adopted by the UN in 1966. A crowd of definitions fills the available space. It looks like there is no limit to creating new rights if the need arises. Despite its formal legal attire, however, these covenants are political statements with little ado with the establishment of 'absolute' rights.

> ... documents such as the ICESCR assign obligations to signatory states. This implies, however, that non-signatory states are under no obligation to respect or meet the requirement of the rights, and that the obligations created by signing and ratifying covenants are special, and not in fact universal. It follows that neither are the corresponding rights.[27]

As it has been elucidated, the universality reclaimed by international covenants and conventions is as bold in principle as challenging to enforce in practice.

> ... these ambiguities are apparently resolved in favour of assigning obligations to states party, that is to the signatory states. This approach has apparent advantages-and stings in its tail. The first sting is that states that do not ratify a Covenant will not incur the obligations it specifies: not a welcome conclusion to advocates of universal human rights, since these states thereby escape obligations to respect, let alone enforce, the rights promulgated. The second sting is sharper. The obligations created by signing and ratifying Covenants are special, not universal obligations. So the rights which are their corollaries will also be special or institutional rights, not universal human rights. Once we take a normative view of rights and obligations, they must be properly matched. If human rights are independent of

institutional structures, if they are not created by special transactions, so too are the corresponding obligations; conversely if obligations are the creatures of Convention, so too the rights.[28]

Moreover, the more 'absolute'—the pun is intended—a right, the more it becomes disconnected from the social and political domains it is supposed to operate.

> There cannot be a claim to rights that are rights against nobody, or nobody in particular: universal rights will be rights against all comers; special rights will be rights against specifiable others … . If we take rights seriously and see them as normative rather than aspirational, we must take obligations seriously. If on the other hand we opt for a merely aspirational view, the costs are high. For then we would also have to accept that where human rights are unmet there is no breach of obligation, nobody at fault, nobody who can be held to account, nobody to blame and nobody who owes redress. We would in effect have to accept that human rights claims are not real claims.[29]

The difficulty of giving rights an 'absolute' nature is also counterintuitively apparent in the 2000 *EU Charter of Fundamental Rights.*

At first sight, the Charter seems to address, if not all, at least many of the criticisms raised against its predecessors. Firstly, the Charter is a treaty binding directly on the signees by limiting their national sovereignty. Secondly, it sets the perimeter for the legislative activities of the EU institutions. Lastly, its enforcement is made effective by the judicial redress to the European Union Court of Justice. In short, the Charter works as a constitution. Only it is not.

On 5 May 2020, the German highest court, deciding a controversy about the 2015 bond-buying programme launched by the European Central Bank, also challenged the reach of the European Court of Justice.

> Controversially, the Karlsruhe-based court also defied a previous decision by the Court of Justice of the European Union, saying that the EU judges in Luxembourg had acted 'ultra vires,' or beyond their competence. This raised concerns that the German ruling could encourage other countries like Poland or Hungary, which are locked in a rule-of-law battle with Brussels, to also question the authority of the top EU court and argue that national law should stand above EU law.[30]

The nightmare that the German decision could encourage the other EU Member States to follow this lead did not take too much time to become real.

On 14 July 2021 and 7 October 2021, the Polish Constitutional Court affirmed the supremacy of domestic law over the Community's binding powers, whether manifested in directives, regulations, or decisions of the Court of Justice.

The EU Commission reacted on December 2021 by starting an infringement procedure against Poland based upon the claim that the domestic rulings violated Article 19(1) of the Treaty of the European Union.[31]

As much as this reaction was correct in political terms, there are doubts about its legal soundness. That is because, as said, the process of creating a European Union as a sovereign and independent political entity is still ongoing. Therefore, the Polish Constitutional Court is hardly challengeable in purely normative terms. It enforces a formal criterion that classifies the hierarchy of sources in the international sphere and places the member State interests above those of the EU as Germany has also done. The matter would have been different had the EU achieved an actual and *superiorem non-recognoscens* political status, becoming a federal state's sovereign entity.

It is worth recalling that EU legislative rule is based on a delegation of powers and not on their irrevocable transfer. Therefore, the source of its authority is the system of treaties which are essentially international agreements. Their domestic enforcement should constantly go through a prior compatibility check with national constitutions. In other words, also in 'delegated matters', a Member State maintains the power (and the duty) to verify whether the EU provisions are compatible with its own Constitution and, more importantly, if they respect the *national interest* that is a *political*, not a *legal* category. In other words: an EU legislative primacy based on treaties allowed Brexit by invoking a contractual clause (or even forgetting about it). By contrast, the existence of a European Constitution would have required the UK to wage a war of secession. Therefore, the rights acknowledged by the Nice Charter may well be called on paper 'fundamental' but hardly 'universal' or 'absolute'.

Human rights between moral superiority and state sovereignty

A common trait of the absolute/fundamental/universal/human rights emerging from the multitude of international covenants and rulings on the matter is the assumption that, whatever their name, they are considered a sort of 'genetic' attribute of the human being. They come first and before any normative acknowledgement by a sovereign power and are *morally* grounded. This is, however, a *petitio principii* built upon the belief in the *ontological* nature of human rights and their *intrinsic* superiority because of the ground on which they are built. This attempt to explicitly set common ethics is instrumental in supporting the reboot of the 'natural' law approach in its current 'human rights' disguise.

In this conceptual framework, the State is no more necessary to affirm an (absolute) right. The role of parliaments and courts is limited to notarising their existence and behaving accordingly, adapting the domestic regulations to enforce them. They exist because they exist. Human rights—as natural law—are stateless. This fits perfectly with the characteristics of transnationality and globality, which are the main attributes of digital rights.

Notwithstanding the pressure of international bodies and global activism movements, rights still require sovereignty, and sovereignty presupposes the existence of a social group that behaves according to shared rules within a political jurisdiction.

There can be no legal rights without a State with the power to command their respect, just as there can be no legal tender without a State that guarantees its value or no army without State's border and a community living within. In other, more concise terms, sovereignty is the basis on which a social group is built and its functioning regulated. Hence, the need to use the law as an instrument of mediation between opposing instances that find a mediation in the provision (legislative power), in its application (executive power) and its adaptation to the changing conditions of a given historical period (judicial power). As Santi Romano wrote in his 1918 seminal work, *L'ordinamento giuridico*:

> The whole concept of law must be linked to the concept of society in two reciprocal senses, which complement each other. What does not go beyond the purely individual sphere, what does not go beyond the individual's life as such, is not law (ubi ius ibi societas). Furthermore, there is no society, in the true sense of the word, without the manifestation of the legal phenomenon in it (ubi societas ibi ius). ... Society is not merely a relationship between individuals ... it is an entity that constitutes, even formally and extrinsically, a tangible entity, distinct from the individuals comprised in it. And it must be an entity actually constituted ... The concept of law must, secondly, contain the idea of social order; this serves to exclude any element that is to be traced back to pure arbitrariness or mere, i.e. unmanaged, force.[32]

It is worth repeating two core points of Romano's thought: law presupposes the existence of social order; 'pure arbitrariness' and 'unmanaged force' are incompatible with the idea of law.

This legal theory might seem outdated if compared to political-economic scenarios that emerged from the ashes of WWII, the rise of transnational ideologies, and the necessity of managing international relations. Economic and financial globalisation, as well as technologies such as those backing cryptocurrencies and *defi*, have progressively de-sovereignised rights or, better, have separated sovereignty from the exercise of the prerogatives which are (were) proper to it. Treaties and conventions—including those on human rights—have become the instruments to manage national interests or pursue geopolitical goals. On the opposing front, the rise of transnational activist movements has been facilitated by the technology of information. That also severed the connection between legal rights as a *domestic* social regulatory tool and the system of values upon which they are built. The progressive lack of connection between the powers-that-be and citizens allowed a surreptitious transition towards ruling by ethics instead of law.

> When new digital solutions become available, there are often only very general rules applicable to them, e.g. rules on privacy, safety, advertising, and so on. Want to use Artificial Intelligence? Go ahead, no specific rules apply. Want to use facial recognition? Same thing. Deploying robots, Internet of things applications, etc.? No specific rules in place...
>
> However, a lack of specific rules does not relieve you of your responsibilities. Every time you deploy a digital solution you have an opportunity to gain the public's trust, but there's also a risk of losing it. Make no mistake, society at large will be looking at you to do the right thing. Whether it be your users, customers, politicians, or the general public; they will all be looking at you to properly implement that brilliant, but somewhat scary, digital solution.
>
> Doing the right thing regardless of whether whatever you are doing is governed by laws and regulations, brings you in the domain of ethics. Doing so with regard to digital solutions, that is the domain of Digital Ethics. It is focused on responsible use of digital solutions.[33]

The oddity of this tenet is apparent. Firstly, the alleged 'lack of rules' for AI, facial recognition, and other 'new', technology-connected phenomena are at least questionable. Major Western legal systems enacted statutes punishing harms caused by wrong or reckless design of (software-run) machinery. Threats or harassment by abusing messaging systems or social network profiles remain threats and harassments. *How* they are committed does not change their criminal nature. If facial recognition is (ab)used against an individual, there are plenty of criminal provision to invoke. Invoking the 'do no harm' legal principle is always possible if no specific legal rules are available. This conclusion is not meant to affirm the *absolute* lack of need for new regulations, as it only invokes a more generous wielding of the Occam's Razor. Notwithstanding its ubiquity, the 'technology is faster than law' *mantra* is often ungrounded.

Secondly, even if specific provisions are lacking, 'doing the right thing' would hardly be an alternative. In a Western democracy, ethics belongs to the private domain. Ethically-based individual choices are not relevant to law *until they breach it*. Therefore, claiming that if regulations are absent, a *moral* decision should orient a choice with *legal* consequences nonetheless creates an apparent short circuit. It injects *personal* beliefs into *social* regulations. Commonly shared ethical beliefs relevant to a constituency are *already* incorporated into statutes or part of a public debate to have them acknowledged as legal rights.

However, the spreading of the technology of information allowed to move the concept of 'right thing' to the next level. Not only executive powers reclaimed the 'right to disregard rights'. Even single individuals began to demand that their personal views become mandatory because 'they said so'.

Über-rights

The Big Tech sector's business strategies exploited a paradox called 'herd-individuality'. Products and services are sold under the pretence of making people—customers, actually—feel unique. This uniqueness, however, is an illusion, for the customer is but 'another brick in the wall' as Pink Floyd sang back in the 1970s. He must sit tranquil where the profiling machine has put him. At least until he can afford it, he must enjoy the freedom of living in a walled garden or a golden cage. Like all humans 'living' sealed in the satchels of *The Matrix* had to do was to produce energy for the machines, he must work to produce wealth and transfer it to the garden keepers (or cage masters) in exchange for a crown. The individual is proclaimed king behind the invisible but insurmountable fences made by social media profiles, app-centric life, and high-pressure nudging surrounding him. A puny king, but a king nonetheless. As a supreme ruler of a one-man non-existent country, the individual is morphed into a customer, and then a user reclaims the absolute power of telling right from wrong and doing justice in his evanescent kingdom.

A disruptive effect of this state of the matter is the growth of the *über-rights*—the diffuse belief that individual creeds or demands should deserve to be acknowledged as legal rights just because one says so. Cancel culture, private online vigilantism and policing, blaming of lifestyles and beliefs, and denial of the authority of the State are but a few examples of *über-rights*. They can hardly be considered legal—let alone fundamental—rights; however, they are perceived as such because of confused and abused exploitation of the *digital* adjective.

Like the word cyberspace, which meant nothing to his creator, the association of the word 'digital' to whatever other term immediately blurs its meaning, weakens its understanding, and opens the door to irrationality, greed, and self-gratification.

This clear symptom of the deranged relationship between technology and society indicates how legal rights are losing their *raison d'être* in the growing dismantling of social bonds. A once again illusory, technology-mediated

50

hyper-individualism favour the practice of 'isolation capitalism': a model (on which, *infra*) built upon the induced perception of being part of a society when all that lasts is a man in a room, a computer, and an Internet connection.

Big Tech and digital rights

Über-rights' adverse effects are matched, in parallel, by the aggressive and systematic Big Tech appropriation of the power to tell 'what is a right'. It is where the peruse of the 'digital' adjective becomes essential to divert the goal of rights towards the satisfaction of a private need—be it financial gain or lobbying effort.

Big Tech and, at large, corporations have a vested interest in defining (digital) rights, as elucidated by the following examples regarding the right to privacy, *post-mortem* wills, copyright, and free speech. They all have in common the commodification of legal rights into *a quid pro quo*.

Right to privacy

Apple shapes legal concepts according to its marketing needs and promotes the former to pursue the latter. A partisan reading of the right to privacy is at the core of the unique selling proposition of the advertising campaign for its products.

> Privacy is a fundamental human right. At Apple, it's also one of our core values. Your devices are important to so many parts of your life. What you share from those experiences and who you share it with, should be up to you. We design Apple products to protect your privacy and give you control over your information. It's not always easy. But that's the kind of innovation we believe in.[34]

One may agree with the proposition that the right to privacy is about *control* of information—a thesis, by the way, that this author has advocated for years. However, that control should be balanced with competing interests. It should find a mediation outside the domain of the right to privacy. Administering justice requires the possibility of infringing the privacy of the investigated person. In this case, however, she is protected by due process and defence rights, not by a non-existent right to confidentiality. Notwithstanding, in the 2016 investigation of the San Bernardino mass shooting, Apple invoked (its reading of) the right to privacy as a legal basis to refuse to cooperate with the FBI in a criminal investigation.

Asked by a journalist about civil liberties being the reason for this refusal, Apple CEO Tim Cook answered adamantinely:

...if this All Writs Act can be used to force us to do something would make millions of people vulnerable, then you can begin to ask yourself, if that can happen, what else can happen? In the next senate you might say, well, maybe it should be a surveillance OS done. Maybe law enforcement would like the ability to turn on the camera on your Mac. But it wasn't clear at all. ... And also the act itself doesn't look at the crime, it doesn't look at the reason the government wants it. It looks at the burden to the company that it's asking to do it. So this case was domestic terrorism, but a different court might view that robbery is one. A different once might view that a tax issue is one. A different one might view that a divorce issue would be okay. We saw this huge thing opening and thought, you know, if this is where we're going, somebody should pass a law that makes it very clear what the boundaries are. This thing shouldn't be done court by court by court by court.[35]

As it is apparent, Apple's refusal is not based on choosing a peculiar reading of the All Writs Act that precludes the State from asking for cooperation. Opposing the court order was a political decision: the company challenged the court order based on its private view of the right to privacy and how it should be balanced against other competing rights (more, on that, in Chapter 4).

Last will

A similar approach emerged concerning the right of heirs to access data and information stored in a device or remote storage of a person who passed away. Different jurisdictions regulate the matter differently. In the USA, a person is free to—literally—give all his wealth to his cat. In Italy, the freedom to manage one's patrimony is limited because the law assigns a portion of the wealth to *eredi legittimi* (wife, husband, parents, descendants). Be it as it may, it is out of the question that under Italian law, once a person becomes a legitimate heir, he acquires the ownership of the whole assets of the deceased, including the right to recover data and information stored online. Notwithstanding, Apple refused to let heirs access the data stored in the iCloud account of the *de cuius* because it contended that only a judicial order would have allowed it. The heirs took the matter to court, and on 10 February 2021, the Tribunal of Milan granted the right to access the data stored in the online repository.

Apple sustained its refusal by claiming that the defunct person was entitled to its (its, not his) right to privacy, even being dead. Moreover, Apple dictated the conditions under which it would have complied with the ruling. Firstly, it invoked the application of the US Electronic Privacy Communication Acts. Secondly, it asked the court to specify that the defunct was the actual owner of the accounts connected with the involved Apple IDs, and the claimants were 'agents' or 'legal representatives' of the defunct. Lastly, the company required the court to issue a specific order to provide support in recovering information that might also involve third parties.

The Italian court granted the injunction against Apple with a three-strikes decision.

First, it is impossible to invoke the direct enforcement of foreign (namely, US) legislation in the Italian jurisdiction. The second was that there was no evidence that the person who passed away did not want to allow access to its data. The third was that even if a deceased person is not a data subject according to the data protection regulation, their family may have some legitimate interest in accessing this information.

The court could have granted the injunction without invoking the EU general data protection regulation. Once a person is given the heir legal status (because the *de cuius* did so in the testament or, by contrast, because lacking the last will declaration, the person is *erede legittimo*), she does not need further authorisations to acquire the possession of goods that now wholly belongs to her. However, putting aside the quibbles of inheritance law, what matters is that, once again, a private company reclaimed the right to tell what a (fundamental) right is.

Copyright

Apple is not the sole and only to show this gentle but predatory approach to digital rights, as the evolution of copyright legislation elucidates.

The 1886 Berne convention is called the 'copyright convention'. Its actual denomination, though, is *Convention de Berne pour la protection des œuvres littéraires et artistiques* (Berne Convention for the Protection of Literary and Artistic Works). Its Article 1 verbatim states that 'the countries to which this Convention applies constitute a Union for the protection of authors' rights in their literary and artistic works'. Notwithstanding the clarity of the Convention's goals, the industrialisation of culture (i.e. the transformation of the artistic expression in a bookshelf product) affected its reading by domestic legislation. Draconian provisions did not protect authors. They were meant to empower publishers and, in general, those who secured for themselves the development rights of artistic work. In theory, authors can file legal action to assert their moral rights. However, a significant body of laws is more concerned with protecting the developers' interests. This conclusion is apparent if only considering what constitutes a copyright offence and who can claim their punishment. Over time, many countries fined (even with criminal punishment) the unauthorised duplication and sharing of artistic works. The legislation imposed pre-emptive levies on digital storage regardless of whether they were used to memorise non-copyrighted work. They deprived de facto the legitimate user of the right to make a backup copy by allowing the enforcement of (privacy-infringing) digital rights management systems (DRM), criminalising even the abstract research on methods exposing the weakness of copyright protection technologies (see Chapter 4).

Ironically, the search for 'digital rights' on academic papers' search engines and online bookstores often mainly provides results about digital rights management rather than those of authors and individuals.

The high level of legal protection granted to those who market an artistic work does not match the effectiveness of the redress given to authors and audiences to protect their rights.

One of the last examples is the EU Copyright Directive 2019/790 passed on 17 April 2019[36] whose Whereas 72 reads

> Authors and performers tend to be in a weaker contractual position when they grant a licence or transfer their rights, including through their own companies, for exploitation in return for remuneration, and those natural persons need the protection provided for by this directive to be able to fully benefit from the rights harmonised under Union.

Despite the declared good intentions, the core of the directive is, once again, protecting the economic interest and enhancing the legal remedies for copyright holders. They influence and affect the activity of parliaments and public institutions in several ways. By contrast, authors and—this is what they are called nowadays—'content creators' remain without effective protection. Their works are routinely abused by 'pirates of the web' and those on the 'right side'. The devaluation of individual creative work is now a fact. Content sharing services ask users to publish their work for free, assuming that exposure is suitable for their professional careers. Publishers do not even consider paying people to write columns, taking for granted that the contribution to a newspaper or a magazine is paid in visibility. The situation is aggravated by the incipient ability of AI platforms to create texts, images, videos, and sounds of such quality to replace human creations. Some have even gone so far as to theorise that AI should have a copyright on the files they produce. As it will be explained further in Chapter 5, this statement is meaningless because software, no matter how complex, is an inanimate object and, therefore, cannot and cannot have rights.

In reality, however, deciding whether or not an AI should have the copyright on an image or any other product is irrelevant. In a purely business context, where content is a product, it doesn't matter who built it but who has the right to sell it. So whether an image is the result of a creative act or the application of parameters to an automated process is not a matter of copyright.

Copyright is inextricably linked to the creative act. The work is protected not as such but as the final act of an intellectual process. This explains, for example, why Lucio Fontana's *Cuts*, Jackson Pollock's drips, or Marcel Duchamp's *Ready made* were given artistic status.

On the contrary, from the user's point of view, all this is irrelevant because only the type of aesthetic experience elicited by the work counts. Therefore, whether a painting was made by the real Rembrandt or the Next Rembrandt[37] is irrelevant. If this AI produces a good enough result to satisfy a person's aesthetic sense, that's enough to give this painting an economic value—a price. Eliminating the role of creativity in producing content to which to attribute economic value is a way to exclude an element—that of the artist—from the value production process and, therefore, maximise profits. It is clear that, in this context, technology companies have a vested interest in taking control of the meaning of copyright. In this, they are greatly aided by the 'technological modernism' that afflicts legal scholars worshipping the idea of 'digital rights'.

Free speech

The 2022 announced acquisition of Twitter by Elon Musk makes Big Tech's invasion of the law and rights landscape more concerning.

> Elon Musk buys Twitter in order to guarantee freedom of speech that, according to him, was too curtailed by previous management. Analysts embark on complicated reasoning to understand the financial impact on the social network. Some jurists question the appropriateness of allowing individuals to express themselves without restrictions. This is the vulgate. The merits of the question, however, remain largely ignored. By becoming the owner of Twitter, Musk will not guarantee the right to freedom of expression but will impose his own concept of free speech. In other words, Musk has bought the right to decide what is a right, conditioning people's lives on a par with a legislator.[38]

The venture proved challenging, and after a series of controversies and mutual accusations, it finally landed in court and still has to be decided.

That social networking platforms or other protagonists of the Big Tech sector strongly influence individual opinions and intervene in freedom of expression is certainly known. At least on paper, this happens discreetly, applying clauses of the terms and conditions to limit users' activity or claiming the right to act at their discretion because the services are free (but are they really?).

More than Apple, Microsoft, the entertainment industry, and other stakeholders of the online sector, Musk cut off civil society from having a say and bypassed parliaments.

What makes Musk's decision different is its reason why: to protect freedom of expression as a whole. In this, Musk found himself on the same side as former US President Donald Trump. After Facebook and Twitter deactivated his social profiles, Trump funded the creation of Truth Social, a platform meant to be a forum from which to harangue users.

The two initiatives, however, are very different. Trump's is 'only' an attempt to create a tool for expressing one's views without any control by any 'supervisor'. Musk's action, on the other hand, is fuelled by the belief that he has the right to protect the freedom of expression of thought. Instead, what makes them similar is the conviction of 'being right', thus claiming for themselves the power to 'know best' how a right should be shaped.

The point, then, is not whether Musk or Trump are 'on the right side' but that, based on individual convictions or commercial strategies, thanks to their strength and wealth, they could readily have endorsed entirely opposite views, regardless of the merits of their choices.

Loss of relevance of judicial regress

In what is more than just a legal easter egg, a 2016 review of Amazon in-house game engine Lumberyard's terms and conditions introduced clause 42.10 waiving a restriction of use

> in the event of the occurrence (certified by the United States Centers for Disease Control or successor body) of a widespread viral infection transmitted via bites or contact with bodily fluids that causes human corpses to reanimate and seek to consume living human flesh, blood, brain or nerve tissue and is likely to result in the fall of organized civilization.[39]

This *Zombie Clause*—as it has been nicknamed—is deeply nested in a 26,000 words agreement. A document so ponderous that it is improbable a customer would read it entirely.

> Clauses like this one don't actually encourage us to read the terms of service. Instead, they mostly work to make a joke of our failure to do so. A few publications that have reported on the zombie clause have taken the story as an opportunity to point out other, less sexy, details from the document. Ars Technica's Kyle Orland, for example, notes that the engine collects information about where, how, and when it gets put to work. It's not clear, though, that this is especially sinister, let alone that different from the data collection practices of other software companies.[40]

Legal documents linked to online products—service agreements, data protection policies, licenses, fair-use regulations—are as ubiquitous as ill-considered, particularly if they are designed to be complicated or tiring to read. The result of this deliberate choice is that the relationship between a Big Tech and its minuscule counterpart is reduced at its bare terms: money (or data) in exchange for service or goods. A 'user'—this is what human beings are commonly called—will not sue Amazon, Meta, or any Big Tech if they fail to comply or infringe his rights. 'Customer support' takes over court, 'terms and conditions' override statutes and norms. As soon as the contractual obligations are met, the rest does not matter.

Out of ruthless pragmatism, one might conclude that this model works good enough and that the complexity of the legal texts is just a necessary collateral evil. A sacrifice on the altar of the legal bureaucracy. That conclusion, however, does not consider that nugating the possibility of understanding a right is a way to deprive it of its meaning and function.

Right to ignorance

Big Techs are not the only one that can profit from the legal rights' loss of importance or that gave way to this phenomenon. Lawrence Lessig's Creative Commons project[41] has been a revolutionary way to approach copyright's complicated issues. He designed a set of standard licenses with descriptive icons and 'machine-readable' instructions. He made handling copyright licensing easy for non-jurists. He possibly did not factor in the collateral consequences of his proposal. People started patching Creative Commons labels on their work without actually understanding their meaning and carelessly using these contents. There was no need to actually 'read the fine prints'.

Legal trolling—exploiting obscure terms and conditions against somebody who initially agreed on them—is gaining momentum in the online sector. In 2022 an American student received a copyright infringement notice and a payment request because he failed to comply with the licensing terms of a photography available on a repository hosting creative common-licensed contents.

> Popular Creative Commons sites such as Wikimedia, Flickr, Pixabay include hundreds of thousands of photos and images that you can use for free if—and this is the big big IF—if you comply with the photo's Creative Commons license, which usually is listed alongside the photo. Sometimes that just means you have to include the photographer's name. Sometimes it means you can't significantly alter the original image or can't make a profit off of it. Whatever it says, if you want to use a Creative Commons photo you must take the time to read and comply with the license requirements or risk being sued for copyright infringement. Unfortunately, some

photographers and companies are now intentionally taking advantage by including very specific or complex licensing terms that they know most—or at least many—users probably won't comply with. Let's call it what is: a trap. And once a user falls into their trap, a demand letter soon follows.

In this case, the photo was that of a generic medical syringe. Like pretty much every news organization on the planet, this student media group was writing about COVID19 and they wanted a basic, no-frills image to illustrate their article. ... Unfortunately, they didn't read the license requirements further, which required that users also link to a specific page on the photographer's website and include licensing terms in the photo's file credits, which they didn't do. So they were out of compliance with the Creative Commons license and now the photographer is demanding over $5,000 for his simple, generic photo.[42]

From a pure defensive advocacy perspective, several issues should be considered in this case: is a generic picture taken with no creative purpose entitled to (full) copyright protection? Is the payment demand fair? Should the photographer provide evidence of the damages he incurred because of the license terms infringement?

The parties' counsellors will handle all these questions and maybe in court. However, what matters for this book is the attitude of those who downloaded the picture and the comment quoted above. The blame is on the right holder, not on the (alleged) infringer. Why would somebody be justified in infringing somebody else's rights because he entered into an agreement without reading—and understanding—it in full? Why would setting specific license terms would be necessarily a 'trap'? Why would it be unfair to demand a restoration for the (actual, if proved) damage caused by the breach of a contract?

It may be argued that this claim for a 'right to legal ignorance' is an issue affecting 'just' copyright matters. Therefore, the critic might continue, being copyright not a 'fundamental right', it would not be possible to generalise the conclusion.

Firstly, maybe copyright is not a fundamental right; however, it is an *absolute* right with constitutional ties, being connected to free speech, freedom to teach and practice art and science, and private property.

Secondly, the same 'right to ignorance' is also claimed in other legal domains that unquestionably belong to the 'fundamental rights' realm.

The ubiquitous 'Data protection and Cookie policy' popping out from websites and mobile apps are often templates provided by third-party services. The wording is vague or, in contrast, heavily detailed. They are useless or impossible to read. They are accepted without even trying to understand them. Is the data subject entitled to complain against the mis-treatment of his personal information because he did not care to read and *understand* the data controller statements?

Do we need 'new' digital rights?

Cyberspace and digital rights are actually two faces of the same coin. One cannot exist without the other. The induced pretence of living in an alternative reality of absolute freedom gives 'digital rights' a sort of legitimacy in sharing the same anti-system, anti-corporation ideology of cyberspace doctrines.

The intrinsic *über-rights* explosive anarchist charge turns digital rights into ordnance. Once exploded, its fragments are supposed to create an indefinite number of individual claims and the demand for them to be acknowledged as legal rights.

A recently published paper acknowledges the matter thoroughly.[43] The reasoning is correct in the parts in which it recognises that many new rights are, in reality, articulations of existing ones. However, even in this case, there is a cultural misunderstanding of believing that a 'digital reality' is distinct from the physical one. It results in some contradictions supporting the conclusion that new—let alone 'digital'—rights are unnecessary.

Some of these 'new rights' are already there. What is called 'right to Internet access' exists since 2002 in the EU as 'universal service directive'.[44] Contrary to the invoked 'right to Internet access', the EU provision is technically neutral. It does not endorse a specific protocol (such TCP/IP) or device. 'Right to disconnection' is labour law basic. An employee is bound to work during working hours. Any extra time must be compensated and cannot be imposed. 'Right not to know' is well established in healthcare legislation. Oviedo convention grants the person the right not to be informed of his status. 'Right to clean and safe digital environment' fall within general environmental and criminal legislations. The peculiarity related to the technology of information is a matter of 'how' and not of 'if'. 'Starting over with a clean digital slate' can hardly be considered a right in itself. It is already regulated through financial credit scoring, actuarial mathematics in the insurance sector, court, and criminal records. These information—whether processed manually or electronically—are meant to stay in the public interest. Their processing is regulated way before data protection became an issue. As per the deletion of voluntarily shared information, that law already allows their deletion. Rights to 'expiry dates of data' and 'know personal data value' are already implied by the data protection regulation. The problem is not acknowledging these 'rights', but granting an *effective* way to enforce them. Once again, it is a matter of 'how' and not of 'if'.

Other proposed 'new rights' such as the right to 'change your mind' are hard to understand. As the cited paper acknowledges, agreements are based on parties' will. Their will, once manifested, cannot be changed unless it has been previously agreed upon or the law says so. Outside this perimeter, if the 'right to change your mind' has something to do with clearing previously recorded preferences to get clean information from digital platforms, it looks more like a 'right to be profiled differently'. Once again, a matter of data protection regulations.

Of course, while there is no need for new 'digital rights', nothing prevents legislators from deciding to acknowledge them anyway. While waiting for this to happen, one fact is certain: 'digital rights' are a concept of no use for the lawmaker or the jurist.

Digital rights are not a legal metaphor because they lack explanatory power. When talking about 'legal sources' to define the hierarchy of laws, the metaphoric nature (and effectiveness) of the word 'source' is self-evident. 'Digital rights' do not share the same characteristics.

Neither digital rights are effective as legal fiction. Unlike legal person or corporate criminal liability, acknowledging an autonomous legal status to digital rights does not add further or better protection to constitutional or international covenants-given rights.

Notwithstanding their cultish status, digital rights can be, at best, considered an umbrella word. A shortcut to define a set of constitutional prerogatives belonging to individuals when they interact with the technology of information.

If so, instead 'digital rights', it would make more sense to speak of rights-affecting technologies.

It can be observed that all rights are affected, in one way or another, by technological achievements and that, therefore, the idea of rights-affecting technology is as weak as the notion of digital rights. This objection, however, would not stand.

Focusing on how technologies affect rights, instead of invoking a right for every technological gimmick put on sales, allows for the correct application of Occam's Razor. It prevents the tail from wagging the dog. It is not meant to create 'new rights' but to identify those most affected by technological transformation. It does not apply only to 'human rights' but also to business rights and public policy.

This approach is also more efficient in describing regulatory and jurisprudential problems caused by the pervasiveness of information technologies and, therefore, more functional in providing guidelines to policy and decision-makers. It brings the dialectics between Power and Rights back on the correct axis. It helps understand how Big Techs seized control over fundamental rights. It exposes how States stepped back from their duty to balance public prerogatives, business interests, and citizens' rights. It shows how the 'isolation capitalism' has severed the fibres of our society.

The following chapters try to put this conceptual framework at stake by analysing the impact of three primary technologies at the core of the 'digital ecosystem': social networking, encryption, and robotics/AI.

Notes

1 Iberdrola *Digital rights, essential in the Internet age* https://www.iberdrola.com/innovation/what-are-digital-rights visited 25 May 2022.
2 Iberdrola *Digital rights, essential in the Internet age* https://www.iberdrola.com/innovation/what-are-digital-rights visited 25 May 2022.
3 Weber 2015: 24.
4 European Commission *Declaration on European Digital Rights and Principles* 26 January 2022 https://digital-strategy.ec.europa.eu/en/library/declaration-european-digital-rights-and-principles visited 25 May 2022
5 Azali, Kathleen *What are digital rights?* 3 August 2020 https://coconet.social/2020/digital-rights-exploring-definitions/ visited 25 May 2022.
6 Wacks, 2015:3.
7 Longhin, Diego. 'La lezione ironica di Piero Angela: 'La velocità della luce non si decide a maggioranza', *Repubblica.it* online edition 13 May 2018 https://www.repubblica.it/speciali/robinson/salone-libro-torino2018/2018/05/13/news/la_lezione_ironica_di_piero_angela_la_velocita_della_luce_non_si_decide_a_maggioranza_-196298981/ (visited 10 January 2022).
8 Wacks 2015:144.
9 European Commission High-Level Expert Group on Artificial Intelligence *Ethics Guidelines for Trustworthy AI* 8 April 2019 https://ec.europa.eu/newsroom/dae/document.cfm?doc_id=60419 visited 10 May 2022.
10 Wacks 2021:145.
11 Monti, Wacks 2021:81.
12 Brooks, Rosa *Rule of law in the gray zone* 7 February 2018 https://mwi.usma.edu/rule-law-gray-zone/ Visited 26 May 2022.
13 Agamben *ibidem.*
14 Agamben 2005:4.
15 Alemanno, Spina 2014:444-445.
16 Monti, Wacks 2020:110.
17 Council of the European Union *Council Decision (CFSP) 2022/351 of 1 March 2022 amending Decision 2014/512/CFSP concerning restrictive measures in view of Russia's actions destabilising the situation in Ukraine* 1 March 2022 https://eur-lex.europa.eu/legal-content/EN/TXT/?uri=CELEX:32022D0351 visited 9 April 2022.
18 A subtle exercise in statutes-embedded diplomacy and a challenging walk on the thin ice of the legal interpretation would allow the EU to have a say in the defence policy of member states. However, it can not go as far as to assert the EU authority to take stands that might lead individual countries to a state of war. Notwithstanding, EU institutions de facto reclaimed the power to set the agenda of the political sanctions and (tried) playing a conditioning role over individual members.
19 Langford 2018:72.
20 Altwicker 2020.
21 Samson 2020.
22 Mutua 2008.
23 Nasr, Leila, *Are Human Rights Really 'Universal, Inalienable, and Indivisible'?* 14 September 2016 https://blogs.lse.ac.uk/humanrights/2016/09/14/are-human-rights-really-universal-inalienable-and-indivisible/ visited 10 April 2022.
24 Donald, Gordon, Leach 2012:91.
25 UK Ministry of Justice Press Release *Plan to reform Human Rights Act* 14 December 2021 https://www.gov.uk/government/news/plan-to-reform-human-rights-act (visited 20 April 2022).

26 Amnesty International UK *What is the European Convention on Human Rights?* 21 August 2018 https://www.amnesty.org.uk/what-is-the-european-convention -on-human-rights visited 27 August 2022.

27 Biggar 2020:28.

28 O'Neill 2005: 431.

29 O'Neill 2005: 430.

30 von der Burchard, Hans. *Commission threatens to sue Germany over EU law supremacy dispute* Politico online edition 9 June 2021 https://www.politico.eu /article/commission-sues-germany-escalating-battle-over-supremacy-eu-law/ vis- ited 30 April 2022.

31 Press Release of the European Union Commission. *Rule of Law: Commission launches infringement procedure against Poland for violations of EU law by its Constitutional Tribunal* 22 December 2021 https://ec.europa.eu/commission/ presscorner/detail/e%20n/ip_21_7070 visited 30 April 2022.

32 Romano 1918-1977: 25-26.

33 Deloitte *The domain of Digital Ethics* 2019 https://www2.deloitte.com/content /dam/Deloitte/nl/Documents/risk/deloitte-nl-risk-digital-ethics-ethical-techology -and-trust.pdf visited 26 May 2022.

34 Apple *Privacy* https://www.apple.com/privacy/ visited 30 March 2022.

35 Gibbs, Nancy – Grossman, Lev *Here's the Full Transcript of TIME's Interview With Apple CEO Tim Cook* 17 March 2016 https://time.com/4261796/tim-cook -transcript/ visited 28 April 2022.

36 *Directive (EU) 2019/790 of the European Parliament and of the Council of 17 April 2019 on copyright and related rights in the Digital Single Market and amending Directives 96/9/EC and 2001/29/EC* Official Journal of the European Union L130/92 17 May 2019 https://eur-lex.europa.eu/eli/dir/2019/790/oj vis- ited 30 April 2022.

37 https://www.nextrembrandt.com/ visited 29 August 2022.

38 Monti, Andrea *Musk, Twitter and the power to buy rights*. Italian Tech 5 May 2022   https://www.repubblica.it/tecnologia/blog/strategikon/2022/05/05/news /musk_twitter_e_il_potere_di_comprare_il_diritto-348210970/ visited 7 May 2022. English translation by Andrea Monti.

39 AWS Service Terms https://aws.amazon.com/service-terms/ visited 6 May 2022.

40 Brogan, *Jacob Amazon Hides a Zombie-Outbreak Reference in New Terms of Service. Hilarious.* Slate 11 February 2016 https://slate.com/technology/2016/02/ amazon-hides-a-zombie-outbreak-reference-in-new-terms-of-service.html visited 8 May 2022.

41 Creative Commons *About CC Licenses* https://creativecommons.org/about/ccli- censes/ visited 26 May 2022.

42 Mike Hiestand *I just got a bill for a Creative Commons photo we used. What gives?* 26 May 2022 https://splc.org/2022/05/charged-for-a-creative-commons -photo/ visited 26 May 2022.

43 Custers, Ben. 'New digital rights: Imagining additional fundamental rights for the digital era'. *Computer Law & Security Review* Volume 44, April 2022 https://doi .org/10.1016/j.clsr.2021.105636 visited 29 August 2022.

44 Directive 2002/22/EC of the European Parliament and of the Council of 7 March 2002 on universal service and users' rights relating to electronic communica- tions networks and services (Universal Service Directive) https://eur-lex.europa .eu/legal-content/EN/ALL/?uri=celex%3A32002L0022 visited 29 August 2022.

3

SOCIAL NETWORKS AND RIGHTS

The previous chapters hinted at the disruptive impact of social networking platforms on individual perceptions of rights. In particular, it pointed out the distorted relationship between ethics and law caused by the belief that 'cyberspace' was real. However, another part of the big picture deserves to be analysed: the progressive loss of decentralisation of social networking technologies and its consequences on legal rights.

Initially, computer-based social networks were 'just' technologies. Everybody could have set up an IRC or newsgroup server and run it. If a group or a channel disappears from one facility, it will reappear in someone else computer. By contrast, contemporary social networks are intrinsically *centralised*. They are social networks because they allow linking people to each other; however, they are not a network because they are, essentially, a *single, non-fungible, centrally owned, and managed* service.

This results from the superimposition of the triple meaning attributed to the words. As Chapter 2 elucidated, *in absentia* social networks existed way before the Internet. In this meaning, the technology that allowed the connection is irrelevant because the focus is on people, not communication tools. By contrast, when the words 'social network' refers to a centralised platform, the accent is on the technology that becomes the enabler of inter-personal exchanges. However, the faithful—and often forgotten—meaning of social network is *'company'*. Social networks do not live an autonomous existence nor appear as an epiphany of divine will. They are a technological platform designed by a company for profit. In short, a *commercial service*. As such, their purpose is to generate revenues for the stakeholders. Their goal is to maximise the valuables that customers can take in exchange for the bare minimum or—ideally—nothing at all. Once depicted this way, social networks lose all of their appeal made of 'virtual space', 'online life', 'digital personality', and all the carefully crafted marketing buzzwords of the trade. They are *just* a server to which customers connect to use some computer-based services.

Nonetheless, the huge number of people they attracted, the time users spend on the platforms, the change of individuals' daily routine to match

DOI: 10.4324/9781003373636-3

the 'need' of the platform, and their 'demand' to be heard made social net-works—as a technology and as a business endeavour—an essential inter-locutor in the 'digital rights' discourse.

Not a day goes by without reading about the risks to privacy or freedom of expression posed by the overwhelming power of platforms and states' impotence (or connivance). Cries arise against platforms' tolerance of radi-cal content on the pretext of guaranteeing freedom. Others stigmatise their 'no qualms attitude' about censoring content and depriving citizens and even heads of State of the right to engage in politics via social network pro-files and pages.

However, these are only manifestations of a more structural phenomenon.

More than anything else, social networks confront us with a harsh real-ity: the actual product of our times is no longer the result of industrial activ-ity or the ability to offer a service. The actual product is the individual. All the activity generated around the dystopian ecosystem of IT-based services aims at one goal: making a profit by turning our lives, values, and behav-iours into a commodity that can be traded.

Whether this has happened in implementing a diabolical plot or simply as a side effect of the IT-based industrial revolution that we have failed to understand and govern is not essential. What matters is the transformation of the individual into a product.

As something to be bought and sold, this different role assigned to the individual has significantly impacted the system of rights and the conception of law itself. We have moved from acknowledging a right through a public debate to a dimension in which a limited number of Big Tech determine the meaning and latitude of rights. It is certainly nothing new, but the phenom-enon's extent, depth, and speed of propagation have few, if any, historical antecedents. It should make us wonder to what extent we can continue ignoring our condition's seriousness.

As said, States, executives, and international rulers also have a vested interest in depriving the people of their legal sovereignty. The shift from the rule of law to the rule by law as a public policy standard practice made possible by international covenant, universal charters, and conventions is getting momentum. By contrast, Big Techs have a more mundane goal: appropriating rights is instrumental to pursuing financial gain. The indi-vidual becomes an enabler: he is the reason why needs are created to be satisfied and, therefore, goods to do so. On the other hand, however, the individual is also an annoyance. An entire system based on massive profil-ing and data collection at any level has problems dealing with rules that impose at least an obligation of fairness on individuals. It is not only a mat-ter of transparency required by the legislation on protecting personal data. The broader issue is the role of the individual's rights, which are perceived almost as an obstacle to pursuing economic objectives.

The diversity of goals pursued by governments and companies is not Manichean. States have an interest—or are forced—to delegate essential parts of the management of critical sectors to Big Tech. The latter is also interested in influencing decision-makers by imposing their own technological choices.

As important as a legal analysis of the technological impact on decision-making processes is, focusing only on this issue yields partial results. It misses the fundamental nature of the phenomenon to put under the microscope: rights no longer serve to protect the individual but encourage him to work and relentlessly spend his salary. Indeed, even consumer protection laws can be seen as a way to set a 'fair' limit to consumers' exploitation; a tool to take away as much as possible from an individual without endangering his capability to create wealth and transfer it to somebody else, like in the era of Robber Barons.[1] The evolution of social networks provides a better understanding of how far we have gone.

Why do social networks exist?

Social networks exist because humans live in communities. A network is about people, not machines. Indeed, there is nothing new about modern social networks because their origins go back to the dawn of interactive communication technologies. The telephone network, the Internet, FidoNet, and packet-switched networks were born—or were even used clandestinely—to get people talking to who had something to say to each other. In other words, electronic communication services and interactive electronic communication technologies are meant to enable information exchange. All the essential functions of network operating systems were and are designed to empower this interaction. All services built on these functionalities could only implement this purpose.

In the cathedrals that housed mainframes, technicians in white coats only had to ensure that electronic mastodons, whose sole purpose was to process information, were continuously fed with energy and data. By contrast, humans accessing a network, no matter how small or primitive, sought to exchange information.

This anthropological characteristic of the early social network users played an essential role in defining the core of what would later become digital rights, but which were actually 'only' the result of a reflex triggered by the new possibilities of interaction among human beings.

Apart from the criminal phenomena, early users of these systems were people of very different backgrounds, ages, and social conditions. However, a tight bond united them: the desire to communicate and, above all, the irrelevance of differences in age, sex, wealth, and education. In his 1997 article titled 'Soul and Body', Giancarlo Livraghi explained precisely the nature of computer-mediated communication:

We get to know someone that we can't see or touch. Before we meet that person physically, we know his or her personality, style, mood and feelings. A relationship builds up, mutual interest, sharing of thoughts and emotions; we want to meet "in the flesh", and sooner or later we do. Very often the question is: "How different am I from what you imagined?"

The process is the reverse of the usual: first we meet the soul, then the body.

It's not necessarily true that we know each other better if we first meet physically. Appearance can prevail over substance. There are people that have been together for decades, maybe sleep in the same bed, but don't really know each other. ... Interesting things happen on the net. There are people that told me in e-mail very private things about themselves, emotions, doubts, feelings that they may have been less ready to discuss if we were in the same room. The absence of a physical body often leads to greater sincerity; people seem less embarrassed in dropping their defenses, less worried and scared, in the apparently abstract world of disembodied words.[2]

With a prescient intuition, he also anticipates the paradox of videoconferencing and, *a fortiori*, the metaverse. They promise a 'natural' interaction that turns out to be more artificial and less spontaneous than text-based communication.

Maybe one day the net will lose its magic. Maybe with much larger bandwidth, and better software, than we have today, we shall meet in video; once again appearance will prevail, and in a phony way, because a projected appearance is often more constructed than direct physical contact.[3]

The emphasis on the message, rather than the person who delivers it, is also fundamental in the new rise of individual rights in interactive electronic communication mediated through social networks or, that is a horse of different colour, social *media* (on that, though, later).

The condition of anonymity, confidentiality, and freedom experienced by users of the early interactive communication systems led them to develop a reasonable expectation of freedom in how they used the technology of information, however, not in terms of legal rights but as a factual condition and psychological state of mind. It is an anthropological datum explaining why the Internet has, from the outset, carried a libertarian component that has brought fundamental rights to the fore. This fundamental element explains why we continue to talk about a free Internet, network neutrality, and similar topics in a very hypocritical way.

All this has an origin in this initial nucleus of people who experience for the first time psychological and behavioural freedom that in other forms of more physical and social interaction was not allowed to them.

The forerunner of social networking started in 1980 and was called the Usenet

> ... a giant bulletin board that is divided into hierarchical sections, called newsgroups. Newsgroups are to Usenet what subforums are to web-based forums, and each one deals with a particular topic. For example, rec.sport.soccer is dedicated to discussions about soccer. Usenet netizens are supposed to use their clients to subscribe to the newsgroups they want to be active in, in much the same way they would subscribe to a mailing list. Subscribing to a newsgroup means that your client will pull new messages from the newsgroups each time you connect or at regular intervals, depending on your client. Despite the name, newsgroups are actually discussion groups. Newsgroups got their name because they were originally intended to host news.[4]

Not all servers contained all or the same newsgroups because some contents were unavailable everywhere for various reasons (from technical ones to preemptive censorship). After its initial creation, a newsgroup lost its 'originator' nature because it began to replicate and synchronise continuously as its clones were fed independently by users. This meant that shutting down a news server did not stop the circulation of messages.

As is easy to imagine, newsgroups became one of the first frontiers of freedom of expression and privacy issues. True, there were groups such as sci.astro.seti dedicated to the NASA research of extra-terrestrial intelligence, but in the 'ninth hierarchy', there were also newsgroups that were much more controversial, dealing with extreme political views and borderline psychopathological topics. In the, shall we say, 'dark' part of the newsgroups, there were contents that challenged the unconditional support for freedom of expression. This is why newsgroups were the first to pose the problem of balancing the individual rights of the individual and the impact that the collective exercise of these rights has on society.

If Usenet is the forerunner of social networks, IRC—Internet Relay Chat—is the progenitor of instant messaging systems. Like its modern iterations, IRC allowed people to create groups (the 'channels'), talk directly to someone thanks to the DCC (Direct Client-to-Client) sub-protocol or exchange files. One significant difference to the present is that anyone could set up an IRC server free of constraints.

Running an IRC server would still be possible today. An individual would only communicate with whomever he wanted in safety. Freely available IRC servers were also plenty and available to miscreants. Notwithstanding, controversies were dealt with *locally*, not centrally.

Social networks and rights

Traditionally, in the public law context of Western democracy, rights are a one-to-one relationship between citizen and state. The extent and impact of a right are factors affected by the scarcity or the limited number of subjects involved. When, on the other hand, the same right is exercised by many persons and perhaps even from different jurisdictions, cracks begin to appear in the system. First, from the point of view of sovereign powers, there is a substantial difference between even harsh political criticism fomented by an individual or a limited group and the same criticism coming simultaneously from hundreds of thousands of people (belonging, by the way, to different countries). Indeed, as the Vietnam War protests teach us, activists did not need digital platforms to organise mass protests even at the international level. However, newsgroups made it easier, faster, and, above all, possible to protest even where a repressive apparatus would have nipped any initiative in the bud. A notable example is how newsgroups helped European and US Chinese students in supporting the Tiananmen protesters in their home country[5]

Newsgroups were the precursor of what has been called 'public engagement industry' or the 'facilitation services aimed at engaging the public and relevant stakeholders with organisations in more intensive ways than traditional, one-way public outreach and information'.[6] They were probably the first case in which it was necessary to discuss the necessity, advisability, or importance of investigating the *collective* exercise of *individual* rights.

Despite the chance of using technologies that allow better respect and rights' balance we persist in using centralised services over which we have no control and which, on the contrary, guide our behaviour in a way Pavlov or Skinner could never have imagined.

The narrative that wants the Internet as a borderless reality where anyone can reach anyone else expresses all the forcing of behavioural change induced by the supremacy of centralised systems.

From passive expression to guided interaction

Geocities, created in 1994 and discontinued in 2009, was perhaps the forerunner of social networks via the Web and marked the beginning of a change in how interactive electronic communication services were designed, marketed, and sold. Before the Web, as mentioned above, interactive electronic communication services were essentially a domain of people with a fair technical competence and little interest in graphic interfaces. Geocities, by contrast, made it possible to publish a website even for those who did not have great technical skills. It was structured in 29 'neighbourhoods'—it would be better to call them 'categories'—which were associated with contents consistent with how they were named. Alternatively, the user could

68

choose the 'neighbourhood' according to the topic he was interested in or, simply, where he preferred to 'live'. As a rule, but not necessarily, theatre enthusiasts 'settled' on Broadway, while those interested in art chose SoHo. Although this was 'simply' a way of classifying content posted by users, the use of the metaphor—a recurring theme in this book—overwhelmingly stimulated users' reactions. When it was dismissed in 2009, Geocities hosted around 38 million sites: a considerable number, considering the historical period. Although shortly after its launch Geocities' creators also added messaging and chat functionalities, its initial mode of operation, also due to technological limitations, was essentially passive. Geocities was the first large-scale, non-'geek-only' service that went from interaction, from the bilaterality of electronic communication to a passive, TV-like 'show'. Humans began their mutation into a web audience.

> When the World Wide Web was first introduced, it was used chiefly to send information to relatively passive readers, in a similar manner in with which newspapers and books were made popular. The content of each website was written, edited, and published by a selected group of people. The concept of 'ownership' of websites was strong, and the owners were responsible for the content. It was not very interactive as it was mostly used for reading, so users who accessed this kind of websites did not participate or contribute to creating the content.[7]

A pivotal point to consider is that Geocities' marketing strategy aimed to increase hosting services' sales. Therefore, tracking residents' whereabouts—collecting personal information and profiling them—was not at the core of this business model.

The progressive decline of Geocities matched the rise of 'different' social networks. Among the many projects hitting the market with various fates, Myspace—launched in 2003—deserves a particular mention as it is credited as Facebook's forerunner. MySpace was similar to Geocities. It included instant messaging and comment features. Its core strength and success factor was the high level of profiles' customisation. It allowed unprecedented freedom in creativity. However, it still relied more on content than interaction, as LinkedIn (2003) and YouTube (2005)—the latter being initially a sort of video-on-demand platform that lately allowed people to run personal broadcasting even in real time.

The focus on *network* and connections is what made Facebook (now Meta)—finally available to a broader user base in 2008—disruptive. Its initial mottos dating back to 2004 and 2006 described the platform as a (dull) *tool*: an online directory to connect people at schools. However, in 2008 the slogan changed to 'Facebook helps you connect and share with the people in your life'. In 2009 it turned into 'Facebook's mission is to give people the power to share and make the world more open and connected'. The current slogan is slightly concerning: 'Connect with friends and the world around you on Facebook'. It depicts Facebook as a gravitational mass capable of attracting everybody's life and becoming the only gateway to our social life.

Changes in its mottos match the three-stage evolution of Facebook's networking features. The early version allowed limited interaction.

> First, it didn't really give me access to anything I didn't already have in my life. ... Second, there was a finite amount of content—there are only so many prom photos. Third, regular users don't have the resources to generate "high-quality" content ... In this world, the connections were relatively weak, in the sense that they do not optimise for intense and ongoing engagement that keep me using Facebook. [8]

However, the 'issue' was soon dealt with.

> ... Facebook solved this problem by bringing on millions—and eventually billions—of users and then facilitating global connections. Suddenly, through the stronger network effects of a larger user base, users with niche interests could connect and reach a critical mass. ... There's another important shift that's happened, too. As Facebook has evolved, it has begun to rely heavily on indirect network effects. Instead of peers reciprocally generating content for one another, a large user base of content consumers incentivises the 'professional' content producers to keep pushing out content, and the professional content keeps the large user base on Facebook and engaged. [9]

In short, Facebook's business strategy—lately becoming the golden standard for all others players—was to create relationships and profit on them. So, where 'old school' social networks offered individuals a chance to *express* themselves, new platforms focused on *networking*. Where MySpace and Geocities mainly offered self-referentiality, Facebook and its competitor promised *interaction*.

> ... we can study different types of social media interactions. However, 'interactions' can also refer to many things. ... there are conceptual distinctions here between channel-centred approaches (focused on the hardware and software) and communication-centred approaches (the process of interactions afforded from access to devices). At a basic level, someone's level of interactions on social media may be determined entirely based on the device they are using to access it (e.g., smartphone, laptop), followed by what

specific social media app they may be using (Facebook, Instagram). Beyond this, we can obtain a more ingrained perspective of how 'social' they are being from things like what features on these specific social media sites they may be using (e.g., messaging, commenting, timeline posts), and finally with whom they are engaging (individuals, groups, broadcasting) and how (text-based, multimedia, synchronously etc).[10]

Social networks did not keep their promise because they failed to specify that what they meant was neither a *free* nor a *libre* way to connect people. The price people pay—and the prize companies get—is the handover of entire pieces of life in the form of electronic data.

Personal information as a *currency* and a *quid pro quo* is still debated. However, the point was already made in early 2000 by the Italian market regulator and the Data Protection Authority. The *Autorità garante per la concorrenza e il mercato* ruled that a claim advertising as *gratis* a service that can be used only by granting consent to processing personal data is deceptive because the lack of a payment in legal tender does not allow to qualify the service as free of charge.[11] In a parallel investigation, the Data Protection Authority hold that data subjects may trade their personal data in exchange for a service, provided that they are given all information to express an informed consent.[12]

The substantial lack of user growth of WT Social is the best demonstration of how successful is the strategy of anesthetisation towards compression of individual rights. Launched in 2019 by Wikipedia founder Jimmy Wales, as the non-toxic social network 'where your data isn't packaged up and sold', it promises not to turn users into the classic goldfish in a bowl, make them live in a sort of 'Truman Show', or perform 'algorithmic nudging'. However, to date, WT Social has a very scarce user base and does not show signs of improvement. Compared to other emerging platforms such as Clubhouse (about 28 million users) and Be Real (about 10 million), about half a million WT Socialites look like an endangered species.

There can be three main reasons for this radical difference. The first is that WT Social is based on a system of economic contributions paid by users. Paying for the service is not mandatory, but the quid pro quo is clear, and users accustomed to paying in personal data instead of in legal tender are not comfortable in throwing out the money in exchange for the possibility of writing what they want. Furthermore, the second reason is that what is published on WT Social can be modified by other users, according to the same scheme—and therefore with the same issues—as Wikipedia. It does not matter if somebody is an academic, ill-informed, or conspiratorial disinformer. Nobody would accept that his freedom of expression could be curtailed by somebody else, no matter how correct the edit is. Finally, as it has been remarked,

By declaring war on fake news and clickbait, the Wikipedia creator's new site is spurning the very things that help social media networks succeed. Remember: it wasn't only Facebook's ad model that caused the spread of fake news in 2016, but also the public's genuine interest in those dubious stories[13].

Profile by design

The objective of locking the user in a cage made up of confirmation bias and manipulation of his behaviour makes profiling a structural element of how a platform of this type is conceived.

A deluge of ink has been used to analyse the complex strategies behind designing a social network. They involve—as this book advocates—the commodification of rights. Such a result, however, is achieved through a subtle and massive deployment of psychological manipulation techniques at *the design* level. Social *media* users are controlled through a complex machine of behavioural psychology, interface design, and marketing techniques.

Legislators, regulating authorities, and privacy activists focus on the danger of unscrupulous personal data collection and misuse. They are concerned about what 'algorithms' and 'artificial intelligence' could do with our data.

No-holds-barred profiling is, of course, a real problem. However, it is not the only one and, counterintuitively, not the most relevant. Indeed, before selling users something or manipulating their behaviour, profiling them serves to *design* a social network platform according to their personality traits and preferred communication channels.

Profiling is the foundation, not (only) the outcome, of a social networking platform. It allows the application of 'Warhol's Law' through the artificial creation of hierarchies and social scoring associated with the use of the platform (number of 'likes', 'friends', views, and shares) and behaviour's homologation.

> Social media platforms are using the same techniques as gambling firms to create psychological dependencies and ingrain their products in the lives of their users, experts warn. These methods are so effective they can activate similar mechanisms as cocaine in the brain, create psychological cravings ... 'Facebook, Twitter and other companies use methods similar to the gambling industry to keep users on their sites,' ... 'In the online economy, revenue is a function of continuous consumer attention – which is measured in clicks and time spent.' Whether it's Snapchat streaks, Facebook photo-scrolling, or playing CandyCrush, ..., you get drawn into 'ludic loops' or repeated cycles of uncertainty, anticipation and feedback—and the rewards are just enough to keep you going.[14]

Regardless of their commercial success, Twitter, Instagram, Soundcloud, TikTok, Clubhouse, and the myriad of vertical platforms dedicated to writers, photographers, musicians, sportsmen, and athletes relied upon a *different* kind of interaction. Each social network targets an audience in terms of age, interests, communication channels, and content creation tools. Young people hardly own a Facebook profile, which is considered a 'boomer thing'. TikTok users of every age only interact through a mobile device. Instagram, Snapchat, and Twitter users 'live fast' and burn content. Some like visual communication. Others are more attracted by spoken or written messages.

Thematic social networks aimed at professionals are often advertised as where one can potentially be spotted from—say—the company that needs a photographer or a record label looking for new talent. Maybe there is even some more or less real success story to show that if someone publishes a poem on that specific platform, a prominent publisher might notice him and make him the new Dante Alighieri. So a person is induced to spend money to use a social network from which he expects a return in professional terms that will most likely never come. In the meantime, he falls for the 'pat on the back syndrome': putting 'likes' on somebody else's work to solicit reciprocity and get likes back. Getting a few hundred or a few thousand 'thumbs-up' may be gratifying or flattering. However, at a second glance, it is easy to rationalise that having all these likes does nothing to enhance one's professional standing. A like is the equivalent of the distracted gaze of a passer-by who is briefly attracted by a busker's performance. He looks at the artist for a moment, he might even think 'bravo', and then moves on, minding his business. The same is true for a five-star rating on a personal profile.

The ubiquitous, vague, and hard-to-understand 'privacy policies' promise that we get a better 'user experience' and a more efficient service in exchange for our intimate life, that being the actual prize. In reality, however, the purpose is to create a hunting reserve to which no one has access except the landlord, the owner of the hunting reserve who decides whether today he hunts foxes, tomorrow roe deers, and the day after wild boars. Therefore, creating a social network is closely linked to the concept of clusters—the possibility of grouping several individuals into specific categories.

Understanding how people 'work'—or rather, convincing them that they work as if they were machines—is the prerequisite to controlling them.

So far, this result has been achieved by collecting data about personal preferences, political views, and orientations. Behaviour-related information have also been processed but mainly through mouse and keyboard tracking.

The increased computing power, Internet bandwidth, ubiquitous mobile connectivity, and networked biosensors available to final users make it possible to take existing technologies and use them to allow large-scale processing of biometric and physiological information.

Eye-tracking technologies for the civil market were already available in the early 1990s. In 1992 the venerable Canon EOS 5—a *film* camera— was already capable of detecting in the *optical* viewfinder where the photographer was looking and focus accordingly. The video games industry invested huge figures into systems to map, collect, and digitise athletes' biometric information to create clones that can replicate their 'signature move'. Nowadays, Canon Free Viewpoint Video System[15] promises to 3D digitise reality by giving users the possibility to *pick* also viewpoints they would never had access to, such as flanking a goalkeeper or facing the opponent in a tennis or boxing match. The increased availability of wearable sensors and the ease of processing their data flow in shorter and shorter timeframe made possible to expand the *quantity* and *quality* of data up to conceive a social network based on biometric data and physiological response[16]. It will not take too much before the wearable-based studies on baboons' social networks[17] translate into the human realm.[18]

> The biometric data collected from metaverse users will make the privacy issues around in the current online environment seem like child's play. Tracking clicks and keystrokes pales in comparison to tracking emotions through biometric data. Beyond the implications to the individual of gathering of private information, there's the matter of whether the companies that have dominated social media through their dominance of data will similarly dominate biometric data and use it to crush new metaverse entrants.[19]

Achieving this result implies accessing our very personal sphere, the one we do not share with anyone and which does not necessarily correspond to the public version of ourselves that we use to interact with others.

In Greek tragedy, *persona* was the mask worn by the actors. It represented the play's character—a god, a demon, a ghost. Once worn, the *persona* gave the actor its identity. He *became* the persona. Similarly, everyone has at least a public and a private persona, as explained by how Japanese society relates to this issue. Social interaction starts from an individual's own exclusive sphere, accessible not even to loved ones. Then there is a slightly wider sphere that includes the family. Then there is the social circle and, finally, the *tanin*, the strangers to whom there is no relationship.

Profiling is not meant to control the public person because that is easy enough (and not very useful, indeed). The profiling's goal is to break into the inner circle, the one that contains our most intimate, most personal individuality, the one that drives our behaviour and orients our choices.

The more publicly exposed behaviours, the more they appear rational. Students go to class because they have to take an exam, whether or not they like the teacher. People work to earn wages. Public actions are—or are supposed to be—rationally goal-oriented. However, the closer one gets to the true nature of one's self, the less rational decisions become. As trivial as the example may be, shopping is one domain where the line between rational and impulse-driven choices becomes thinner. More so when deciding whether a person can become our 'friend'—in particular, an *online* friend. Indeed, decisions about the individual and personal sphere become even less rational and more instinctive when made through social networks.

In short, the goal of profiling is to control the person's intimacy. This is why biometrics and physiology data are of the utmost importance. They do not lie. They allow the understanding of what is hidden behind the mask and—literally—*inside* a person. This knowledge makes it easier to direct her towards a target, whatever that may be.

Modern, and therefore centralised, social networks are based on the idea that people can be categorised to predict and direct their behaviour. Social networks become social *media*—something similar to broadcasting platforms—to which users should be exposed without the chance of reacting or, in the best-case scenario, with limited, pre-determined interactive options.

In other words, where newsgroups and IRC were based on the freedom of the person to be what he or she wanted, to relate to others as he or she preferred, today, social networks create yet another gilded cage. Depending on the point of view, it may be a cage but gilded, or it may be gilded, but a cage nonetheless.

Such centralised systems are built upon the anthropological assumption that people are like (perhaps a little more evolved) Pavlov's dogs.

This conclusion challenges the idea that contemporary social *media* allow people to interact *freely* because the omnipresent 'algorithm' tells them what they should read, see, or listen to. Way before that, behavioural control happens through the interface design that affects the quality and kind of interaction. Indeed, there is a direct connection between the design of a social network and the latitude of rights' exercise.

Nudge and control by design

For a social network to be effective, it must work and be accessible from everywhere. Users must be able to use it from wherever they are but be trapped in a lock-in so they cannot easily leave it.

A paper about how a social network is made and how its users interact pointed out that

> In interviews and survey responses, participants explained that the design of an online space can support having challenging conversations constructively and in ways that could not occur face-to-face, especially when initiating conversations. However, they simultaneously described other common properties of online spaces that interfere with the delicate process of working through a challenging

topic and strip away important cues that occur in face-to-face contexts.[20]

It appears that (even a relative) anonymity fosters participation because 'it alleviates fear and avoidance … asynchronicity facilitates thoughtfulness … privacy and channel switching facilitate authenticity … users value less moderation and censorship from a platform'.[21] These examples show how controlling the interaction design empowers or limits the possibility of reclaiming a legal right. Indeed, the cited paper provides helpful suggestions to *improve* the users' experience. Giving a user a second chance by allowing the deletion of content, blocking accounts of people behaving inappropriately, allowing the disclosure of personal information, and moving a conversation from public to private and vice versa allow emoticons to better define the non-verbal component of the message, automated preemptive warnings about tone and length of a post, delaying the response time to allow cooling down before doing something and even—the topic surfaces once again—monitoring biometrics parameter[22]' … these *control* features may improve the quality of interaction. However, the very same suggestions may be turned 180° and become a roadmap for behavioural control.

Whatever the choice, its implementation happens through an *interface* acting as the gateway between the individual and the platform. Hence the need to control how interfaces are designed, which *behaviour* they allow, and which *rights* they make enforceable.

Interface control can happen (as in the case of Apple) either by imposing one's hardware and how one writes programmes or (Google) by controlling the operating system that runs on the terminals of manufacturers that have chosen not to invest in that software component. The concrete result of these strategies is the obliteration of diversity. A person from Bangalore could not be more different in terms of culture and individual sensibility from fellows from Tijuana or New York; however, when an instant messaging notification arrives, they all do the same thing. They all make the same gesture. This is the power of the interface. A power that can affect people's behaviour and the possibility of exercising their rights.

Suppose a functionality is added to the interface of a messaging platform that enables the deletion of a message even on the recipient's terminal. In that case, it is the one who controls the platform and has unilaterally decided to give the user the possibility of deleting messages sent by mistake. If, on the other hand, the platform owner decides not to make this functionality available or limit its capability, he also unilaterally deprives the person of his right not to suffer the consequences of not being given a chance to prevent or limit a potential problem.

WhatsApp and Snapchat have different policies. They both have messages lasting at least 24 hours before disappearing. On the other hand, Signal—the privacy-committed messaging platform—is far more flexible.

Signal now supports the ability to preconfigure all conversations you initiate with a default timer. Users can now set customer timer durations on their conversations so that some content can be gone in 60 seconds and other exist for 18 minutes or 4 weeks. On the other hand, you have to manually set the disappearing message on WhatsApp or all individual chats. The app also does not offer a custom timer and the chat will disappear after 7 days. Whereas, the Telegram users will first have to enable secret chats on the app to use the disappearing messages feature.[23]

As it is apparent, different ways of enabling such feature make a considerable difference in exercising individual rights.

Another example of how control by design works is whether or not to include a thumbs-down icon in the interface of a webpage.

Some social platforms have this functionality but use it differently.

The ambivalence towards these reaction buttons, which are now an integral part of the language of social networks and which are also perceived as causes and symbols of abusive virality, misinformation or perverted egos, reflects the uneasiness of the digital companies that have developed them. Although they are aware that they must make efforts to fight against online violence, they are still dependent on the information that these features are able to collect.[24]

YouTube opted to show dislike only to the content creator to avoid 'bashing'.

While the removal of public dislikes could help the creators, there is the argument this is also about helping YouTube by getting more eyeballs on videos – even ones that could disappoint some viewers. The lack of 'dislikes' means there is no quick public review of the user-generated content.[25]

TikTok followed a different path

testing a way to let individuals identify comments they believe to be irrelevant or inappropriate. This community feedback will add to the range of factors we already use to help keep the comment section consistently relevant and a place for genuine engagement. To avoid creating ill-feeling between community members or demoralise creators, only the person who registered a dislike on a comment will be able to see that they have done so.[26]

LinkedIn, Instagram, and Facebook (which also experimented with it in the past) have not activated the button for expressing dissent.

Dislikes have a much greater significance and effect than expressions of appreciation than likes do. Likes associated with a specific content do not tell how many people disliked it and why. As in political elections, one can only be sure how many votes individual candidates got. Conversely, as far as abstentionists are concerned, no one can say for sure why they did not go to vote and whom they would have chosen. Similarly, the number of supporters of a piece of content does not tell how many other people have a different opinion on that. Of course, there are always comments that might provide some hint. However, the small number next to the icons conveys an incredibly more direct and perceptible message without the need to go through hundreds and hundreds of opinions. There is no need to do complex reasoning in front of 12 or 12 million likes (at least, in the first instance). The numbers associated with an icon speak to the gut, not to the mind. Indeed, the possibility of expressing dissent can be a way of expressing a legitimate opinion on the merits of content. However, as YouTube's 'conservative' choice suggests, it can also allow attacks on a person's dignity. Hence the justification for making the thumbs down private by compressing the freedom to express one's opinions or restricting its operation.

These choices result in the imposition of arbitrary limits on freedom of speech and the exercise of political rights far more subtle than the macroscopic 'censorship' of posts and comments.

The blocking of content or the deactivation of an account for violating the terms and conditions is a macroscopic event, immediately perceivable and therefore quickly challenged by the interested party and the 'community' of users. Sometimes—as in the case of the iconic photograph entitled Napalm Girl denouncing the horrors of the Viet Nam war—the platform is forced to backpedal.[27] Many other users, however, are denied, without any real possibility to appeal, express themselves, or even use the service.

On the contrary, the interface's control translates into the power to select 'what' and 'how' to allow users. This is a much less perceptible control. It affects the concrete exercise of a person's rights not through laws or judicial rulings but on private, non-transparent decisions taken outside any regulation, at least contractual.

The consequences of these technological choices in exercising political rights are worrying. Suppose the government announces a particular course of action on its official profile. For the sake of simplicity, let us further assume that the profile only registers accesses of real people expressing themselves in good faith and blocks bots or other forms of automatic manipulation, such as the 'like factory'. Finally, suppose tens of millions of citizens use the dislike button to express their dissent on the government project. At this point, for the sake of consistency, the executive would have to respect the people's will and backpedal or even admit that it has been

78

defied. Or the government could ignore the dissent and go straight ahead applying its announced policy. Or again, suppress the protests by suppressing the dissent.

Whatever the choice, such a situation would mean the end of the system based on representative democracy, with the aggravating factor that the facilitator of this process is in the hands of a private entity and—compared to many countries—not even subject to that specific jurisdiction. Citizens might not need a thumbs-down on an executive's social profile to criticise its actions. Other effective online tools allow expressing dissent, such as a trivial, old-fashioned 'mail bombing' or joining online petitions. This is true, but nothing replaces the impact of a deluge of protests addressed directly to the executive. Interestingly, the websites of the American and British governments—countries where freedom of expression is protected almost like a religious creed—have made diametrically opposite choices. The White House does not allow one to comment directly on the site's contents but contains the ubiquitous social sharing buttons that link to official profiles. Downing Street, on the other hand, not only does not allow any public comment—even in the form of a like—but does not even allow official social profiles, which do exist. However, both of them appear as not having a counter to acknowledge people 'like/dislike' sentiments on various matters.

If a political party decides to use an online platform as an alternative to the mechanism of local, regional, and then national congresses to define its policies, this is not a problem because these are internal choices in the democratic dynamics of the functioning of social aggregations. It is not necessarily so when political representation happens through a privately-managed technological proxy.

The company that runs it does not care about the identity or the ideological allegiance (if any) of those who express their opinions (at least, until these opinions do not endanger the business). On the contrary, it has every interest in having them living in a 'social singularity' condition to polarise reactions better and generate a deluge of data to be collected. Social singularity is the pretence (or the delusion) of being part of an online 'community' while being not. Being a community member means sharing values, being ready to help and work for the common benefit, and protecting each other. By contrast, living in a social singularity condition (favoured by social networking platforms) turns an individual into a part of a swarm whose only reason to team up with somebody else is a personal motive, whether logical or irrational. Counterintuitively, that causes the disappearance of originality of thought and the loss of individuality. It is, by the way, paradoxical that that is happening when respect for diversity is a watchword. Indeed, cultural homologation in terms of rituals, behaviours, and social relations is pre-determined by the commercial and industrial interests of a small number of actors.

Secure universal access

Statistics allows conclusions from a relatively small population in terms of numbers, provided the sample is balanced and the other principles of this scientific field are respected. However, from the point of view of behaviour control, numbers count most. If the aim is to monitor people to change their behaviour, it is intuitive that many users are needed to achieve the result.

The bigger the user base, the more influential the steering can be imposed. In other words, sample-based statistics may be helpful for *prediction*, but significant figures are necessary to *exert control*. Controlling the interface and the inner working of 'smart devices' cancels diversity and standardises behaviours. These strategies are also instrumental in expanding as much as possible the target's size.

Achieving a global spread of the same platform, its interface, and the device to use it reminds that of large multinational chains. Many people, wherever they are in the world, look for familiar fast-food or international cafeterias. They are familiar places because they are at least an element of certainty abroad. So, instead of enriching themselves with the new experience of going to a never-seen-before place, people go to the other side of the world to end where they know everything beforehand, without even having to visit it physically.

The global availability of access to an Internet connection and hardware tools is another component of the strategy to get a large number of users.

To this end, an ideal condition for a social network would be to control the entire chain of the data cycle from creation to collection. That would require controlling the entire technological chain, from software running on 'smart' devices and computers to Internet access and traffic data and, finally, to the user's interaction with the platform.

Not being (initially) possible, these platforms had to think of an alternative. They entered into deals with hardware manufacturers to install their software on the devices, with Internet Service Providers to host their servers and telecommunication carriers to attract users.

The unwritten pact between platforms and manufacturers of computers and smart devices included the possibility to get information generated by users' interaction with the devices and software. For years, that has been a standard business practice outside the social network business. Big corporations and small software manufacturers hid behind a thick wall of legal clauses enforce their 'right' to collect data about the device on which their product would be installed. Nowadays, as the next chapter elucidates, it is not even possible to *avoid* being remotely controlled by a software manufacturer through mandatory 'online activations', 'online centralised accounts', and 'anonymous data collection'.

However, the balance between software/hardware manufacturers and platforms cracked when the former started to encroach, at least partially, on the sectors of the latter. On the one hand, platforms want as much data as possible from terminals purchased by users due to 'social appeal' of these slates. On the other hand, manufacturers are increasingly interested in having exclusive access to their users' data—or preventing others from exploiting them. An example is the evolution of Apple's line of services and the role of the 'right to privacy' as marketing leverage.

> Apple's tracking-optional mobile operating system update is coming to iPhones ... and the new privacy-preserving features will give users the ability to opt out of being followed around the Internet via trackers in their apps. Facebook—which makes the vast majority of its money from data collected through those trackers—really doesn't like Apple's new features. Now Facebook is considering suing Apple ... Facebook CEO ... said ... that 'we increasingly see Apple as one of our biggest competitors,' accusing Apple of using its 'dominant platform position' to push its own apps while interfering with Facebook's. Zuck added that Apple may frame this as a privacy service to its customers, but it's really only in Apple's own best anti-competitive interests.[28]

For a long time, the ability to run platforms and services in the data centres of Internet providers allowed services to be launched without having to invest in expensive infrastructure. However, with time, being an *over the top*—a platform deployed *on top* of access, transport, and data-centre services—has become more a problem than a resource. The initial cost-effectiveness of this solution soon exposed a collateral effect: depending on third parties to allow final users to access the data-transport networks implies a lesser strict control over the technical operations and the data flow. More prominent players became de facto Internet service providers or telecommunication carriers. They started building their own data centres and networks, and even deploying undersea, transoceanic cables. This choice has increased their autonomy from other telecommunications operators, although, at least for the moment, a complete disengage from the latter is unlikely.

Particularly concerning the mobile sector, the ability to access social networking, streaming, and content-sharing platforms is an established component of voice and data service offerings. There is, therefore, a mutual interest in using social networks to attract customers to purchase mobile services and in using mobile access 'special offers' to drive users to the platforms.

Those who did not witness the early development of Internet access might not remember when billing was based on connection time and/or volume of data exchanged, and access was mainly a stationary matter. By contrast, contemporary mobile, flat-fee-based billing models push users into always staying on even when a landline connection is unavailable.

Nevertheless, is it indispensable? The continuous availability of network access does not imply that access has to be permanent, as can be understood by asking whether all the time spent with an active data connection is linked to fulfilling a concrete need.

On the one hand, it is evident that when society evolves towards a complete service remotisation, a permanent, secure, and always available network access with adequate performance is no less than mandatory. However, this global availability is only used to a small extent for things people need, such as paying bills, purchasing goods, and interacting with civil services. Most of the time, people stay online simply because the data connection remains active even when there is no need. Meanwhile, the smart device, its controller, continues to collect data even when it is not necessary. Those who advocate for access to the Internet to be acknowledged as a fundamental 'digital right' should think twice before pushing the campaign ahead.

Exploit 'Warhol's Law'

The generalised hedonism induced by social networks' business models reinforces social differentiation based on how one looks *on screen*, not on how one is. This primal need to communicate is beginning to turn into something else. It becomes the need to be recognised as a living being *through a screen*. Indeed, one of the reasons for the success of social networks is that they give a certificate of being alive to people whose existence could otherwise go completely unnoticed.

This statement may sound melodramatic, but it is not so once given a second thought. What is the point of so many people's public social profiles? Why should the world be interested in strangers who have nothing to say except about their (surely no longer) anonymous daily lives? It certainly makes sense to share one's profile with people one knows or meets. Nevertheless, why should this be of interest to anyone else?

The first answer might be: why not? After all, letting anyone come across, even by chance, a profile with no particular interest can be a way of starting a new relationship or expanding one's social network. However, the evolution of web-based social networks suggests a more articulate reflection.

In 2007 the Italian comedian Corrado Guzzanti expressed the paradox of the universality of the Internet with a sarcastic one line. Commenting on the enthusiasm of those who told him that thanks to the net, he would even be able to talk to an Aboriginal, he said: *Aborigeno, ma io e te, che ci dobbiamo dire?*—Aboriginal, but you and I, what will we ever have to say to each other?

From his point of view, that of an individual, Guzzanti was entirely right in asking the question. On the other hand, the possibility of being exposed to an 'international audience' is a powerful source of social network's appeal. It promises everybody to become famous even for a day or a minute, and in a very restricted circle but famous nonetheless. Those who, having no particular talent, go 'viral' nonetheless are the best example of this dynamics. Their 'performance' gets a hit of visualisations and sometimes even ends up in the mainstream media. In a few moments, though, they disappear as fast as they popped up a few moments earlier on top of the posts' feed.

According to 'Warhol's law', everyone, at least once in their life, will have 15 minutes of fame. This line by the father of Pop Art explains the 'nudge' used by social networks to increase their user base. Although Warhol's law was conceived in a world where celebrity came through television, it perfectly works still today. Indeed, social networks have even amplified their effects on people's irresistible desire to receive a certificate of existence through a few likes.

Turning an interactive technology into a TV-like platform is a process initiated way before modern social networks, with the spreading of the Web. The focus on the passive use of the ubiquitous WWW was so concentrated that the Web was wrongly considered a synonym for 'the Internet'.

Of course, many people still connect to the Internet to use in its more essential way. However, a considerable majority just stare at a screen, not caring whether it shows a television programme or a YouTube real-time broadcast. There is no difference between a monitor and a TV set because they both are a screen. And where is a screen, somebody is always looking at it. An audience, in other words.

Create artificial values

Another artful exploitation of the fame-machine comes from the *ex nihilo* creation of social values and hierarchies associated with the platform.

The transformative power of language plays an essential role in this process because words affect the meaning, and meaning alters behaviour. Friend is an important word that should not be associated with someone who happened to pass by and ask for a link just because he is interested in seeing the things we post. That is not a 'friend' and not even an acquaintance, like a LinkedIn 'connection' is often a way to exploit somebody else's 'network' or get indirect credit for having 'illustrious' interlocutors. When disconnected *from* why people want to be informed about news coming from a content creator, a 'follower' is often a way to get a free pizza by promising the restaurant the release of a story on one's profile rather than a measure of personal success.

The consequences on individual behaviour in terms of homologation and social dynamics are no longer only confined to the platforms. Take note of how many people who, instead of realising where they are, walk around looking at their mobile phones or take selfies and videos for 'immediate release' while doing things—such as driving or street crossing—that would require some attention.

Keep State's power at bay

What else does a social networking platform need to achieve its goals? First and foremost, the autonomy of state powers. A company cannot wait for authorisations from ministry X or authority Y. It cannot limit its strategies because the regulators' bureaucracy requires it to fill out forms and amass a stack of papers. There is no reason it should incur higher taxation related to the profits.

Powers-that-be must be kept at bay.

The intricated Web of connections among individuals, companies, and even civil services makes it very unlikely the probability of a State to ban a social network entirely. The consequences of shutting down profiles, pages, and all the related, indirect business would negatively affect the economy but, firstly, would probably cause protests, riots, and social disturbances.

However, relying only upon the *status quo* is impossible to be safe from States' reach, so a multi-level public relation strategy is necessary. Ideally, lobbying should prevent specific regulations from being passed. Just in case, 'Plan B' should secure that they are passed in the least afflictive way possible, 'Plan C' that they are passed as late as possible, and 'Plan D' is that they are passed in the least afflictive way and as late as possible.

The strategy of lobbying legislators and regulators is flanked by mitigation—and possibly elimination—of the importance of individual rights to reduce judicial redress and, hence, public powers' scrutiny (see Chapter 2).

In other words, beyond the normative construct and the perception of the importance of rights, what matters is that people's urge to use a given service must be stronger than the perception of the importance of the rights that are compromised in the use of this service. This is why it is incorrect to claim that 'data are new oil'. Data collection is a means, and lowering the perception of the importance of people's rights is the end. What becomes marketable are rights, not data.

From being absolute, fundamental, universal, or whatever, rights become a commodity like the next product on the shelf of a mall. When a person consents to social network profiling, she is not authorising access to her data. She agrees to give up a right.

To complete the process, another step is necessary: eliminating trust in the justice system or—that is the same—making it ineffective.

Suppose that the judicial redress of a dispute concerning a platform's use or decision requires time, substantial disbursement, and has an uncertain outcome. Putting aside class actions or claims initiated for political reasons, who would file a suit for a censored post or a deactivated account?

If, by contrast, the controversy is decided through the platform, going before a judge becomes pointless. The worst-case scenario is that case is lost—as it might have been in a tribunal. However, it happened fast and cheap. Who needs a court anymore?

The dark side of this approach is apparent. A content removal is decided by some obscure moderator located in some lost place in the world, if not by an automated content analysis system. The content is so controversial that the account is automatically suspended. This is done overnight. The user finds himself without an account and has no one to talk to. He activates the internal procedures. There is an initial review of the case, and if they *tell* him wrong, there is no other option but to comply with the platform reading of its terms and condition or stand for his rights and take issue in court, if he can afford it. In the meantime, the whole universe of contents made available through any of these platforms suddenly disappears irretrievably.

Turn people into 'nomadic monads'

Standard definitions for social network dystopia include 'surveillance' or 'control' capitalism. However, it looks like 'loneliness capitalism' is a better option.

Loneliness is the main characteristic of interaction with social networks. People get the false perception of being connected, of having a social life. However, in reality, they are alone, locked in a room in front of a monitor or wearing 'metaverse-enabling' goggles.

The political and legal impact of such a consequence is clear. If direct interaction between people is lost, the concept of society is lost because the importance of the role we have given to rights is lost.

In other words, rights established through a parliamentary debate are needed if we interact with someone else. If this 'else' is not at arm's reach anymore, there is no need to regulate his interactions. Therefore, the bond that creates society breaks, rights become useless, and only the jungle law remains. By contrast, claiming back the role and respect of individual's rights means rejecting the concept of nomadic and monadic life, refusing to live disengaged from society, with the sole perspective of producing to spend.

Move everything 'to the cloud'

Although omnipresent in everyone's life, social networks are only part of the process of removing the individual from control over his rights. The transfer 'to the cloud' of essential parts of a person's life, such as the relationship with civil services, the administration of justice, and one's own identity, first of all, translates into discrimination to the detriment of the less wealthy and less literate people. As in the case of 'smart weapons' (see Chapter 5), the insertion of an impassable technological layer between citizens and the State dehumanizes the relationship with institutions. Furthermore, the choice to exercise democracy through technology implies handing the former to those who control the latter.

Big Tech has become a subject that interacts on an equal footing with the States and strongly influences their strategic choices and how the public administration must operate. However, this loss of control over the functioning of the state apparatus is not the only problem.

The enormous amount of data and electronic communications flows that cross networks around the world expose the rights of individuals and the interests of states to criminal attacks and hostile actions by enemy countries. They also represent a great temptation for the public authorities to institute a generalised and preventive control in the name of the greater good or national security. Sometimes, as in the case of the pandemic, this happened awkwardly. Some other times, invoking the war on terror, the choices of the chancelleries have been pursued with greater determination and effectiveness at the expenses of constitutional rights.

State and citizens have, indeed, an understandable desire to ensure that the communication, especially of personal or intimate information, is secure from the prying eyes of unintended recipients, miscreants, and offenders. They differ, however, on the extent and limits of this expectation.

The role of cryptography is fundamental in this debate, which has been reignited by its use on a global scale to commit serious crimes and, paradoxically, to facilitate mass and individual surveillance. Historically, the public debate on cryptography has been handled by opposing extremisms. On the one hand, privacy advocates raised the flag of 'digital rights'. On the other hand, those who called for mass control as a preventive solution to all problems gathered in the name of national security. Between the two, Big Tech intervened with an ambiguous position, playing on both fronts at the same time, to become the real policy maker.

This is the topic explored in the following chapter.

Notes

1 Josephson, 1934
2 Livraghi 1997.
3 Livraghi 1997.
4 Llorente, Rubén *The First Social Network* Linux Magazine 217/2018 https://www.linux-magazine.com/Issues/2018/217/Usenet visited 29 May 2022
5 Yang 2009:28–29
6 Lee, 2015:56.
7 Can, Kaya: 2016, 484
8 Wu, Andy *The Facebook Trap* Harvard Business Review online edition, 19 October 2021, https://hbr.org/2021/10/the-facebook-trap visited 28 May 2022
9 Wu, Andy *id.*

10 Kaye, 2021: 2

11 Autorità garante per la concorrenza e il mercato, *Bollettino settimanale Anno X numero 7*, 6 March 2000 https://www.agcm.it/dotcmsdoc/bollettini/7-00.pdf visited 2 june 2022.

12 Autorità garante per la protezione dei dati personali, *Reti telematiche e Internet - Consenso consapevole e libero per il trattamento dati per l'erogazione del servizio Internet gratuito 'Libero' di Infostrada S.p.A.* Provvedimento 30911 del 13 gennaio 2000 https://www.garanteprivacy.it/web/guest/home/docweb/-/docweb-display/docweb/30911 visited 2 June 2022

13 Chandler, Simon *Why Wikipedia Creator's New 'Facebook Killer' Is Doomed to Fail* 23 September 2020 https://www.ccn.com/why-wikipedia-creators-new-facebook-killer-is-doomed-to-fail/Visited 31 August 2022

14 Busby, Mattha *Social media copies gambling methods 'to create psychological cravings'* The Guardian online edition 8 May 2018 https://www.theguardian.com/technology/2018/may/08/social-media-copies-gambling-methods-to-create-psychological-cravings visited 20 June 2022

15 Canon Global Technology *Technologies for Visual Expression Create a Brand-new Viewing Experience* https://global.canon/en/technology/frontier18.html visited 20 June 2022.

16 Kanis, Marije et al. 2005. Toward Wearable Social Networking with iBand. *CHI '05 Extended Abstracts on Human Factors in Computing Systems* https://web.media.mit.edu/~stefan/hc/publications/Kanis05iBandCHI.pdf visited 2 June 2022

17 Gelardi, Valeria et al. 2020. Measuring social networks in primates: wearable sensors versus direct observations. Proc. R.Soc.A 476: 20190737 https://doi.org/10.1098/rspa.2019.0737 visited 2 June 2022.

18 Farseev, Aleksandr et al. Tweet Can Be Fit: Integrating Data from Wearable Sensors and Multiple Social Networks for Wellness Profile Learning. *ACM Transactions on Information Systems* Volume 35 Issue 4 October 2017 Article No.: 42 pp 1–34 https://doi.org/10.1145/3086676 visited 2 June 2022.

19 Wheeler, Tom, *If the Metaverse Is Left Unregulated, Companies Will Track Your Gaze and Emotions* Time Magazine online edition 20 June 2022 https://time.com/6188956/metaverse-is-left-unregulated-companies-will-track-gaze-emotions/ visited 20 June 2022.

20 Baughan et al, 2021:8

21 Baughan et al, 2021: 9–12

22 Baughan et al, 2021: 14

23 TimesofIndia.com *Signal improves its disappearing messages feature, here's how* The Times of India online edition 12 August 2021 https://timesofindia.indiatimes.com/gadgets-news/signals-latest-feature-makes-disappearing-messages-the-norm-4-weeks-to-30-seconds/articleshow/85268967.cms visited 22 June 2022.

24 Reynaud, Florian – Croquet, Pauline *On social networks, the ups and downs of the 'dislike' button*, Le Monde online edition 2 May 2022 https://www.lemonde.fr/en/pixels/article/2022/05/02/on-social-networks-the-ups-and-downs-of-dislike_5982245_13.html visited 20 June 2022

25 Suciu, Peter, *YouTube Removed 'Dislikes' Button – It Could Impact 'How To' And 'Crafts' Videos* Forbes online edition 24 November 2021 https://www.forbes.com/sites/petersuciu/2021/11/24/youtube-removed-dislikes-button--it-could-impact-how-to-and-crafts-videos/?sh=cfc46fd5a53c visited 20 June 2022.

26 Keenan, Carmac *New ways to foster kindness and safety on TikTok* TikTo Newsroom 13 April 2022 https://newsroom.tiktok.com/en-us/new-ways-to-foster-kindness-and-safety-on-tiktok visited 22 June 2022.

27 Kleinman, Zoe *Fury over Facebook 'Napalm girl' censorship* BBC News 9 September 2016 https://www.bbc.com/news/technology-37318031 visited 22 June 2022.

28 Morrison, Sara *Why Facebook and Apple are fighting over your privacy* VOX 1 February 2021 https://www.vox.com/recode/22254815/facebook-apple-privacy-ios-14-lawsuit visited 22 June 2022.

4

ENCRYPTION AND RIGHTS

Social networks have strongly affected the very nature of legal rights and the possibility for individuals to claim their enforcement. As the previous chapter pointed out, they have even triggered mechanisms that have called into question the practical utility of legal protection. Social networks are neither the only nor the first to have significantly exposed the limits of traditional principles such as separation of powers and the rule of law.

Before modern social networks, cryptography was at the centre of endless and still unresolved questions about the limits of its use and—not only in regimes powered by 'variable democracy'—even the legitimacy of protecting itself from state control. On the one hand, human rights advocates see encryption as an essential tool for protecting privacy. Therefore, they are unwilling to accept restrictions on the use of this technology. On the other hand, members of the national security structures and the investigative and judicial sectors argue that it is necessary to sacrifice individual rights to enable the state to protect citizens and secure perpetrators to justice.

This approach is quite simplistic and conceptually—as in the theological confrontation between two monotheistic religions—admits of no solution other than to elide the opposite faith altogether. However, if different cults have an interreligious dialogue, it is clear why 'cryptographic monotheism' is not a viable option.

Indeed, the most controversial early cases involving cryptography, particularly the PGP affair, which will be discussed in the following pages, dealt with its role as a potential facilitator of social unrest and crime. However, the progressive digitisation of human activities, from creative acts to remote interaction with civil services and private platforms, has only been possible thanks to cryptography. Over time, cryptography (public-key cryptography, in particular) has become essential in ensuring the security of economic transactions, remotely identifying individuals, attributing the paternity of content to its creator, and preventing others from accessing it or modifying it without leaving a trace. Encryption has been and is essential to secure the economic interests of copyright stakeholders. Content Scrambling System, Digital Rights Management, Trusted Platform Modules ... these names

DOI: 10.4324/9781003373636-4

sound familiar to both the copyright industry and the activist (but also criminal) communities developing methods to circumvent these protections for the sake of sharing culture—or gain illegal profits.

Cryptography is also the basis of technologies such as blockchain, cryptocurrencies, and NFT, which, although most likely yet another speculative bubble, attract multimillion-dollar investments and provoke (unhinged) reactions from politicians and legislators.

The application areas of cryptography are very different and, at least apparently, unrelated. Seemingly, there is no connection between the risks caused by a technology that makes it possible to conceal evidence of a crime and the making of computer programmes that circumvent the locks to copyrighted digital works or sports events broadcasted in streaming. Similarly, the link between tools to verify a person's legal identity and, simultaneously, to make him or her wholly anonymous is not that obvious.

The variety of these topics might lead one to think that they can be analysed legally independently of each other. There is, however, a red thread linking these and other cryptography uses. Nothing, like modern cryptography, embodies the paradox of a knowledge that, at the same time, is essential for the survival of powers-that-be, fundamental for the protection of legal rights and indispensable for the industrial and economic development of the modern world. These interests are in direct competition with each other and, at least until now, have been balanced empirically. No one has yet managed to find a regulatory solution to meet the needs of all parties involved, and maybe nobody will.

The history of the relationship between cryptography, legal rights, and judicial or intelligence investigation is full of episodes that could be material for a book specifically dedicated to the subject. To go into detail on how and why cryptography has evolved is beyond the scope of this book. However, it is necessary to briefly recall some of the stages of this evolution to understand its consequences.

Without claiming to be exhaustive, the following pages describe a series of events primarily relevant for their symbolic and illustrative value. They show how a single invention—public key cryptography—changed the world.

Public-key cryptography revolutionises the scenario

Since the early 1970s, the mathematics of public key cryptography, developed by the UK Government Communications Headquarters (GCHQ), had remained classified. Its purpose was to guarantee the secrecy of message exchange via an insecure channel by definition, overcoming traditional cryptography's fundamental limitation: entrusting the message's inviolability to a single decryption key. Around the same time, civil research independently produced a similar system: in 1976, Whitfield Diffie and Martin Hellman published an architecture based on asymmetric cryptography.[1] The next year Ron Rivest, Adi Shamir, and Adleman published an influential paper representing the core of the public key algorithm named after them.[2] That was the beginning of a revolution.

Initially, it was designed to communicate information over an insecure channel without exchanging the decryption key. Subsequently, its applications have not only become a fundamental element in the functioning of the Big Internet but have affected many aspects of everyone's life. Indeed, public key cryptography has redefined concepts such as documents and signatures that underpin contractual relationships. It has changed the notions of identity and identification. It has allowed the state to take away prerogatives that were previously its own. Public-key cryptography has become a tool used to undermine the concept of representative democracy, laying the groundwork for the construction of a system of direct democracy that would lead directly to chaos.

Executive powers attack

The 1993 attempt of the US government to pass a regulation imposing the embedding into communication devices of a specific component named 'Clipper Chip' is an archetypal example describing the complex relationships between state needs, the protection of constitutional rights, and the interests of the technology industry.

The so-called 'Clipper Chip', whose functioning depended crucially on the use of public key cryptography,[3] was

> a cryptographic device purportedly intended to protect private communications while at the same time permitting government agents to obtain the 'keys' upon presentation of what has been vaguely characterized as 'legal authorization.' The 'keys' are held by two government 'escrow agents' and would enable the government to access the encrypted private communication. While Clipper would be used to encrypt voice transmissions, a similar chip known as Capstone would be used to encrypt data.[4]

The events connected with the design of the Clipper Chip and the enactment of the Communication Assistance for Law Enforcement Act are a testament to the importance that the US public security apparatuses attribute to the convergence of eavesdropping and cryptography in the non-military sphere, two sectors that can hardly be considered as separate worlds any more. The overall impact of these two proposals on the balance between individual rights and the state's powers is to change two longstanding fundamental legal assumptions: that phone calls are not inherently suspicious and that telephone companies are not law enforcement or secret service officer.

In 1987, the enactment of the Computer Security Act required the reali-sation of a new encryption standard to replace the retiring DES, so far the standard in the US administration. One of the main reasons for the gov-ernment's decision was the concern that the incipient obsolescence of the venerable algorithm, coupled with the absence of a new federal standard, would cause telecommunications and information technology companies to migrate to more modern and robust (non-government-controlled) prod-ucts, thereby irreparably undermining the interception capabilities of law enforcement agencies (FBI in the lead).

The US National Institute of Science and Technology immediately set to work, turning to the National Security Agency (NSA), which in turn worked out in the utmost secrecy the so-called EES (Escrowed Encryption Standard) based on Skipjack, a double-key algorithm to be used with a dedi-cated microprocessor (the Clipper for telephony, the Capstone for comput-ers) installed by the manufacturers in every device meant to interact with the telecommunication networks.

On 16 April 1993, US President Bill Clinton proposed EES as the new cryptographic standard, causing alarm among civil rights associations over the 'authorship' of the algorithm and its implementation. On the one hand, there were concerns that under the pretext of national security needs, the NSA does not allow the public release of algorithms that it cannot decipher. On the other hand, suspicion aroused that although the Computer Security Act involved the private sector, the entire operation would have been cov-ered by almost absolute secrecy for security purposes.

In May 1993, thanks to the Freedom of Information Act (FOIA), Computer Professionals for Social Responsibility—a civil rights association linked to the prestigious Massachusetts Institute of Technology—obtained proof that during the design of EES, the National Security Agency had done everything in its power to thwart (and succeeded in doing so) the attempts of those who wanted to subject it to public scrutiny.

There was enough to give rise to the most varied concerns. Findings dis-covered by CPSR (which had in the meantime been joined by another civil rights NGO, the Electronic Frontier Foundation) raised protests. The events suggested the existence of hidden functions in the Clipper and/or EES that would have facilitated the interception and deciphering of communications. Alongside these noble concerns were the more 'mundane' ones of the com-panies in the telecommunications sector, worried about the reactions of for-eign customers who would certainly not have bought a product based on protections that US investigative agencies could easily circumvent.

However, from a legal perspective, it is the very name of the standard that causes concern: the word 'escrow' means 'to hand something over to someone'. The 'something' is the two keys that allow the message's deci-phering. The 'someone' is two entities that should only hand over the keys to investigators in the presence of a warrant. Theoretically, this would protect communications from abusive eavesdropping (because Clipper renders them unintelligible) and allow the authorities to always know who is saying what to whom. From another angle, though, this means deliberately weakening the confidentiality of the entire communications system in favour of one party, law enforcement, and intelligence entities, weakening the right to a fair trial way before the right to the confidentiality of communications.

The civil rights NGOs' battle against EES caused a one-year delay in the release of the standard. It also turned into a fierce confrontation with the government, at the end of which many companies declared that they would have preferred the RSA algorithm developed by RSA Data Security, which was very robust and devoid of any 'institutionalised weakness', to EES.

On 4 February 1994, despite the enormous joint efforts of this atypical alliance of companies and civil rights associations, the Clipper chip became the federal standard for telephone communications, while—sad consolation—it was not made compulsory in the private sector. However, in 1996 the Clipper chip initiative was eventually dismissed. As the recent leaks by Manning and Snowden, punctually amplified by the media, confirmed, this did not mean the end of attempts by the US and more technologically advanced countries to exploit their own or more or less cooperating companies' interception and surveillance capabilities.

Although the Clipper chip case is now more interesting for cryptography historians than modern policymakers and jurists, it still has a lot to teach. Indeed, it contains all the elements that would later mark the political debate on encryption, from the necessity to impose upon a suspect the compulsory handover of his encryption keys to law enforcement up to the latest events related to the push for a de facto end-to-end encryption dismissal once and for all.

Activists strike back

As long as computers and programming languages were only used in companies and public institutions, the mathematics of cryptography was a subject reserved for a few researchers who were mainly concerned with civil and military communications security. So, apart from dabbling in puzzles, the rest of the world had little need for cryptography. Of course, organised crime and gang members used (and still use) low-tech coded languages[5]— such as those found in Cosa Nostra's Pizzini[6]—to hide information on the proceeds of extortion, betting, and other illicit trafficking or covertly communicate between those who serve jail time and other acolytes.[7]

However, resorting to low-tech to hide or make messages not readily available does not mean easy code-breaking. It took more than half a century to crack the code used by the Zodiac Killer—the still anonymous serial murderer from the late 1960s—who, without computing power, manually devised a transposition cypher strong enough to resist for decades.[8]

The situation changed dramatically when computers and, later, access to telecommunications networks made the tools to build serious cryptographic applications and services widely available also to 'common people'.

Within a few years, theoretical studies multiplied that produced algorithms based on the public-key cryptography revolutionary approach, and, in the early 1990s, Philip Zimmermann, a then unknown computer programmer, made them available to anyone who wanted 'Pretty Good Privacy' (PGP)—this is the name of Zimmermann's piece of software.

PGP was, indeed, built upon a mix of symmetric and public-key cryptography. It brutally brought governments face to face with a harsh reality: mass cryptography can no longer be handled with the old-style approach of when secret codes were the prerogative of embassies, the military, and a few other categories of actors.

Zimmermann's goal was to create software to protect the confidentiality of communications. Despite PGP being named after the 'privacy' word, Zimmermann was more concerned about creating something to protect political activist working in life-threatening places. In a 1996 interview, he clearly stated:

> PGP is used all over the world by human rights groups, human rights activists who are documenting the atrocities of death squads, interviewing witnesses and using that to keep track of human rights abuses, and they encrypt that stuff with PGP, and they tell me that if the government there could get their hands on it they would round up all the witnesses and kill them, after torturing them first ... We need encryption. ... If a future government inherits a technology infrastructure that's optimized for surveillance, where they can watch the movements of their political opposition ... if the incumbency has that political advantage over their opposition, then if a bad government ever comes to power, it may be the last government we ever elect.[9]

From Zimmermann's words, it is pretty clear that privacy, understood as the right to be alone, was not entirely at the top of the list of reasons that prompted him to create PGP. Moreover, it is pretty clear that Zimmermann did not have a precise perception of the difference between privacy as a person's right to control his or her information and confidentiality as a practical necessity to prevent unwanted entities from snooping into the activities of an individual. Not being a legal expert, he cannot be blamed for confusing different concepts. That, however, does not demote the incredible contribution Zimmermann gave to democratising cryptography.

The events that followed the computer programme's release showed that protecting personal information was not the only legal right at stake.

94

When PGP became available outside the US in 1993, the US authorities tried to block its distribution by applying the International Traffic in Arms Regulations (ITAR). Software that used keys longer than 40 bits was considered 'war ammunitions' and therefore subject to export under government licence. PGP did not use keys shorter than 128 bits, so, at least formally, the accusation was well-grounded. However, Zimmermann cleverly exploited the US Constitution's First Amendment protection of free speech by printing PGP's source code in a book[10] and claimed that selling it worldwide did not infringe the weapons' export control regulation.[11]

Zimmermann's defence was not subjected to the stress test of a trial because the US government dropped the charges after the relaxation of the limits on the export of cryptography. Nevertheless, it was the first case to short-circuit the national interest in control over knowledge and technology and the US constitutional right to freedom of expression.[12]

In 1997, to reduce the risks associated with intellectual property claims made on the algorithm implemented in PGP, the OpenPGP standard was published, which would have allowed other software to be developed independently and which could exchange files with the 'original' PGP. Thanks to the adoption of this standard, the Free Software Foundation made GNU Privacy Guard (GPG) available in 1999, adopting the same 'free' licensing model that governed the use of its other pieces of software. It made GPG free from any possible intellectual property claim.

PGP did not remain an isolated phenomenon and the sole nightmare for law enforcement and intelligence agencies. It has shown that an average person could access complex theoretical notions and the tools to turn them into functioning and efficient pieces of software. In the years to come, this realisation gave rise to countless projects whose aim was to protect the rights of the individual from everyone, including the state.

About in the same period, between 1997 and 2000, Julian Assange, Suelette Dreyfus, and Ralf Weinmann launched a project based on the concept of deniable encryption, also known as 'rubber hose encryption'. Deniable encryption contains nested encrypted file systems not immediately apparent to the interrogator. It is, therefore, possible for an individual to deny the existence of the wanted information. However, if forced to disclose the deciphering key under duress—hence the reference to the rubber hose, the beating tool of choice for torturers—the victim could release the key to access certain information, keeping those actually important still hidden and hoping that the Torquemada would not suspect the existence of further information. In 2004 another deniable encryption project gained momentum: TrueCrypt lately evolved into the still active (as far as 2022) VeraCrypt.

The political motivation for creating software with the precise aim of protecting political activists and investigative journalists challenges the common belief that encryption is only instrumental in protecting the right to privacy. In other words, not everything that has to remain secret has to be so in the name of privacy.

This conclusion is reinforced by the events that, in 1993, led a Finnish computer expert named Johan Helsingius to create anon.penet.fi, the first pseudonymous remailer. At about the same time as PGP's birth, Helsingius gave birth to a service that allowed users to send anonymous emails to anyone except the system administrator, who had the option of re-associating the anonymised address with the user who had sent it. Victim of unbearable pressure from local and foreign authorities eager to discover the identity of leakers and far-east regime critics, unjustly exposed by a questionable article published by a British journal as a child pornography 'trade facilitator', in 1996, Helsingius pulled the plug on his server.[13]

As in the case of PGP, that of anon.penet.fi constitutes the paradigm of the clash between public powers and legal rights. In creating his pseudonymous remailer, Helsingius was a victim of the borderless, alternate, jurisdictionless delusional idea of cyberspace. Answering a question during an interview, he said:

> laws don't matter anymore, because the net isn't governed by any country, so the laws of any specific country just don't apply, which is a really big strength. I see it definitely happening where lots of countries try to restrict things, and say, in our country you can't do this and this and this, but there is no way they can stop the network.[14]

It presents, however, a peculiarity deserving to be highlighted. Whereas in the case of Zimmermann's software, the legal dispute was between the author of the computer programme and the US government, in the case of Helsingius, the Finnish government was not directly involved in blocking the operation of the remailer. It bears repeating: the legal actions taken against Helsingius were based on complaints from a private organisation and a far-east foreign government. The former claimed a copyright infringement of their internal documents by a user of the remailer to find out, in reality, who was the author of the criticism. Similarly, the latter was looking for dissidents using the remailer to criticise the powers-that-be. However weak and imperfect, anon.penet.if was a demonstration that cryptography could also play an essential role in exercising political rights.

In 1998 another military research that stemmed from asymmetric cryptography became publicly available: onion routing. Evolved in 2002 into the Tor protocol (and the service of the same name), onion routing is a technology that allows information to be exchanged remotely, via the Internet, in an anonymous and untraceable manner (at least, on paper). Before being used for network access, onion routing was at the core of a new generation of remailers that, unlike Helsingius', could offer anonymity and not just pseudonymity. These remailers have evolved in various forms to guarantee the total anonymity and non-traceability of the sender of a message. Interestingly, in this case, the result is achieved not only through thoughtful approaches to algorithm and software development but also by exploiting the complexity of international judicial cooperation. Launched in 2008, the Mixmaster anonymous remailer was designed to pass the anonymous message through several national jurisdictions. This meant, in case a wiretapping or a seizure warrant issued by a court, going through different judicial rules, a possible lack of agreements for international judicial cooperation and legal conflicts. In other words, the law went hand in hand with mathematics to achieve as much anonymity as possible. Once again, therefore, law and politics were both the impetus for creating software and services that could protect the individual and a structural element for computer programme design.

The spread of cryptography and the tools to use caused the progressive loss of centrality of the law as a tool for asserting and protecting rights. The activists most sensitive to the political use of freely available technologies and information understood there was no need to ask parliament to protect this or that right. It was much simpler and faster to take the law into their hands by creating the necessary tools and confronting the executive with a fait accompli. The problem with this approach is that the decision to use a specific technology to protect an individual right is taken not based on the traditional democratic dialectic but, often, in the name of an ideological, fideistic, and religious conception that admits of no compromise. The so-called 'right to privacy' is the clearest example of this trend, which the passage of time would later confirm.

A similar approach would characterise Big Tech's strategies in the years to come. Only the motive for taking over the power to shape a legal right through technology was profit, not ideology.

Big Tech raises

The evolution of the cybersecurity market shows that as long as the Internet remained a tool for academics, public institutions, and large private companies, the technology industry did not worry much about data integrity and confidentiality of online information. In the civil sectors, backup and business continuity were more relevant concerns, excluding strategic areas where 'the enemy is listening', and information secrecy was indispensable.

Admittedly, the first firewalls and antiviruses date back to the late 1980s. However, it was only with the massive online shift of services directed at the individual that computer security became a product to be sold. To interact remotely with a vast number of customers—be they buyers of gadgets on e-commerce sites or bank account holders who have to make payments—it is essential to secure the connection, the identity of the parties involved, and the content of the transaction. The most severe issues stemmed from Internet services based on the IPv4 protocol, which was developed without particular attention to security. This design choice required adding software and equipment to mitigate the problem.

The growing concerns about the possible illegal trespass to computer systems and monitoring of the Internet's passive use, such as the browsing of contents and the use of services, led to the design of a multi-layered approach heavily relying upon public key encryption. Virtual Private Networks (VPN) allow Internet access (theoretically) unmonitorable by third parties. Secure DNS prevent snooping requests to connect to websites. Messaging platforms such as Signal or Tutanota do not store any information about the user using them and, like Protonmail, encrypt user-generated content locally.

Like all inventions, asymmetric encryption, onion routing, Tor, and its various applications, VPNs and alike are far from perfect. Nonetheless, they further exemplify the dialectic between the needs of the state, the interests of individuals and, last but not least, private industry.

Directly or through funding from international working groups and standardisation bodies, telcos, software houses, and hardware manufacturers develop encryption standards, protocols, products, and services. They integrate them into packages available to companies and institutions and the personal paranoia of those who think they have to protect themselves from the phantom, ubiquitous, all-knowing Big Brother (or Central Scrutiniser) instead of more common and actually dangerous miscreants.

At the same time, the growth of over-the-top services (OTT) based on content-sharing platforms and the spread of personal communication devices required to offer users perception of anonymity. It did not happen so much to protect their privacy or allow a free expression of their thoughts. Instead, this strategy (willingly or not) produced a sense of impunity from the consequences of inappropriate or illegal behaviour. The EU mantra 'what is illegal offline is illegal online'[15] is just the latest demonstration of the cultural and legal damage caused by crediting the cyberspace narrative of a 'place' where ordinary rules do not work. It has resulted in inducing the perception that behaviour carried out through telecommunications equipment and systems (much less glamorous names than 'smart device' and 'metaverse') has a different legal regime from that governing the same behaviour carried out by less technological means. Providing tools and services that guarantee—or claim to guarantee—anonymity and privacy have little to do with empowering people to exercise their legal rights and more with business strategies. Big Tech pushed this approach to the edge. Certain products are natively designed not to be accessible even to law enforcement. Moreover, those who design 'picks' to open these locks will likely be sued (on that, later).

Big Tech has consistently demonstrated a ruthless pragmatism that led them to consider rights as a mere element of a product's design and sales strategy. Their choices are not according to sacred and untouchable principles but strategic needs. In this context, encryption served not so much to protect users' privacy as to allow only certain parties to economically exploit the enormous amount of data generated by individuals who use the Internet daily while excluding all other potential stakeholders. Encryption became a way to implement marketing strategies based on the concept of 'none of your business', but only to a certain extent.

Tracking users who link to a website can be done in many ways. One of these consists of adding additional instructions to the URL that allows access to a page. These instructions aim to track the user for as long as he or she interacts with the site. As of June 2022, browsers such as Firefox have activated the URL stripping functionality. In a nutshell, this functionality removes additional commands from the URL, leaving only the part that allows the user to reach the desired content. To block this functionality, Facebook started to encrypt the entire URL of its pages[16] claiming that it had been done to prevent 'data scraping' and furtherly protect its users' privacy.[17] URL stripping is a clear example of how essential encryption is to protect the data-driven business models of Big Tech. The latter promises invisibility in the eyes of anyone but the lord of the platform.

On the other hand, certain services also use encryption, but with limitations on the overall design. Big Tech can claim that it keeps user-generated data away from prying eyes. The other part of the story is that it nonetheless keeps relevant data. The encryption used to deliver the service is undoubtedly robust; therefore, one can legitimately claim that communications are 'secure'. However, the system as a whole still allows relevant data on users to be captured. Indeed, Big Tech deserves credit for its cleverness in jointly exploiting marketing, law, and technology.

A paradigmatic example is 'differential privacy',[18] a mathematical method devised in 2006 to prevent the truth value of a single piece of information from being known while preserving—on an aggregate scale—the statistical value of the results. Its goal is to allow mass data collection without violating the confidentiality of individual subjects. In 2017, Apple announced[19] its implementation of a differential privacy model to support the collection of its users. Although seductively titled using the word 'privacy', this mathematical method has little to do with protecting personal information.

Suppose asking a certain number of people (selected to constitute a statistically valid sample) to express their voting intention. It is intuitive that, at an aggregate level, it is impossible to know 'who' votes for 'whom'. However, this association is always possible by keeping the raw data (the individual results of the questionnaire). The risk of privacy imperilment skyrockets.

To overcome this problem, Apple designed the process to introduce controlled errors in the earliest data collection phase. This solution would make it impossible to know whether the answer associated with the specific person is true or false and, at the same time, would preserve the statistical value of the aggregate analysis.

As it is easy to see, what is called 'differential privacy' does not precisely guarantee privacy protection, but only the impossibility of knowing with certainty whether a particular piece of data is connected to a specific person. Moreover, if a question is asked in a black/white form—e.g. 'in the candidate selection run, will you vote for A or B?'—the meta result of the political orientation of the individual respondent remains intact. So true is this that the cited Apple's document takes the trouble to state that 'The records arrive on a restricted-access server where IP identifiers are immediately discarded, and any association between multiple records is also discarded'.[20] Therefore, it is possible to conclude that differential privacy without proper anonymisation techniques does not guarantee the entire confidentiality of personal space.

The emphasis on the word privacy is undoubtedly attractive to users and reassuring to legislators and national protection authorities. However, in this context, the marketing-oriented wording of the message tells the truth concerning a single issue but does not tell the whole story.

Another example of marketing-oriented legal hairsplitting is WhatsApp's description of how it secures messaging exchanges:

> End-to-end encryption ensures only you and the person you're communicating with can read or listen to what is sent, and nobody in between, not even WhatsApp. This is because with end-to-end encryption, your messages are secured with a lock, and only the recipient and you have the special key needed to unlock and read them.[21]

A deeper analysis of how the service works, thus not limited to the simple protection of message exchanging, shows that despite cryptographic protection, WhatsApp does not guarantee a complete impermeability to the company's control.[22] So, it is true that the exchange of messages is secure, but it is not necessarily (entirely) private. In other words, the possibility of someone on behalf of WhatsApp accessing messages, metadata, and traffic analysis means that messages are protected against third parties. At the same time, though, users should be aware that it is legally possible that the company providing the service retains the power to access them, albeit under certain conditions.

Google provides another example of this clever exploitation of the difference between the security of message transit and the complete impossibility of accessing users' data.

'We never sell your personal information' claims Google in its privacy statement[23]. That is, for sure, technically correct in the sense that its users' data remains within Google's control only. However, Google's interest is not in selling data but in the results of the analyses that can be carried out. So, from the point of view of privacy, it makes little difference whether Big G keeps on its users' personal information or sells them to one, a hundred or a thousand entities. What matters is that Google can exploit that information with effectiveness unattainable by anyone else. Once again, data being inaccessible to others does not mean the individual's rights are fully protected.

The same careful approach to the legal significance of marketing claims is apparent in the recently launched Google One VPN service announced in 2021. It is a further example of the subtlety of which a marketing strategy is capable when dealing with the law.

Such a service promises to protect the privacy of users' Internet connections by acting as an 'intermediary' between the user and the big Internet. The promise is alluring, but a deeper analysis highlights certain limitations and structural criticalities.

Firstly, geolocation tracking is still possible. Moreover, notwithstanding the VPN, Google can still provide 'personalised services'. In other words, individual profiling remains active despite the encryption of traffic and the anonymisation of the users' IP. The help pages of the service, in fact, clearly state three things. The first: it is possible to reduce online tracking by hiding an IP address ('reduce', therefore, not 'eliminate'). Secondly, the IP is hidden and not fully anonymised. Thirdly

> while VPN by Google One secures your device connection, it does not affect how Google collects data when you use our other products and services. For example, depending on your sync settings, Chrome will continue to store your Chrome browsing history on your Google Account.[24]

In other words, the connection is protected, but accessing the user's data (stored in his account even during protected sessions) might be possible to reconstruct the association between the accessed network resource and the user's identity. Thus, based on an order from the judicial authorities or the secret services, it would be possible to access this information and, in theory, exceed the level of anonymisation promised by the service.

Around the same time as the announcement of Google One VPN, Apple announced the availability of a service called 'Private Relay'.

Strictly speaking, Apple Private Relay is not a VPN-based service. However, it attains (on paper) similar results thanks to a new and (mind the words) still non-standard protocol called Oblivious DoH (OdOH).[25]

Developed with Internet giant Cloudflare and Edge Cloud Computing Platform Fastly, ODoH has been proposed to overcome a side problem affecting the use of VPNs: the open availability of DNS queries.

As said, VPNs prevent (at least in theory) anyone from intercepting the traffic in transit over an insecure channel. It can also hide the origin of the user, who shows up on other networks with the IP of the VPN exit point. However, this only solves part of the problem.

Connecting to any Internet service requires querying a DNS server that transforms the human-understandable address of a network resource—say, www.routledge.com—into the corresponding IP number (in this case, 104.16.182.86) and allows the connection accordingly. These DNS queries are, by default, in clear text and can be accessed in various ways. This issue led to the adoption of the DoH protocol (DNS over HTTPS) to encrypt DNS queries' transit. However, the DNS server maintains the association between the two. Therefore, whoever controls or has more or less legal access to it can still gather the information that may lead to the user's identification. ODoH protocol has been designed to overcome this further problem.

By adding a layer made of public-key encryption and a series of proxies

> The target sees only the query and the proxy's IP address; the proxy has no visibility into the DNS messages, with no ability to iden-tify, read, or modify either the query being sent by the client or the answer being returned by the target, Only the intended target can read the content of the query and produce a response[26].

Although ODdoH is not yet an accepted standard by the Internet Engineering Task Force, Apple, and Cloudflare have made it available to the public. The former is part of the Private Relay service, the latter a feature of an OpenDNS service.

One might wonder whether this effort was made solely for users' privacy. Something suggests that this is not precisely the case. To use Apple's Private Relay, one must have an iCloud account and use Safari, using Apple prod-ucts, in other words. Cloudflare's OpenDNS is gratis; however, it is market-ing leverage to attract privacy-minded (or paranoid) customers and users.

By using a non-standard protocol and forcing (or nudging) people to use it, the two Big Techs have effectively imposed their vision of the right to privacy and its limitations.

Since the 2001 US ruling in the case of *A&M vs Napster*,[27] courts have called into question the ex ante decision to design a system in such a way as to allow also illicit use. However, they have not yet reached a definitive orientation on the liability of information society service providers for the way they design their technological infrastructure. The void concerns, in particular, the use of cryptography in such a way as to obstruct the exercise of state authority in the name of protecting users' rights—or, more realisti-cally, their economic interests.

Things could, however, change as a first, timid signal coming from the Italian Milan court suggests. Issued in July 2022, a preliminary ruling on Cloudflare's failure to comply with the web access filtering order issued by the communications authority states that '... the contribution made by

Cloudflare Inc. in determining the conditions for substantial anonymisation of the sites inhibited ... appears to be confirmed'.[28]

The court order did not concern the legality of OdoH. In broader terms, it chastised that Cloudflare's open DNS allowed the anonymisation of queries and that Cloudflare cannot call itself out from compliance with an order from a public authority, even if not a US one. However, for probably the first time, a judicial ruling established the principle that allowing indiscriminate anonymity without the possibility of enforcing the law contributes to violating it. If confirmed and shared by other courts (also) in other countries, this legal principle could end all those services and products based on absolute anonymity and, thus, on strong encryption.

It is no coincidence that such an attack on the role of anonymity came from the entertainment industry, given its attitude of stubbornly pursuing any behaviour that endangers its economic interests.

On its side, Big Tech has shown an ambiguous attitude towards this strategy. On the one hand, as mentioned above, technology companies are interested in strong encryption to sell mission-critical services and protect their products; on the other hand, they have a softer approach (disguised behind sophisticated wording) when it comes to users. At the tactical level, Big Tech and copyright stakeholders may differ on specific aspects. In strategic terms, they have the same agenda. Protecting their software and forcing users to change hardware is a definite necessity. Encryption proves to be of great use to these ends.

Copyright industry defends its valuables

The strategic compromise on protecting the right to privacy and other legal rights self-appropriated by Big Tech should be well received by the entertainment industry (of which, by the way, Big Tech is also a member). Copyright stakeholders have a compelling interest, on the one hand, in preventing the use of encryption from harming their economic interests and, on the other hand, in having proprietary encryption available for themselves.

Controlling access and circulation of content is of strategic importance for copyright stakeholders. These strategies were applied without considering other personal rights, such as the right to education, freedom of thought, and freedom to teach. As a result, any study and research into the vulnerability of encryption used on copyrighted content have been made illegal by laws skewed towards the interests of one party.

In the early days of digital content—then still sold on physical media such as laser discs, CDs, and DVDs—copyright stakeholders' business models were already based on regionalisation. The world was divided into five zones, and audiovisual products were constructed so they could only be viewed in the cleared zone. As there was not yet the possibility of performing these checks remotely and in real time via the Internet, as large platforms such as Netflix do today, control was achieved through a crypto-graphic algorithm, the content scrambling system (CSS). CSS was embedded in players' firmware and digital code stored on non-rewritable media. Controlling the circulation of digital content with the CSS allowed the multiplication of licence agreements on a territorial basis and, before that, the power to decide if and when to make it available in other countries. Those who wanted to obtain CSS-protected digital content had limited options (apart from directly infringing copyright laws and getting an illegal copy): wait if and when the rights holder decided to make a regionalised version of specific content, purchase a digital player sold in the area authorised to reproduce the content (not an inexpensive option, though), crack the players' firmware to make them 'zone free' or use the DeCSS.

In 1999, three programmers, of whom only one's identity was known, released closed-source software to remove the cryptographic protection of CSS. DeCSS (the name of the computer programme) was hardly the only one, as various other pieces of software attaining similar results were—or would have later been—available. The entertainment industry reacted with a barrage of legal actions claiming various infringements of its intellectual property. A core legal issue was that DeCSS was built by reverse engineering the DVD player firmware, a practice deemed illegal also by statutes in the USA and the EU. Notwithstanding the aggressive campaign against the building of computer programmes that circumvent copyright protection, the core of the matter in the DeCSS and similar software was using cryptography to deny the rights of legitimate users.

Users of the Linux operating system did not have software available to view CSS-protected DVDs because nobody had developed them. Therefore, the free-software community decided to solve the problem by creating an ad hoc programme. The community's efforts resulted, in particular, in the creation of Libdvdcss, a library that, using various techniques, enabled software using it to make DeCSS ineffective.

The methods used to achieve this result may not be entirely legal. On the one hand, European legislation allows the reverse engineering of software to achieve interoperability. On the other hand, breaking or guessing DeCSS keys might not easily fit with the interoperability exception if it implies gaining access to encryption keys that belong to the manufacturers of DVD players.

One should therefore go into the merits and assess whether the concept of reverse engineering also includes these activities.

To date, Libdvdcss is still available, as are the various software that exploits it. However, a relevant case law is still the 2008 decision of the French Conseil d'État[29] against the complaint filed by an NGO claiming the right to reverse-engineer copy protection systems to allow software interoperability.[30] The ruling has been saluted as a success; however, its reading is far from being clear enough to assert this right judicially. Sticking to the literal meaning of the rules (the European Directive 29/2001), it is pretty challenging to claim that the interoperability exemption covers the cracking of CSS keys. The rule is written as a Catch-22 so as not to be practically applicable. It allows reverse engineering but not if this causes copyright infringement. Since Libdvdcss allows the display of any content, making no difference between legal and illegal copies, those who disseminate and use this software should be sanctioned.

Depending on the point of view, the CSS affair is either a battle for freedom to allow everyone accesses to culture or a crusade to protect the economic interests of private industry.

However, the role of cryptography in securing the industrial interests of copyright stakeholders went further. It extended from content encryption to anonymity restrictions to handle video-on-demand and streaming.

The massive increase in video-on-demand and live streaming services made it essential to protect content broadcasted on the Internet from being viewed by those who had not paid for it and by legitimate users that are denied the possibility to access content by enforcing geolicensing strategies.

Pursuing these goals required sophisticated watermarking and tagging systems made possible by ad hoc encryption algorithms making content uniquely identifiable. They allow to match content with the identity of the possessor and verify if he is or is not a legitimate user. Automated, 'AI-powered' algorithms scan content-sharing platforms in search of (potentially) illegal contents[31].

However, these measures are not enough because good-faith users wanting to pay for access to content can be prevented from doing it if so the Lords of Copyrights want. Two are the ways to take over users. The first is to limit the anonymisation of their identity. The second is to prevent the concealment of their location. It all boils down to preventing VPNs or only authorising the use of services that, like Google's VPN and Apple's Private Relay, allow copyright controls to be applied.

This new way of enforcing regionalisation through geolocalisation affects individuals' rights in substantially different ways. Pre-internet regionalisation operates on the medium containing the digital content; it does not require collecting information about the person to be effective. Geolocalisation, on the other hand, operates on the natural person because it works by collecting the IP number and perhaps other information on those who are connecting to a specific platform. It directly affects the Internet connection, the software the user uses, and the computers that run it. It enables the collection of data that is not needed to protect copyright but to support commercial strategies.

Using cryptography to protect copyright is not only limited to the world of entertainment. Hardware and software manufacturers have pursued the same goal and can be said to have paved the way for expanding this mode of operation.

Initially, anti-copying systems worked based on serial numbers encrypted in the programme, so the user could not abuse them. Then the anti-copy features were built directly into the operating systems. Then they became more invasive via the 'Internet activation' method and the control of the subscription validity, now ubiquitous in the software industry. Finally, they became physically installed in the computer hardware thanks to crypto chips called Trusted Platform Modules (TPM) that, under the guise of protecting the user, deprived him of control over his computer. It ominously evokes the ghost of the 30-year-old Clipper chip.

In the case of TPM, marketing also played an essential role in deflecting attention from the impact of this technology on rights.

The marketing emphasis built around TPM is all about the concept of security. So, according to the industry coalition that designed and maintain this technology, it makes it possible to

> protect critical data and systems against a variety of attacks, enable secure authentication and strong protection of unlimited certificates, keys, and passwords that otherwise are accessible, establish strong machine identity and integrity, help satisfy regulatory compliance with hardware-based security ... provide more secure remote access through a combination of machine and user authentication, protect against data leakage by confirmation of platform integrity prior to decryption, provide hardware-based protection for encryption and authentication keys used by stored data files and communications (email, network access, etc), protect in hardware Personally Identifiable Information, such as user IDs and passwords, protect passwords and credentials stored on drives.[32]

Reading through the lines of the official wording, however, reveals a few more details about the concrete consequences of using TPM.

This technology allows manufacturers of software and operating systems to take complete control of the computer, of which the user should, in theory, be the sole owner. Depending on the manufacturer's will, the TPM can be used to decide which software can run and which cannot. On the one hand (although other systems are now used), it can directly serve to protect copyright. On the other hand, it can force a person to buy a new computer to use the latest operating system version. The availability of free operating systems, such as Linux, makes it possible to breathe new life into hardware rendered obsolete by commercial strategies. However, regarding at least the interaction with civil services, it is not yet possible to rely exclusively on free software. This might not be a severe problem was it not because online services often require the latest versions of operating systems and applications to function. That has nothing ado with 'security', as TPM can be used to enforce business strategies to the detriment of consumers.

Officially, Microsoft Windows 11 requires the presence of TPM version 2.0 to work. Therefore, computers that do not have the latest crypto chip on board cannot use the new operating system. There are ways to 'trick' the software into thinking that TPM version 1.2 is still enough. If the computer does not even have the old TPM but still has connectors for an external crypto chip, it may be possible to buy one, but there is no guarantee that it will always work.[33]

Apple's TMP equivalent, the T2 chip (whose features are now 'embedded' in new M-generation processors), only allows certain versions of Microsoft Windows to run natively. Moreover, it affects users' right to repair because only authorised service providers own the proper tools.[34] It is not easy to draw a line between the need to guarantee the security of a system and the interest in controlling what a user can make of a piece of hardware, of which, in theory, he is the sole owner. There are ways to get around the blocks in computers, enabling installing other operating systems or software that is no longer supported. Using them, however, could violate the manufacturers' intellectual property. Thirty years later, the unresolved issue raised by the DeCSS case comes up again. More than in the past, at stake, is the compression of property rights. Although there may be differences in individual legal systems, property right implies the possibility of doing what one wants with the purchased object without anyone being able to prevent it. By contrast, a computer becomes useless because a third party owning the software decides that it should no longer work. It is a limitation of the personal property right that has no legal justification. It questions the very fact of being able to consider oneself the owner of something.

Remote control over computers—be it for copyright control or whatever else the reason—increases the power of Big Tech over governments and civil services in the USA, EU, and elsewhere in the world. It would limit the sovereignty of foreign countries, making them in need of Big Tech support also in managing vital interests of the state, such as administering justice and managing national security. This is why Russia banned TPM-equipped computers and China built its own version of the chip, the Trusted Cryptography Module,[35] also known as the Hengzhi Chip.[36],[37] They cannot accept public powers being limited by private actors who can decide whether, how, and when superior interests can be protected.

States and courts push for compulsory key disclosure

Some Eastern European and Eastern Asian regimes have explicitly adopted very restrictive rules on using cryptography for the sake of national security and delivery of justice. Western governments, however, cannot afford the same luxury as they are subjected to the rule of law and bound to respect legal rights, at least just yet.

The foundations of the Western criminal trial are the right to silence, the prohibition of self-incrimination, and the 'innocent-until-prove-guilty' standard, i.e. the state's duty to prove the responsibility of the accused. These principles prevent convicting someone without evidence and using torture—or less harsh but still unacceptable methods, such as denying a person the assistance of a defence counsel—to obtain a confession. However, as any defence lawyer knows, there can be huge differences between theory and practice. The experience of criminal investigations teaches that when faced with certain guilt or the need to find a culprit at all costs, rules bend in the name of the greater good. Thus, even without actual clues, a person may be searched, justifying ex post the 'suspicion' that called to action by the result obtained (the discovery of, say, drugs or weapons).

Similarly, during an interrogation, the 'good cop-bad cop' game is instrumental in creating empathy with the suspect. If he is clueless enough, he will compromise his defence by answering the investigators' questions before his lawyer arrives (assuming he has been informed that he is entitled to do so). Locking a suspect in custody in a prison wing populated by dangerous convicted felons may, technically, not be termed 'torture'. In reality, however, this is an unscrupulous method to induce a person to reconsider his or her decision on invoking, for instance, the right to silence.

Of course, a criminal investigation cannot be done with white gloves. There are cases in which the use of force is unavoidable, as in the case of someone who does not want to be arrested or tries to escape. Similarly, minimal use of force may be authorised when collecting a suspect's fingerprints and a DNA sample or taking a photograph of him or her for inclusion in forensic databases.

This reasoning, however, cannot be applied analogically to an act such as forcing a password or decryption key. A fortiori, this cannot be permitted when it comes to forcing the release of biometric data when the direct consequence of this action is the acquisition of circumstantial or full-weight evidence.

Notwithstanding, national courts and legislation also imposed on suspects to grant the police unencrypted access to the data held. France passed such legislation in 1999 as a quid pro quo for the unrestricted use of strong encryption. However, it was not alone because the UK established similar obligations with the Regulation of Investigative Powers Act of 2000. Lately, Ireland, Croatia, and Belgium followed the same path.[38]

Recent EU member states' case law[39] has different views on the legality of compulsory password handover provisions. Some consider it a violation of the right to remain silent or an infringement of the self-incrimination prohibition. Others adopt a more nuanced approach introducing subtle distinctions citing *Saunders vs UK* according to which [the right to not self-incriminate] does not extend to the use in criminal proceedings of material which may be obtained from the accused through the use of compulsory powers but which has an existence independent of the will of the suspect such as, inter alia, documents acquired pursuant to a warrant, breath, blood and urine samples and bodily tissue for the purpose of DNA testing.[40]

In 2018 a Dutch court deemed it lawful to use moderate force to compel a suspect to put his finger on his smartphone to unlock it. The seriousness of the investigation, said the court, had justified such a measure.[41]

There are similar argumentative contortions in American[42] jurisprudence supporting the legality of compulsory password or cryptographic keys hand-over and use of force to achieve the result. In 2022, the US FBI obtained a warrant to 'force' a suspect to unlock his smartphone by putting his face in front of the camera[43] according to a trend that is gaining momentum in the USA[44].

Banning compulsory compliance as a method to obtain evidence should be non-negotiable. If not, it would be challenging to set a limit separating 'force' from 'coercion' or 'torture'. Moreover, as the Dutch court did, by applying the criterion of the case's exceptionality or the community's superior interest, the risk of making this boundary disappear is too high.

Simply put, 'prohibition of self-incrimination' is a synonym for 'right not to facilitate investigations'. Therefore, when it comes to passwords and secret keys, it makes little sense—as courts did—to draw an artificial line between material that exists independently of the suspect and information that depends on his will or clutching at other straws to solve this problem. The key point is that a suspect cannot be forced to confess, nor can he be forced to cooperate with the prosecutor. If police discover or seize things, biological leftovers, or information, they can use them as incriminating evidence. However, it is up to the prosecution to make sense of these things for the trial. This means, in other words, that the prosecution has every right to use any tool to access the medium or device that contains helpful information for investigations. Just as it is justified to break down doors or force locks, it is just as legitimate to crack encryption keys or passwords to access accounts and information in possession of the suspect. However, it is not always possible to decrypt the information quickly or do it at all. Sometimes this happens because the suspect makes the most efficient use of the software tools at hand. Other times investigation activities are blocked because certain products and services are designed to prevent decryption or otherwise hinder attempts to retrieve information from those not possessing the proper key.

As repeated ad nauseam, a suspect has no obligation to help the investigation. The same cannot be said of anyone else, a natural person or company, who is not involved in the case. These individuals must cooperate with the investigation. Sometimes, as in the case of Internet providers, cooperation is mandatory by law. In other cases, prosecutors and courts can order anyone to lend their technical expertise. However, what happens when a product—and, more often, a service—is designed to prevent this collaboration?

Big Tech's ambiguity on anti-forensics

A seemingly insurmountable obstacle to information gathering for law enforcement and intelligence purposes is the choice of companies like Apple to design products and services powered by encryption that even the manufacturer cannot crack. Two cases that, in the USA, involved the iPhone maker and two more involving Canadian companies involved in criminal trials for selling (allegedly) unbreakable encryption-powered communications services help investigate a crucial topic: the responsibility of hardware and software manufacturers in marketing products based on such strong encryption and how this design choice affects their duty to cooperate with investigators.

The marketing strategies adopted by Apple concerning security and encryption are a fascinating case study. They help understand the relationship between technology, industrial policy, and the appropriation of rights by Big Tech (the latter, a constant feature of the behaviour of technological giants).

Privacy and security are two longstanding pillars of Apple's corporate identity. Its commitment to these matters has its root in the secrecy culture that, over decades, has become a landmark of the company. Way before thinking of creating secure products for its customers, Apple enforced an incredibly tight internal security management system to prevent leaks of confidential information on products and strategies.[45]

In 2016, the US Drug Enforcement Agency (DEA) and the Federal Bureau of Investigation (FBI) obtained warrants from two different courts that obliged Apple to cooperate with investigators to recover encrypted data inside suspects' iPhones.

Apple objected in both cases, arguing that it could not cooperate with the authorities because the product was designed so that even those who had built it could not breach its security. Moreover, Apple denied the possibility of building specific tools to circumvent the security measure of its smartphone, as ordered by the court.[46]

Both cases did not produce conclusive results. The Californian one was not decided because, in the meantime, the FBI found a way to overcome the iPhone's protections without Apple's cooperation (which raises other issues that will be examined in a moment). The one in New York favoured Apple. However, the court ruled on a procedural issue: the non-applicability of the All Writs Act of 1789 to the case.[47] Thus, there was no analysis specifically directed at whether Apple's defences were correct. However, what Apple publicly told its users about the matter is far more interesting and revealing.

Apple's then CEO, Tim Cook, addressed his customers with a master-piece of public relations.[48] In its essence, Apple's opposition against the court orders was based on the following arguments that are going to be analysed head-to-head with critical counterarguments.

Claim: the refusal to build a backdoor-equipped operating system (à la Clipper Chip) prevents exposing our (whose, actually?) privacy and safety at risk. Rebuttal: designing on purpose less secure products would have increased the risk of non-compliance with data protection regulations (in the EU) and led the company vulnerable to complains and even civil actions. A high level of security is, firstly, an effective legal shield and a powerful marketing leverage.

Claim: there are concerns about possible future expansion of mandatory surveillance features such as conversation recording and location tracking. Rebuttal: Internet service providers, telecommunication companies, mobile operators, and data carriers are bound by law to support criminal investiga-tions by providing geolocation and metadata and—of course—eavesdrop-ping services. Moreover, court-authorised malware capable of sneaking into smartphones to record conversation and exfiltrate contents are now a stand-ard investigative tool also in Western countries. It is challenging to affirm that Apple should be granted an exemption from these mandatory duties.

Claim: the need to raise the security against malicious actors led to design an 'Apple-proof' security. Rebuttal: law enforcement and crime prevention are exclusive duties of the executive power. Deciding what and when should be prevented is a prerogative of the parliament. A private company has no direct 'jurisdiction' over policy issues and cannot supersede the state. In other words: Apple—as every individual, NGO, or company—can lobby for its interest, hire spin doctors, and engage in public awareness campaign. Only parliament, however, can have the final word on what is 'safe' and what is not for individuals and the country as a whole. Agreeable or not, France and other countries already dealt with this topic by imposing manda-tory password disclosure.

Claim: the refusal to create the tools the authorities need prevents its exploitation for illegal purposes. Rebuttal: this would mean that picks should be illegal as they can also allow criminal offences.

Claim: there are concerns that once devised the method to bypass or weaken the security of the operating system, that would lead to countless alike software also if its specific implementation were destroyed. Rebuttal: correct, and this is what is happening nonetheless. Like other manufactur-ers, Apple's products are not immune to flaws and vulnerabilities. From time to time, indeed, bug hunters—computer experts making a living from finding software flaws—have discovered ways to circumvent the protections of software considered impenetrable. Apple itself runs an extensive 'Security

Bounty' programme[49] offering substantial money—up to one million US$ per single bug—to those who find vulnerabilities affecting its products. This challenges the statement that Apple cannot overcome its products' security. Moreover, specialised companies are constantly developing tools that enable police and intelligence agencies to take control of smartphones and computers. When this happens, like in the case of RCS Lab's Hermit malware, Apple releases versions of its software that prevent the exploitation of its devices or tightens controls over authorised app developers.[50] Moreover, like in the case of the Israeli firm NSO that created spyware called Pegasus, Apple reacted by suing these companies. The complaint it filed with the Northern District of California, San Jose Division[51] contains a mix of claims based on privacy infringements, national security imperilment, and—the only one that should directly concern the company—the attack on a core unique selling proposition: verbatim 'Apple is synonymous with security'.[52.]

Chastising the defendant's behaviour, the complaint states:

> Defendants seek to operate with impunity by hiding behind their unnamed customers. Indeed, in response to another lawsuit brought against NSO and Q Cyber by other victims of their attacks, NSO and Q Cyber argued that they should enjoy some form of 'sovereign immunity' based on the status of the governments to whom they claim they sell their products and services. But as the Ninth Circuit recently held, NSO and Q Cyber are not sovereigns and are not entitled to sovereign immunity. See WhatsApp, Inc. v. NSO Group Technologies Ltd., No. 20-16408 (9th Cir. Nov. 8, 2021). Nor do they enjoy any other form of immunity for their unlawful commercial and tortious activity directed at Apple and its products, platforms, servers, and users in this country.

As it is apparent, the defence of NSO and other software producers similar to Pegasus is based on selling their services only to governmental entities in compliance with technology export regulations.

In pure theory, regardless of the merits of the matters, a claim against this kind of company could be built around—say—problems with the validity of the export licence, compliance with the conditions laid down by law, and a thousand other issues, including intellectual property infringements. However, if the letter of the law is respected, the responsibility for using such a piece of software should lie solely with the entity that purchased it. Otherwise, the arms manufacturer should be held responsible for their use by governments authorised to purchase them. This might be a relevant ethical or political issue. However, it has no merit in court.

It can be assumed that this strategy avoided diplomatic conflicts with other sovereign states. If, as would have been more logical, Apple had contested the unlawful use of spyware by other states and the court had confirmed that foreign powers had taken aggressive actions against the USA, the consequences would have gone far beyond those of a court dispute and the blacklisting of individual companies.[53] Be that as it may, the core of the legal action brought by Apple is the liability of the spyware producer, not the entities that used it.

The major flaw of this argument is that it is a double-edged sword.

Firstly, US software houses—or foreign manufacturers under US orders— could build spy products to be used to protect American national interests. Contrary to what one might think, this is not just a hypothesis. Until 2018, the Swiss company Crypto AG, actually a covert joint venture between the CIA and German intelligence, has been selling weakened cypher machines to governments and entities halfway around the world.[54] Therefore, applying the same logic backing Apple's complaint, these companies should also be subject to legal actions even if they worked (clandestinely) for the USA.

Secondly, designing an 'anti-forensics by default' product and actively patching it to maintain its robustness might constitute aiding and abetting an offence. This might be true, in particular, when the product is designed with the specific purpose of defying law enforcement investigative tools.[55]

In what can be seen as a broader public relation and marketing strategy, Apple implemented in its latest operating systems a set of features called *Lockdown Mode* and funded public initiatives against state-sponsored malware

> Apple today detailed two initiatives to help protect users who may be personally targeted by some of the most sophisticated digital threats, such as those from private companies developing state-sponsored mercenary spyware. Lockdown Mode—the first major capability of its kind, coming this fall with iOS 16, iPadOS 16, and macOS Ventura—is an extreme, optional protection for the very small number of users who face grave, targeted threats to their digital security. Apple also shared details about the $10 million cybersecurity grant it announced last November to support civil society organizations that conduct mercenary spyware threat research and advocacy.[56]

Lockdown mode is a further enhancement, based on encryption, of Apple devices' resistance to external attacks. With the already high levels of security that had already challenged the US authorities in 2016, Lockdown Mode further reduces the possibility for criminals and public authorities to compromise a device.

All that considered, if—like Apple claims—it is true that anyone who produces software used by the authorities of a government to carry on criminal investigation and intelligence actions is liable for merely having built it, for the sake of consistency, it should be stated that anyone who makes software blocking police investigations is also responsible for obstructing them. Indeed, one could go so far as to argue that while providing malware to states restricts its circulation and use for the sole purpose of protecting national interests, making forensics-proof products indiscriminately available that prevent law enforcement activities has no justification. This is precisely the charge brought by the US authorities against Phantom Secure in 2019 and Sky Global in 2021, two providers of encrypted communication services. The CEO of the former was convicted 'for leading a criminal enterprise that facilitated the transnational importation and distribution of narcotics through the sale of encrypted communication devices and services'[57]; in 2021, two of the latter's managers were targeted by an arrest warrant based on the charge of racketeering and knowingly facilitating the import and distribution of illegal drugs through the sale of encrypted communications devices.[58]

Intuitively, it is clear that the Phantom Secure and Sky Global cases are radically different from those involving Apple. The prosecution office's official statements made clear that the responsibility of Phantom Secure and Sky Global would lie in having designed the entire delivery process to ensure anonymity and plausible deniability for suppliers as well as the non-traceability of customers. This does not apply to Apple, which operates in the open at every stage of marketing its services.

Suppose the US attorneys' thesis in law were correct. In that case, one could conclude that when it comes to a possible justice obstruction, it is not technology per se or technology alone that should be illegal. Instead, the overall context in which specific technology is used would make the difference between compliance and violation of the law. This argument has its merit, although it might not provide definitive guidance. Following this line of thought, in order to assess whether a product or service was consciously constructed to obstruct investigations or intelligence activities, one would first have to check whether there were technological alternatives that could meet regulatory requirements. For instance, in 2010, the Canadian firm Blackberry, whose marketing was heavily based on the encryption-based security features of its infrastructure, shared with law enforcement the secret PGP keys to decrypt users' information, thus cracking down on criminal rings.[59] It was done without introducing backdoors, reducing the system's security or other hideous features. It 'only' needed handing over a master password. Moreover, Blackberry's troubles were caused by a mistaken read of market trends. There is no evidence that its more open attitude towards cooperation with law enforcement contributed significantly to its failure. The example of Blackberry shows, therefore, that allowing prosecutors to disable encryption securing particular communications does not necessarily translate into the systematic and massive violation of the rights of all users. Therefore, it could be possible to conclude that, in balancing opposing interests, allowing the exercise of state duties should be a requirement of technological product design. This principle is neither new nor strange in any Western legal system. The law requires the design of industrial machines, power tools, vehicles, household appliances, and—in the future—software with a high level of operational autonomy (so-called 'AI') that considers the safety of those who interact with them. Nevertheless, when this reasoning lapses the use of cryptography, it reignites the eternal debate between supporters of civil rights and those of the prevalence of state interests.

In this context, as long as these positions are fideistically entrenched, it will be impossible to find a general compromise. No activist will be willing to accept weak encryption; no government authority will be willing to see its operations restricted. Each Big Tech company will maximise its interest according to the field in which it chooses to stand.

The difficulty in getting out of this stalemate has three causes.

The first is the 'Hegelian' approach to the matter, based on the contrast of absolute ideas, which is a contradiction. As monotheism teaches, there can only be one absolute. In the case of plurality, other absolutes must be either reconciled with the only true faith or eliminated. The second—a direct consequence and landmark of the Digital Rights narrative—is that rights are confused with individual ethos (or greed). Hyperindividualism leads to über-rights: claiming that individual absolute(s) should be acknowledged by everybody else. The third is that rights no longer need the law to be asserted because technology is a better fit for the purpose.

As the facts show, however, this approach has proved unsuccessful. It has radicalised the positions of the parties involved. It has weakened the role and value of the law. It has forced case-by-case solutions that, as the comparison of the Apple suits on the one hand and the Sky Global and Prometheus investigations on the other, do not provide clear long-term solutions. By contrast, addressing the legal rather than technological and 'cultish' problems might offer a viable way out of the stalemate just highlighted.

As the marketing of Apple's Lockdown Mode paradoxically demonstrates, not everyone needs the same level of security and confidentiality. Most people need to protect themselves from criminal acts, poorly constructed software that damages or lets personal information slip through the cracks, and—contrary to that—from the constant prying eyes of platforms, not from state interference. On the contrary, those who need extreme protection are a minimal number of people. A sufficiently robust, but not necessarily invincible, encryption is more than adequate to protect the rights of the vast majority of citizens in the free world. People with special needs are certainly entitled to more sophisticated protection. However, under strict control and accountability, state authorities should be able to design or borrow tools and technologies to circumvent it.

However reasonable this position may seem, at least in theory, the first judgements that addressed the issue of accountability in using encryption-bypassing technologies for criminal investigations raise some concerns.

Law enforcement accountability's denial imperils due process

Since 2017, the French Gendarmerie and judicial authorities have been investigating phones that used the secured communication tool EncroChat, after discovering that the phones were regularly found in operations against organised crime groups and that the company was operating from servers in France. Eventually, it was possible to put a technical device in place to go beyond the encryption technique and have access to the users' correspondence.

> In early 2020, EncroChat was one of the largest providers of encrypted digital communication with a very high share of users presumably engaged in criminal activity. User hotspots were particularly present in source and destination countries for cocaine and cannabis trade, as well as in money laundering centres.[60]

In early 2020, having devised how to penetrate Encrochat's security, the French *Gendarmerie* and Dutch police launched an extensive investigation targeting users of this device. There are few details on the method used by the French authorities to achieve the investigative result. However, the information in the public domain allows us to formulate some hypotheses. Instead of directly attacking the encryption used by Encrochat, the French police, with the collaboration of the secret services, appears to have hacked the servers hosted on a French hosting service provider that routed the communications or hijacked the concerned domains, installed malware to be deployed as a software update on all devices, and gained access to a massive amount of messages relating to criminal actions.[61] The idea behind this investigation reminds of a similar method used by the public prosecutor of Bologna (IT) in 2004. By simulating a power outage of the targeted server hosted in a data centre, the law enforcement officer got access to a mail system allowing encrypted messages to be exchanged. Unbeknownst to the organisation (a hacktivist NGO), the authorities eavesdropped for about two months on a specific address belonging to a suspect.[62]

This way of carrying out the investigation caused quite a few protests due to the lack of information on how the results were obtained. As a result, doubts were raised about whether the chain of custody had been respected, whether individual messages could be traced back to each suspect, and whether the evidence acquired was legitimate. However, these issues will be dealt with at a national level, according to the specific rules of evidence. For instance, in 2021, the Federal German Court of Justice acknowledged the possibility of using Encrochat messages collected by the French authorities in criminal proceedings in Germany.[63] A similar conclusion has been sustained by the Court of Appeal in the UK.[64] Italian courts have not been involved, just yet, in Encrochat-related cases. However, in a similar case—the validity of the Falciani List—the *Corte di cassazione* holds that as soon as information are received through the international cooperation channel, they are valid evidence even if initially acquired illegally.[65]

By contrast, the 2022 French *Conseil Constitutionel* ruling in the Encrochat case[66] addresses a different and more general issue: the imperilment of the due process because of the '*secret de la défense nationale* exceptions' invoked by the prosecution to not disclose the technicalities of the investigation.

> French investigators enforced Article 707-102-1 of the Criminal Code—described as a 'legal bridge' between the French police and the secret services—to ask the French security service, the DGSI, to carry out surveillance operations on two encrypted telephone systems, EncroChat and SkyECC.[67]

This decision is the first high-level judicial test in the EU of the accountability requisite involving law enforcement attacks against encryption systems used by criminal organisations. According to the court, the state's interest in prosecuting criminal activities would justify the existence of this rule. The legitimacy of the provision is also sustained by the mandatory annotation of all other details of investigative activities.

The most severe attack on the right of defence is not so much the unavailability of technical information. The subject is undoubtedly crucial because the state is the only one who can guarantee the right to an effective defence, especially in conditions where the chain of custody and inalterability of seized data cannot be ensured without resorting to proper best practices. Therefore, the right to access all information on how investigations were carried out, including their technological components, should be guaranteed to the fullest extent. However, there are ways to circumvent this argument. US Court held that 'the mere possibility of alteration is not sufficient to exclude electronic evidence. Absent specific evidence of alteration, such possibilities go only to the evidence's weight, not admissibility.'[68] The consequences of this principle are twofold. The first is that even if the evidence is not acquired in a technically correct manner, the judge may still evaluate it. The second is that it is up to the defence to prove that the evidence is flawed. In several jurisdictions—certainly in the UK and Italy—if independently acquired evidence confirms the uncertain ones, the latter may be considered reliable by indirect confirmation nonetheless.

The international investigation against the Ukrainian ReVIL ransomware group, the conclusion of which was announced at the end of 2021,[69] replicated the French script, but this time starting from the US. The similarities between the two cases are striking: the prosecutor claimed the investigation was a national security case, the military and secret services were, therefore, involved, and the FBI hacked back the criminal organisation servers and planted software to track the members, private entities have been asked to cooperate, a non-well clarified 'international cooperation' led to arrest of the suspects.[70]

Trends emerging from these cases raise some concern about the possible loss of balance between the state's power and the citizen's right.

Resorting to national security to justify the involvement of the military and intelligence services in criminal investigations is a way to take control over the functioning of justice and, in particular, the use of information technology for investigation purposes. Blurring the line between judicial and intelligence/military domains allows for a much more fluid condition, where information can be shifted from one domain to another according to the moment's necessity. That would be a fatal blow to the possibility of an effective defence.

On a separate account, it has become clear that overcoming cryptography protection requires increasingly getting the information of investigative interest before it is encrypted. In addition to having powerful code-cracking tools, law enforcement needs to access communications and take control of devices through malware. It is necessary, in other words, to put an end to end-to-end encryption.

Politicians advocate the ban of end-to-end encryption (and Big Tech supports it)

As much as end-to-end encryption has recently gained headlines, the concept is nothing new. It simply refers to the process by which a message is encrypted before being sent, instead of relying solely on the security offered by protocols such as HTTPs—the 'lock' icon appearing on browsers' address bar—or IMAPs for emails and FTPs for file transfer. The latter offers a certain level of security to communications in transit, but how tight the security depends on the access provider involved. Either by order of the judiciary or because they are the victim of an attack, the latter may make possible an interception based on the 'man-in-the-middle' technique that would allow the message in transit to be deciphered. If the message is encrypted before being sent, even a man-in-the-middle or a deep-packet inspection would be unable (at least immediately) to capture the communication and turn it into plain text. This is why cryptography exists, indeed.

End-to-end encryption is not an exclusivity of the criminal underground. As said, it is a standard operating procedure for a privacy-minded individual when exchanging private messages and a ubiquitous feature in communication platforms, e-commerce services, and other widely used computer programmes and devices.

As in the case of PGP, as long as end-to-end encryption was a curiosity for a few geeks, it was not a significant source of concern. Since, however, it has been finally included as a feature in commonly available products, things have changed dramatically. The number of potential users has grown to such a level that end-to-end encryption is routinely activated by people outside criminal rings, non-exceptionally versed in mathematics, to protect information on their extramarital intercourses, questionable behaviours, and other personal affairs.

Like it or not, since the enormous availability of data generated by telephone and Internet communications made it possible to use military-derived techniques such as traffic analysis, investigative methods have also been adapted accordingly. Carpet data retention has become a commonly used investigative tool. The European Court of Justice has found it to be a disproportionate measure, but states have not repealed national laws, thus keeping it legal. However, if communications are encrypted during generation and transmission, carpet data retention loses its usefulness. Indeed, even if the authorities have access to traffic data, the combined use of end-to-end encryption, secure protocols, and traffic anonymisation would render the information obtained useless. This is why also end-to-end encryption has led to the attention of lawmakers and Big Tech.

Most prominent supporters of end-to-end encryption curtailing are the USA that took a public standing on the matter in 2020,[71] the UK that did in 2015,[72] reiterated in 2020[73] and still keeps the debate alive in 2022,[74] and, finally, the EU[75] that put challenging end-to-end encryption at the core of its political strategy.

Big Tech joined the panel, although with an ambivalent attitude. On the one hand, as it has been pointed out *supra*, they advocate for unbreakable encryption to be a core component of their product and services. On the other hand, they support—and actively propose—mechanisms to bypass end-to-end encryption to protect minors.

Aware of the extreme difficulty—bordering on the impossible—of dismantling the regulatory apparatus on cryptographic freedom and, most important, the intricate network of interdependencies between civil services, private businesses, and citizens, European politicians are thinking of a different solution,[76] and Big Techs (namely, Apple[77], that finally stepped back at the end of 2022) are thinking of an alternative solution: client-side (or cloud-side) scanning (CSS).

In short, CSS intercepts content locally (i.e. on the user's device) before it can be encrypted, verifies using a 'tagging' mechanism, and compares with a 'blacklist' whether the content in question is legal or legitimate (a not insignificant difference) and, if not, blocks it, possibly reporting the fact to the authorities. In this case, encryption would be irrelevant because the control would occur before the content is encrypted. This is, by the way, exactly how state-operated malware works, only on a global and 'carpet' scale.

In terms of public policy and public relations, the idea of CSS is very attractive. Formally, it does not affect the robustness of encryption. It does not propose installing backdoors or using master keys. Thus, the CSS respects the right to strong encryption.

However, going to the core of the matter, this public policy choice creates more problems than it solves.

In the Encrochat investigation, courts did not challenge the legitimacy of active hacking of unidentified individual devices on the assumption that a large part of users was involved in criminal activities and that only a minority was just privacy-minded. However, despite some limitations, the principle was established that one could investigate using the fishing net method. Take everything that passes through a net and choose what is needed for the investigation. Fishing for criminals may be an efficient method, but this does not demise the need to reinforce safeguards for those outside the investigation and those subjected to it.

If CSS were to become a standard feature imposed by law or, much more effectively, by Big Tech's business strategies, this would take it to another level of preventive criminalisation. All users should be forced to undergo preventive scanning of the content they exchange with others. They would be turned into presumed offenders by default, encompassing even the 'nothing to hide, nothing to fear' argument.

This is yet more proof that when a principle is violated in the name of the case's exceptionality, it is easier to extend the violation to areas for which, initially, it would not have been conceivable.

Making CSS mandatory by law is a choice largely compatible with Big Tech's needs to offer its customers a sufficiently robust level of security that protects them from the attention of (almost) anyone except Big Tech itself.

The convergence of this public policy strategy and commercial necessity calls into question the pillars on which the debate on anonymity rests. It translates into the attribution to private subjects of the power of identification. It challenges the very idea of 'identity'.

Cryptoanonymity steals State's power to certify personal identity

The concept of anonymity is often associated—and considered synonymous—with privacy. In reality, this is incorrect. Just consider that a criminal or an unfaithful partner is interested in not getting caught violating the law or marital duties. Equally certainly, however, they cannot invoke the right to privacy!

Typically, as it has been discussed for a very long time in endless debates, online cryptoanonymisation is thought of as a way to completely hide from the eyes of others. However, complete anonymisation allows us to achieve another result: being someone else without revealing our legal identity and without asking the State to provide a legally valid alias. As such, that severs the connection between persons and powers.

Census and identity management were two elements that served to collect taxes and manage public order and security. It would have been of little use to know all the inhabitants of a nation individually if they could not be recognised with certainty. The idea of a State-issued ID is relatively recent. Census and other methods to list the population or identify particular individuals date back to Greek and Rome. However, it was in the 19th century that, also thanks to the development of biometric techniques, States began collecting information on the population and certificating its identity in a more structured way.

Maintaining tight control over the power to identify people was and still is crucial for the survival of the State. Dictatorships are clearly interested in knowing the identity of possible protesters, rioters, and political foes. They can also deny a person the right to be acknowledged or identified.

However, under a democratic rule, identity is something citizens own. A State cannot take it away. It can only stamp a seal on what is declared in the birth registration statement. However, even if, in strictly legal terms, it is the State that certifies whom we are, wanting to be identified as someone else still has legal consequences, as demonstrated by the complex issue of gender identity.

At least in a democratic state and according to specific regulations, each of us has the right to be identified as we prefer. Nicknames, nom-de-plume and—recently—avatars, and social profiles are proof of the everlasting desire to be identified as we see fit, also if our legally certified self differs.

In the interaction made possible by the platforms, identity certification through State-ID is substantially non-existent. Even in e-commerce transactions, people are indirectly identified via their credit cards. It does not matter who is using it, just that the card is valid and active. Chinese messaging platform WeChat—the one-stop place for almost every online task—uses Voiceprint as a password. Once processed, the user's voice becomes his gateway to the system and his identification (by the public authorities). Also, in the West, computers and other devices can be accessed through biometric authentication to make payments or perform other legally binding activities.

Although it is possible to manage one's identity online independently, in the vast majority of cases, it is necessary to resort to a technological intermediary that becomes the doppelgänger's keeper and master. It is the platforms, or rather, who controls it, that decides 'who' can be 'who' and until when. The identity provider becomes an alternative to the State. It acquires the power—and therefore the right—to do something that not even the State is allowed: to attribute identity to a person instead of merely acknowledging it.

Cryptocurrencies deprive the State of wealth control

Absolute anonymity, which allows us to appear different from what we are or not appear at all, has an essential role in undermining another prerogative of the State: the creation of value and the control of wealth.

The anonymity of transactions is one of the elements that, more than others, have contributed to the success of cryptocurrencies. In reality, it is not always true that cryptocurrencies can be used ultimately anonymously. However, tracing the individuals who participated in the tokens' transfer can be challenging.

Cryptocurrencies have become an instrument of financial speculation, money laundering, and other operations with a questionable level of legality. However, they were born with an entirely different purpose: to deprive the State of the power to create value and control its circulation.

It is of little importance whether a cryptocurrency is an alternative to legal tender or simply an intangible asset to which people conventionally attribute an exchange value in money or other goods. What matters is that, in practical terms, a cryptocurrency works as if it were a real currency. Therefore, if a sufficiently large number of people accept them instead of the legal tender as a tool to abide by payment obligations, this is enough to transform cryptocurrencies into a system of creation and management of value removed from the control of the State.

Again, platforms of various types play an essential role.

Cryptocurrencies do not exist in a vacuum. In order to be created and exchanged, they need to be included in a series of technological platforms. In addition to a blockchain, which constitutes the heart of the system, a vast network of computers is needed: those willing to host the various copies of the ledgers, platforms for trading cryptocurrencies, and interfaces to other platforms that accept tokens as a payment.

Very different specimens inhabit the world of cryptocurrencies. Initially, they were decentralised objects, designed by default not to be centrally managed. Financial speculations have partially altered this condition, but the principle remains intact. Conversely, Facebook's failed attempt to create its cryptocurrency (first called Libra, then Diem, and finally Novi) was based on a completely different assumption. It was meant to centralise in the hands of a single private entity the wealth produced by each individual in exchange for the simple expectation that other people would accept this currency. Although the comparison is not precise, it is like working for somebody that pays the salary with vouchers and owns the shop where (or through which) the worker can spend them.

The Novi project was definitively shelved at the beginning of September 2022. However, this does not eliminate the fundamental problem represented by the attempt to carry it forward. After the VPNs for Google users and the Private Relay for Apple users, the announcement of the latter's exercise of its self-attribution of crime prevention powers, Libra, Diem, and Novi, are yet another iteration of a theme that is as critical as governments and parliaments neglect it: the continuous expropriation of state prerogatives by Big Tech, which has now become the lords and masters of ever more significant and more essential parts of our lives.

When a private entity gain control over ideas, personal identity and the ability to create value for the individual and gives him an 'environment'—one of the many possible metaverses—were to 'live', very little remains in the hands of the State.

There is, however, one final step to undermine the role of rights as an instrument of protection of the natural person. It is the attempt to attribute legal autonomy to the machines and software systems that make them work.

The convergence of interests of scientists in search of fame, companies in search of clients, and futurologists in need of a role have created the subtle perception that machines and software may be entitled to legal subjectivity.

Starting from the semantic deception of the way it is called, artificial intelligence is the end of the path of dehumanisation of law.

This is the subject of the next chapter.

Notes

1 Diffie, Whitfield, Hellman, Martin. 1976. 'New Directions in Cryptography', IEEE Transactions on Information Theory. 22 (6): 644–654 https://ee.stanford .edu/~hellman/publications/24.pdf visited 20 July 2022.

2 Rivest, Ron, Shamir, Adi, Leonard, Adleman A Method for Obtaining Digital Signatures and Public-Key Cryptosystems https://people.csail.mit.edu/rivest/ Rsapaper.pdf visited 20 July 2002

3 The Clipper chip used a symmetrical algorithm for encrypting communications, while a Diffie-Hellman algorithm cared about the distribution of decryption keys among the concerned entities.

4 Electronic Privacy Information Center The Clipper Chip https://archive.epic.org /crypto/clipper/ visited 25 June 2022

5 Olson, Daniel Analysis of Criminal Codes and Ciphers, Forensic Science Communications Vol. 2 N. 1, January 2000 https://archives.fbi.gov/archives/ about-us/lab/forensic-science-communications/fsc/jan2000/olson.htm visited 30 June 2022.

6 Pullella, Philip The Provenzano Code - the Mafia's answer to Dan Brown Reuters Life! https://www.reuters.com/article/italy-mafia-code-idUKNOA8372 4420070308 visited 22 June 2022.

7 The FBI News Cryptanalists. Part 1 Breaking Codes to Stop Crime 21 March 2011 https://www.fbi.gov/news/stories/breaking-codes-to-stop-crime-part-1 visited 22 June 2022.

8 Goodin, Dan Zodiac Killer cipher is cracked after eluding sleuths for 51 years Ars Technica 12 December 2020 https://arstechnica.com/information-technology/2020/12/zodiac-killer-cipher-is-cracked-after-eluding-sleuths-for-51-years/ visited 20 June 2022.

9 Hoffman, Russel *Interview with author of PGP* HighTech Today 2 February 1996 http://www.animatedsoftware.com/hightech/philspgp.htm visited 22 July 2022.

10 Zimmermann,1995

11 Rose, Lance *Just When You Thought It Was Safe To Encrypt Again* Wired.com 1 June 1993 https://www.wired.com/1993/06/just-when-you-thought-it-was-safe-to-encrypt-again/ visited 26 June 2022

12 Levy, 2001.

13 Scanlon, Jessie 'anon.penet.fi RIP', *Wired.com* 1 November 1996 https://www.wired.com/1996/11/anon-penet-fi-rip/ visited 1 July 2022.

14 Grassmuck, Volker 'Don't Try to Control the Network Because it's Impossible Anyway. Interview with Johan Helsingius on Anonymous Remailers' *IC Magazine*, 12/94 NTT Publishing, http://waste.informatik.hu-berlin.de/~grassmuck/Texts/remailer.html visited 20 July 2022.

15 Council of the EU – Press release *What is illegal offline should be illegal online: Council agrees position on the Digital Services Act* 25 November 2021 https://www.consilium.europa.eu/en/press/press-releases/2021/11/25/what-is-illegal-offline-should-be-illegal-online-council-agrees-on-position-on-the-digital-services-act/ visited 22 July 2022.

16 Schneier, Bruce, *Facebook Is Now Encrypting Links to Prevent URL Stripping* 18 June 2022 https://www.schneier.com/blog/archives/2022/07/facebook-is-now-encrypting-links-to-prevent-url-stripping.html visited 22 July 2022

17 Brinkmann, Martin, *Facebook has started to encrypt links to counter privacy-improving URL Stripping* 17 July 2022 https://www.ghacks.net/2022/07/17/facebook-has-started-to-encrypt-links-to-counter-privacy-improving-url-stripping/ visited 22 July 2022.

18 Dwork, Cyntha, Differential Privacy, *Proceedings of the 33rd international conference on Automata, Languages and Programming - Volume Part II* July 2006 Pages 1—12 https://doi.org/10.1007/11787006_1https://dl.acm.org/doi/10.1007/11787006_1 visited 22 July 2022

19 Apple Differential Privacy Team, *Learning with Privacy at scale* December 2017 https://machinelearning.apple.com/research/learning-with-privacy-at-scale visited 22 July 2022.

20 Apple Differential Privacy Team, *cit.*

21 WhatsApp Help Center *About end-to-end encryption* https://faq.whatsapp.com/791574747982248/ visited 22 July 2022.

22 Elkind, Peter, Gillum, Jack, Silverman, Craig, *How Facebook Undermines Privacy Protections for Its 2 Billion WhatsApp Users* 7 September 2021 https://www.propublica.org/article/how-facebook-undermines-privacy-protections-for-its-2-billion-whatsapp-users visited 22 July 2022.

23 Google *Ads that respect your privacy* https://safety.google/privacy/ads-and-data/ visited 24 July 2022.

24 Google One Help *Increase your online security with the VPN by Google One* https://support.google.com/googleone/answer/7582172 visited 22 July 2022

25 Internet Engineering Task Force *Oblivious DNS over HTTPS RFC 9230* https://datatracker.ietf.org/doc/rfc9230/ visited 22 July 2022

26 Verma, Tanya, Singanamalla, Tanya, 'Improving DNS Privacy with Oblivious DoH in 1.1.1.1' *The Cloudflare Blog* 12 August 2020 https://blog.cloudflare.com/oblivious-dns/ visited 22 July 2022.

27 US Court of Appeals for the 9th Circuit *A&M Records, Inc. et al. v. Napster*, 239 F.3d 1004 (9th Cir. 2001).

28 Tribunal of Milan – XIV Branch, Order 8266/22 issued on 11 July 2022 *Sony Music Entertainment Italy S.p.a., Universal Music Italia S.r.l., Warner Music Italia*

S.r.l. vs Cloudflare Inc. 'Rileva il giudicante che ... appare confermato l'apporto fornito da CLOUDFLARE Inc. volto a determinare le condizioni per una sostanziale anonimizzazione dei siti inibiti da AGCom, funzione che di fatto non è contestata in sé dalla stessa resistente.' Unofficial English translation by Andrea Monti.

29 *Conseil d'État, 10ème et 9ème sous-sections réunies, 16/07/2008, 301843, Inédit au recueil Lebon* 'un dispositif mis en place par un exploitant aux fins de permettre l'interopérabilité de systèmes informatiques, dès lors qu'il est rendu possible par la diffusion d'informations par les fournisseurs de mesures techniques, ne constitue pas un dispositif portant atteinte aux mesures de protection au sens du décret attaqué ; que, par suite, les moyens tirés de ce que le décret attaqué interdirait les pratiques permettant l'interopérabilité en méconnaissance des dispositions de la directive du 22 mai 2001 et de la loi du 1er août 2006 doivent être écartés ; https://www.legifrance.gouv.fr/ceta/id/CETATEXT000019216315/ visited 22 July 2022.

30 APRIL, *DADVSI : l'APRIL dépose au Conseil d'État une requête en annulation 21 February 2007* https://www.april.org/dadvsi-lapril-depose-au-conseil-detat -une-requete-en-annulation visited 22 July 2022

31 Grey, Joanne, Suzor, 'Nicolas, Playing with machines: Using machine learning to understand automated copyright enforcement at scale'. *Big Data & Society*. January 2020. doi:10.1177/2053951720919963visited 22 June 2022

32 Trusted Computing Group, *Trusted Computing* https://trustedcomputinggroup .org/trusted-computing/ visited 22 July 2022

33 Yee, Alaina 'You shouldn't buy a TPM for Windows 11. Here's why'. *PC World* 28 October 2021 https://www.pcworld.com/article/545941/you-shouldnt-buy-a -tpm-for-windows-11-heres-why.html visited 25 July 2022

34 Humphries, Matthew. 'Apple's T2 Chip Makes Third-Party Mac Repairs Impossible'. *PC Magazine* 5 October 2018, https://www.pcmag.com/news/apples -t2-chip-makes-third-party-mac-repairs-impossible visited 22 July 2022. Apple recently allowed users to self-replace some components but only with authorized pieces of hardware.

35 Lenovo *Set the TPM/TCM Policy* https://thinksystem.lenovofiles.com/help/index .jsp?topic=%2FX07%2Fenable_tpm.html visited 28 July 2022.

36 People's Daily Online *Lenovo releases China's first security chip* http://en.people .cn/200504/12/eng20050412_180617.html visited 28 July 2022

37 HP Customer Support. *HP Commercial PCs - TPM policy changes in China: October 2021* 9 November 2021 https://support.hp.com/us-en/document/ish _5031710-5031755-16 visited 28 July 2022.

38 Europol and Eurojust *Second report of the observatory function on encryption* 18 February 2020 https://www.europol.europa.eu/publications-events/publica- tions/second-report-of-observatory-function-encryption visited 30 June 2022.

39 Europol, *cit.*: 14

40 Eurpean Court of Human Rights Grand Chamber Case 43/1994/490/572 *Saunders v United Kingdom* 17 December 1996.

41 Eurojust *Cybercrime Judicial Monitor* Issue 4 December 2018:32 https://www .eurojust.europa.eu/sites/default/files/Publications/Reports/2018-12_CJM-4_EN .pdf visited 28 July 2022.

42 Wareham, Jason. 2017. *Cracking the Code: The Enigma of the Self-Incrimination Clause and Compulsory Decryption of Encrypted Media.* GEO. L. TECH. REV. 247 https://georgetownlawtechreview.org/cracking-the-code-the-enigma-of-the -self-incrimination-clause-and-compulsory-decryption-of-encrypted-media/ GLTR-03-2017/ visited 22 July 2022.

43 Brewster, Thomas. 'The FBI Forced A Suspect To Unlock Amazon's Encrypted App Wickr With Their Face'. *Forbes* 22 July 2022 https://www.forbes.com/sites/

thomasbrewster/2022/07/19/fbi-forces-open-amazon-wickr-app-with-a-suspects
-face/?sh=798761a5633e visited 22 July 2022.

44 Brewster, Thomas. 'FBI: You Don't Have To Tell Us Which Body Part Unlocks
Your Smartphone—But We Will Guess Anyway'. *Forbes* 29 November 2022
https://www.forbes.com/sites/thomasbrewster/2021/11/29/fbi-no-consent
-required-for-forced-phone-unlocks-via-finger-or-face/?sh=33be81f71e4e visited
22 July 2022.

45 Schiffer, Zoe. ' Apple's fortress of secrecy is crumbling from the inside'. *The Verge*
30 September 2021 https://www.theverge.com/22700898/apple-company-cul-
ture-change-secrecy-employee-unrest visited 5 August 2022.

46 US District Court for the Central District of California, Case ED 15-0451M
Order compelling Apple, Inc. to assist agents in search https://epic.org/amicus/
crypto/apple/In-re-Apple-AWA-Order.pdf visited 22 July 2022.

47 US District Court Eastern District of New York, Case 15-MC-1902 (JO)
*Memorandum and Order In re Order requiring apple, inc. to assist in the execu-
tion of a search warrant issued by this court* 29 February 2016 https://www.gpo
.gov/fdsys/pkg/USCOURTS-nyed-1_15-mc-01902/pdf/USCOURTS-nyed-1_15
-mc-01902-2.pdf visited 26 July 2022.

48 Cook, Tim *A Message to Our Customers* 16 February 2016 https://www.apple
.com/customer-letter/ visited 28 July 2022.

49 Apple *Apple Security Bounty* 5 August 2022 https://developer.apple.com/secu-
rity-bounty/ visited 5 August 2022

50 Newman, Lily. 'Google Warns of New Spyware Targeting iOS and Android
Users'. *Wired.com* 23 June 2022 https://www.wired.com/story/hermit-spyware
-rcs-labs/ visited 30 July 2022.

51 Apple Newsroom *Apple sues NSO Group to curb the abuse of state-sponsored
spyware* 23 November 2021 https://www.apple.com/newsroom/2021/11/apple
-sues-nso-group-to-curb-the-abuse-of-state-sponsored-spyware/

52 US Disctrict Court Northern District of California San Jose Division *Apple v
NSO Complaint* 23 November 2021, page 3 line 16 https://www.apple.com/
newsroom/pdfs/Apple_v_NSO_Complaint_112321.pdf visited 29 July 2022

53 US Department of Commerce Press Release *Commerce Adds NSO Group
and Other Foreign Companies to Entity List for Malicious Cyber Activities*
3 November 2021 https://www.commerce.gov/news/press-releases/2021/11
/commerce-adds-nso-group-and-other-foreign-companies-entity-list visited
5 August 2022.

54 Newman, Lily. 'The US Fears Huawei Because It Knows How Tempting
Backdoors Are'. *Wired.com* 11 February 2020 https://www.wired.com/story/
huawei-backdoors-us-crypto-ag/ visited 5 August 2022

55 Hatmaker, Taylor. 'Apple confirms that it will seal up law enforcement's favorite
iPhone cracking method' *Techcrunch* 14 June 2018 https://techcrunch.com/2018
/06/13/apple-confirms-that-it-will-seal-up-law-enforcements-favorite-iphone
-cracking-method/ visited 5 August 2022.

56 Apple Newroom *Apple expands industry-leading commitment to protect users
from highly targeted mercenary spyware* 6 July 2022 https://www.apple.com/
newsroom/2022/07/apple-expands-commitment-to-protect-users-from-merce-
nary-spyware/ visited 5 August 2022.

57 Department of Justice - U.S. Attorney's Office - Southern District of California
*Chief Executive of Communications Company Sentenced to Prison for Providing
Encryption Services and Devices to Criminal Organizations* 28 May 2019 https://
www.justice.gov/usao-sdca/pr/chief-executive-communications-company-sen-
tenced-prison-providing-encryption-services visited 5 August 2021

58 Department of Justice - U.S. Attorney's Office - Southern District of California *Sky Global Executive and Associate Indicted for Providing Encrypted Communication Devices to Help International Drug Traffickers Avoid Law Enforcement* 12 March 2021 https://www.justice.gov/usao-sdca/pr/sky-global-executive-and-associate-indicted-providing-encrypted-communication-devices visited 6 August 2022.

59 Khandelwal, Swati. 'How Dutch Police Decrypted BlackBerry PGP Messages For Criminal Investigation'. *The Hacker News* 10 March 2017 https://thehackernews.com/2017/03/decrypt-pgp-encryption.html visited 25 July 2022

60 EU Agency for Criminal Justice Cooperation *Dismantling of an encrypted network sends shockwaves through organised crime groups across Europe* 2 July 2020 https://www.eurojust.europa.eu/news/dismantling-encrypted-network-sends-shockwaves-through-organised-crime-groups-across-europe visited 6 August 2022.

61 Goodwin, Bill Secrecy over police EncroChat hacking is unconstitutional, defence lawyers tell top French court, *Computer Weekly News* 5 April 2022 https://www.computerweekly.com/news/252515556/Secrecy-over-police-EncroChat-hacking-is-unconstitutional-defence-lawyers-tell-top-French-court visited 6 August 2022.

62 Autistici.org *Aruba-Postale 1/Privacy 0* 21 June 2005 https://www.inventati.org/ai/crackdown/comunicato_en_210605.html visited 5 August 2022.

63 Whal, Thomas. 'Germany: Federal Court of Justice Confirms Use of Evidence in EncroChat Cases'. *eucrim spotlight* 19 May 2022 https://eucrim.eu/news/germany-federal-court-of-justice-confirms-use-of-evidence-in-encrochat-cases/ visited 6 August 2022.

64 UK Court of Appeal A, B, D & C v Regina [2021] EWCA Crim 128 20 January 2021.

65 Corte di cassazione, Sezione tributaria Ruling 31085/2019 issued on 28 November 2019.

66 Conseil Constitutionel *Décision n° 2022-987 QPC du 8 avril 2022* https://www.conseil-constitutionnel.fr/decision/2022/2022987QPC.htm visited 6 August 2022

67 'La France affirme que le "secret défense" dans les opérations de surveillance policière est constitutionnel'. *Les Actualité* 9 April 2022 https://lesactualites.news/technologie-et-science/la-france-affirme-que-le-secret-defense-dans-les-operations-de-surveillance-policiere-est-constitutionnel/ visited 5 August 2022. English translation by Andrea Monti.

68 Jarrett, Marshall et al. 2009. *Searching and Seizing Computers and Obtaining Electronic Evidence in Criminal Investigations*. Office of Legal Education Executive Office for United States Attorneys. OLE Litigation Series, p. 202 https://www.justice.gov/file/442111/download visited 6 August 2022

69 US Department of Justice *Ukrainian Arrested and Charged with Ransomware Attack on Kaseya* 8 november 2021 https://www.justice.gov/opa/pr/ukrainian-arrested-and-charged-ransomware-attack-kaseya visited 6 August 2022.

70 Menn, Joseph, 'Bing, Christopher Governments turn tables on ransomware gang REvil by pushing it offline' *Reuters Technology* 22 October 2021 https://www.reuters.com/technology/exclusive-governments-turn-tables-ransomware-gang-revil-by-pushing-it-offline-2021-10-21/ visited 6 August 2022.

71 US Department of Justice, Office of Public Affair *International Statement: End-To-End Encryption and Public Safety* 11 October 2020 https://www.justice.gov/opa/pr/international-statement-end-end-encryption-and-public-safety visited 25 June 2022.

72 https://www.theguardian.com/uk-news/2015/jan/15/david-cameron-ask-us-barack-obama-help-tracking-islamist-extremists-online viisted 22 June 2022.

73 https://www.gov.uk/government/publications/international-statement-end-to
-end-encryption-and-public-safety visited 22 june 2022.
74 https://noplacetohide.org.uk/ visited 10 July 2022.
75 https://eur-lex.europa.eu/legal-content/EN/TXT/?uri=COM%3A2022%3A209
%3AFIN&qid=1652451192472 visited 22 June 2022.
76 Council of the European Union, 12143/20 LIMITE JAI 851, COSI 156, CATS 73
ENFOPOL 256, COPEN 287, DATAPROTECT 106, CYBER 198, IXIM
107 Draft *Council Declaration on Encryption - Security through encryption and
security despite encryption* as reported by Politico.eu https://www.politico.eu/wp
-content/uploads/2020/09/SKM_C45820090717470-1_new.pdf visited 30 June
2020.
77 Apple *Expanded Protections for Children* https://www.apple.com/child-safety/
visited 30 June 2022.

5

AI, ROBOTS, AND (THEIR?) RIGHTS

Robotics, machine learning, and AI are three terms that are often used together almost as synonymous. However, although the areas present common issues, they also have such marked peculiarities that a unified analysis of their impact on law and rights would be challenging. This is true, in particular, for anthropomorphisation, which poses different problems depending on whether it refers to the robot as a replica of a human being, to software designed to operate with high levels of autonomy in parsing data, or to a machine—be a vacuum cleaner, a vehicle, or a weapon—capable of accomplishing tasks without little or any human supervision.

Although still at an early stage of development, robotics and AI add further insights into the relationship between mind and body and what it means to 'be alive'. Advances in genetics and neuroscience have made it possible to understand how to replicate the Shell and how the Ghost that inhabits it—the mind—should operate. In parallel, research in the field of the technology of information has made it possible to divide the attributes of cognitive activity into various components. Until now, public policy and regulatory issues mainly concerned medical research and biology, which are undoubtedly much further down the road to artificially creating life. Since the late 1990s, international agreements such as the Oviedo Convention[1] have set limits on the activities of scientists, industry, and governments in life sciences. Now, at least on paper, information technology is also beginning to be involved in the public debate.

The promising results achieved by synergy in the different fields of study have sparked people's imagination, the media's interest, and the industry's attention.

If one listens to the reports, it might seem that literary nightmares and science fiction dystopias have come true. Confused by the complexity of the topics, by the unscrupulous marketing strategies of the industries concerned, and by a renewed and problematic hyper-activism of philosophers and ethicists, public policies look influenced by literary suggestions instead of pragmatic approaches.

DOI: 10.4324/9781003373636-5   129

The European Union has even proposed recognising the existence of 'artificial beings' and giving them an autonomous legal status of personhood. The autonomous systems' liability debate has gone so far as to consider shifting legal responsibility from the human being to the products of his ingenuity. Scholars and politicians wonder, asking a meaningless question, what ethics should be instilled in self-manning machines or how to prevent an AI from rebelling against its creators.

The entertainment, consumer electronics, and information society services industries have played a central role in this tragicomedy. The symbolic impact of Hollywood films like *I Robot*, *AI*, *Terminator*, or *Ex Machina*—let alone *The Matrix*—is so strong that the suspension of beliefs remains active even when the show is over. It is practically impossible not to be bothered by the image of a robot dreaming of an army of its own kind, not to feel empathy towards the puppet with the features of a child desperately searching for its human 'parents', not to be frightened by a machine capable of deceiving and killing to eradicate humans or win its freedom.

Similarly, the evolution of real-life simulation games such as *The Sims* promised by the metaverse will allow living in alternate psychological realities and being able to show oneself to others with a different appearance or even a different form. Disengaged from the physicality of interpersonal interaction, and thanks to the infantilisation of culture,[2] new versions of Eliza,[3] the incredibly successful Rogerian psychotherapist chatbot of the late 1960s can easily blend in with human beings. Voice interaction with 'personal assistants' embedded in smartphones and other IoT gimmicks unconsciously induces the impression of dealing with real interlocutors, as empirically demonstrated by the tone and attitude each of us displays when using these tools. All this is nothing more than the manifestation, at various levels, of the irrepressible lust to rob nature (or some deity, for those who believe) of the power to create and command life.

Playing God (or forcing its hand)

Building machines capable of replicating and enhancing activities and cognitive processes characteristic of human beings was a clear goal since the dawn of cybernetics in the 1950s. However, discovering and mastering the secret of life is an endeavour that began long before science and technology made it, at least in part, feasible.

Claiming for the individual the power to decide on death and life is an anthropological trait that transcends the peculiarities of individual cultures. Life and death cults are a constant presence in any civilisation. Their physical manifestation has resulted in the creation of methods to kill and heal (sometimes, two sides of the same coin). In contrast, their spiritual expression has given rise to myths and legends about the divine power to create life and the attempt of human beings to appropriate it. Humankind's quest for the secret of life led to different epiphenomena that have often crossed paths. They were based upon the idea of life to be made, not born.

On the one hand, sapiential, alchemical, and religious traditions have focused on the body, its preservation, and reproduction propitiated by esoteric knowledge. A few examples among the many, are the use of Virgil's *bougonia* method to produce 'spontaneous' generation of a magically powerful rational animal that can tell its maker 'all things that are absent'[4]; Simon Magus' power of creating human beings out of the air,[5] Paracelsus' *Homunculus*, sixteenth century Haitian/Caribbean cults, united under the *Voo Doo* umbrella definition, claiming to cast spells through *Jujus*, *hotoke-oroshi*, the Japanese shamanesses' power of summoning the souls of trespassed.

However seemingly baseless, inappropriate, or even blasphemous the comparison may seem, they all share as much the same goal of synthetic biology and genetic engineering: using 'nature' to assert the power to control and create life—or at least some of its essential components.[6] Stem cell research, bioprinting and CRISPR-CASE9, the 'genetic cut&paste' method, mini-brain manufacturing[7], and eggless or spermless embryos growing[8] are conceptually not that far from the alchemists of the past. Sometimes, as in the case of marine biologist Jacques Loeb, it could even be challenging to tell the difference.

Having devised how to induce parthenogenesis in sea urchins artificially, he generalised the discovery into thinking that 'life could be understood—and manipulated—using engineering principles'.[9] In a 1902 famous interview, he claimed adamantly:

> I wanted to take life in my hands and play with it, I wanted to handle it in my laboratory as I would any other chemical reaction – to start it, stop it, vary it, study it under every condition, to direct it at my will![10]

As much as Loeb was criticised and even mocked by his peers for a claim that vividly reminds alchemic experiments of the past, his intuition that biology could be explained by chemistry lately found confirmation.

> Skip forward to 2003, and here's a headline in New Scientist: '"Virgin birth" method promises ethical stem cells'. The article discusses research demonstrating that parthenogenesis can be induced in human eggs by a simple chemical stimulus using the compound called calcium ionophore. The resulting embryos, lacking the genes from sperm that promote full development, can't grow beyond the blastocyst stage that they reach in a few days. But that's far enough to produce embryonic stem cells that can be harvested for research and medicine – without the ethical quandaries presented by taking

stem cells from human embryos discarded in IVF. ... There's more, though, because chemical parthenogenesis might have a real role in research on assisted reproduction.[11]

Rise of the robots

In parallel with the search for the immaterial component of life, mechanistic-oriented visions of the world have materialised in a myth about automata capable of displaying, apparently, human-like (or human-independent) behaviour.

> Long before the clockwork contraptions of the Middle Ages and the automata of early modern Europe, and even centuries before technological innovations of the Hellenistic period made sophisticated self-moving devices feasible, ideas about making artificial life—and qualms about replicating nature—were explored in Greek myths. Beings that were 'made, not born' appeared in tales about Jason and the Argonauts, the bronze robot Talos, the techno-witch Medea, the genius craftsman Daedalus, the fire-bringer Prometheus, and Pandora, the evil fembot created by Hephaestus, the God of invention. The myths represent the earliest expressions of the timeless impulse to create artificial life. These ancient 'science fictions' show how the power of imagination allowed people, from the time of Homer to Aristotle's day, to ponder how replicas of nature might be crafted.[12]

The idea of life to be made, not born, is not exclusive to Greek culture. Freyja, the Norse goddess of war, and Celtic King Nudd could be considered *ante litteram* cyborgs.[13] It is not by coincidence that the Indian Vishwakarma Institute of Technology is named after the Hindu divine architect, builder of automata and other marvellous machines. In India, under the order of King Ajatasatru, spirit-powered, human-shaped warriors—Bhuta Vahana Yantra—guarded Buddha's mortal remains.[14]

The evolution of automata and machines is no less focused on replicating human features or activities. Once again, in no particular order, it is worth mentioning a few examples ranging from the remote past to the 21st century: Mesopotamian's al-Jazari hand-washing servant and musicians, Indians singing birds, Leonardo's mechanical knight, Tommaso and Alessandro Francini's moving statues built for the Royal Gardens at Saint-Germain-en-Laye, Japanese tea-serving *Karakuri ningyō*, Maillardet's Draughtsman Writer. In the 20th century, electricity and more advanced technologies led to a new breed of automata, such as Westinghouse Electric's Elektro, shown at the 1939 New York World Fair.

The development of Wiener's cybernetics (conventionally associated with his 1948 book *Cybernetics: Or Control and Communication in the Animal and the Machine*) and the fast pacing evolution of information technology (eternally indebted to Claude Shannon's studies on information theory published during the same period) ideally turned automata into programmable and (more or less) autonomous machines—robots, in other words. Initially, excluding entertainment phenomena such as Elektro, these machines did not necessarily have a human-like appearance. This does not mean, however, that the dream of creating evolved automatons more and more similar to humans had vanished. Indeed, the technology may still have been too primitive, but the final goal was clear from day one.

On 23 January 1950, the weekly magazine *Time* featured on its cover the Mark III, an electromechanical–electronic hybrid computer built by Harvard University for the US Navy. The title and the image created to illustrate the news leave no doubt about the use for which the machine was designed and built. *Can Man build a Superman?* The magazine asks rhetorically. The claim is surmounted by a parallelepiped-shaped computer with two anthropomorphic mechanical arms tucked into the sleeves of a uniform with Admiral insignia. A hat—also carrying Admiral's rank—hangs over an eye that reads the processing results into the machine. Rarely, as in this case, has a picture been more eloquent than a thousand words.

Equally clear was the Soviet ideological position on cybernetics and computers that gained momentum in the 1950s. It was based on the same criticisms Lysenko formulated years earlier against Mendel's theories: cybernetics, like genetic inheritance, was a reactionary pseudoscience.

> In 1953 an author who wrote under the pseudonym 'Materialist' published the infamous article 'Whom Does Cybernetics Serve?' in a leading journal for ideological and intellectual battles, Voprosy filosofii (Questions of philosophy). Materialist waxed poetic in his rebuke: 'The theory of cybernetics, trying to extend the principles of modern computing machines to a broad variety of natural and social phenomena without due regard for their qualitative peculiarities, is mechanism'.[15]

Even more explicit and harsh was the reprimand contained in the entry 'cybernetics' of the *Concise dictionary of philosophy* published in 1954, according to which this discipline was a reactionary pseudoscience reflecting

> one of the basic features of the bourgeois worldview—its inhumanity, striving to transform workers into an extension of the machine, into a tool of production, and an instrument of war. At the same time, for cybernetics an imperialistic utopia is characteristic—replacing

133

living, thinking man, fighting for his interests, by a machine, both in industry and in war.[16]

In a few years, the Soviet ideological position would radically change. Cybernetics was politically rehabilitated, and even Russian scientists could devote themselves to this branch of knowledge. However, it is worth noting that the criticisms initially levelled by Marxist orthodoxy towards the use of 'thinking machines' are not too different from those formulated today towards Artificial Intelligence by Western intellectuals.

From robots to androids

The US and, in general, the West have not concentrated studies and industrial applications of automated computing on creating anthropomorphic robots. On the contrary, Japan has taken a leading position in this sector. Indeed, the next generation of humanoid robots and androids was mainly of Japanese descent. In 1985, at the Tsukuba World Expo, Waseda university presented Wasubot, capable of reading music and playing it accordingly. Publicly presented in 2000, Honda's Asimo has been an incredible example of engineering ingenuity for over 20 years. However, it was not autonomous, as it needed to be either deterministically programmed or remotely controlled to act.

Ishiguro Hiroshi of Osaka University focused his research projects on creating a full-functioning human replica.

In 2010 he built a clone of himself that could be remotely operated. He chose not to rely upon AI, as the still primitive stage of this technology could not replicate the complexity of human behaviour. In 2014 Ishiguro built two other robots: Kodomoroid and Otonaroid. Like Asimo, the two automata were remotely manned. Nonetheless, they were another step in the evolution of anthropomorphic robots. Alter 3, like the two last ones, is also professor Ishiguro's creation. In 2018 it gained an improved operational autonomy, boosted by a neural network and prosthetics mimicking facial expressions, becoming hot news when it was used to conduct a symphony orchestra. According to professor Takashi Ikegami, a member of the team that built Alter 3, the robot conducts the orchestra but cannot yet assess whether it is following his instructions correctly. However, the musicians felt comfortable following its directions nonetheless. It would be interesting to know, however reasonable it is to guess the answer, if the musicians would have shown the same willingness to follow the directions of a non-anthropomorphic machine composed, for example, of a pair of mechanical arms only.

Remotely controlling an android is a very demanding engineering challenge. Still, it could be considered a simple temporary step, waiting to reach the total autonomy of the machines thanks to AI, but this is not the case.

Remotely controlled androids—and machines in general—can be extremely useful precisely because they can be manned. On the other hand, these androids invoke the dystopian world of *Surrogates*; a 2005 graphic novel later turned into a Hollywood motion picture in 2009, where people live indoors and delegate every component of daily life to remote-controlled robots. We are still far from the moment these machines will be able to interact entirely with the environment by following our orders or operating independently. However, they have reached a stage that leads one to question whether it is desirable to build such anthropomorphic machines.

From Androids to Man

The issue did not pass unnoticed to professor Ishiguro himself:

> In some situations you don't need or want your robot to resemble a person. You don't need an android to vacuum your house if a saucer on wheels can do a better job. And a robotic assistant that helps an elderly person out of the tub probably shouldn't sport a human face. He's also well aware that, although people might better connect with a robot when it resembles another human being, when it gets the nuances wrong it may seem more like a zombie or an animated corpse.[17]

The question was already answered in 1970 by a prophetic essay, *The Uncanny Valley*, authored by roboticist Mori Masahiro. It established a relationship between the robot's exterior appearance and the feelings it evoked in human beings.

As long as robots were destined for industrial production, even if endowed with ever-increasing autonomy, they were 'simply' machines. Therefore, people did not feel any connection with them. By contrast, toy robots like Sony's Aibo—a robotic pet—are *purposely* built to elicit a sense of affinity, even if still clearly non-human.

Things start changing with artificial limbs. Contrary to common opinion, one may think that a realistic prosthetic should increase the affinity with the unfortunate person forced to use it.

> However, when we realise the hand, which at first site looked real, is in fact artificial, we experience an eerie sensation. For example, we could be startled during a handshake by its limp boneless grip together with its texture and coldness. When this happens, we lose our sense of affinity, and the hand becomes uncanny. ...[18]

Another step towards a surprising conclusion is looking at the audience's reaction to *bunraku* puppets. They look pretty human when seen from a distance, and how they are manned enhances this perception. Notwithstanding, as soon as the suspension of belief kicks in, the connection with the puppet might start accordingly. Back to the prosthetic issue, Mori says that even a myoelectric signal-powered artificial hand could create a feeling of unease in healthy persons.

> If someone wearing the hand in a dark place shook a woman's hand with it, the woman would assuredly shriek! Since negative effects of movement are apparent even with a prosthetic hand, a whole robot would magnify the creepiness.[19]

Counterintuitively, Mori proposes *limit*ing robots' 'mankindness' to maximise the possibility of human acceptance. He knows that a more-human-than-humans android (like Asimov's R. Daneel Olivaw) might affect people's acceptance of this technology. In other words, instead of building ever more perfect imitations of a human being, the aim should be to make anthropomorphic machines that are clearly recognisable as such and thus easier to integrate with humans.

By contrast, Ishiguro, although aware of the issue, orients his research towards the perfect automata.

> He is convinced that human-looking robots are a natural interface for humans to interact with and that the uncanny valley idea may be too simplistic to explain people's reactions to robots. We may simply come to accept lifelike androids as we're exposed to more of them and, in the future, rely on them for our care and other needs.
>
> These is exactly what causes problem when it comes to decide if and how to regulate the design, manufacturing and use of these machines.[20]

Fifty years after Mori's writing and over ten years after Ishiguro's statements about the still too early stage of AI development, the debate on the anthropomorphisation of robots is still ongoing. Its new iteration extended the classic topic of human-like exteriority to the embedding into a robot intelligence and autonomous consciousness, allegedly achieved by the AI.

The Ghost enters the Shell

Media are always attracted to anthropomorphic androids and 'intelligent machines' news. Every time a prototype is presented to the public showing some degree of autonomy, sensationalistic headlines multiply. Out of ignorance, recklessness, or, God forbid, the search for sensationalism at all costs, generalist media seldomly deepen the technical components of the news. Invariably, articles go at length into explaining how much machines can now think for themselves, that we are facing a new form of life, and that the moment we succumb to these new gods is closer and closer.

The most obvious and controversial example is the marketing operation built in 2016 around Sophia, a robot manufactured by a Hong Kong-based company named Hanson Robotics.

Within months from being publicly announced, the robot—then just a head and a torso—was declared 'basically alive' by its manufacturer, was presented to the United Nations where it declared 'I am here to help humanity create the future', told the press that it wants to destroy mankind and wanting to have a family. It also received honorary citizenship from Saudi Arabia.[21]

It did not take long for the scientific community to harshly criticise how the Sophia project was featured to the public and the media.[22] The machine was far from being capable of interaction, 'intelligent', and 'self-conscious'. It talked with people through pre-arranged scripts (a fact of which the public was not made aware). It had no autonomous 'Artificial Intelligence', and the claim that it was 'basically alive' was—in the mirror-climbing words of its manufacturers—to be understood differently than the usual meaning associated with the idea of life.

> Digital and robotic entities are not the same as biological entities, so applying words like 'alive' to them is often going to be more misleading than informative.... Currently the Sophia robot—and all other existing robots—lack the kinds of independence and autonomy that are characteristic of biological lifeforms.[23]

Criticisms prompted the various parties involved in using Sophia as a cog of the marketing machine for Hanson Robotics to make a series of clarifications on the fact that they would never have intended to imply that the robot had abilities that it did not possess. These explanations highlight a fundamental aspect to be considered in legal analysis: the difference between possessing characteristics of biological life forms and reproducing their outward manifestations (more on this *infra*). However, they were put forward as a defence against criticism of the commercial project rather than as a purely scientific issue. They did not change the broader consequences of the whole case.

If the impact of Sophia had perhaps stopped in the media, it would not have caused too much damage in terms of public policy and legal analysis. The novelty effect would gradually fade, and the public would lose interest in the subject until the next time. Unfortunately, the Sophia project did much more damage.

Firstly, it may seem like *minutia*, but referring to this object with the pronouns 'she' and 'her' instead of 'it' subliminally induces a change of attitude towards the thing. It is not seen for what it is—an inanimate *machine*—but for what it looks like or, better, for the feelings it elicits from those who interact with it. On 24 April 2014, US President Barack Obama visited Tokyo's *Miraikan*—the National Museum of Emerging Science and Innovation—where he 'met' Asimo. President Obama was obviously aware that he was not interacting with a living being, and indeed he was playing for the camera. However, the expression on his face shows a spontaneous feeling of acknowledgement towards the machine.[24]

Secondly, although the attribution of Saudi citizenship is clearly a marketing stunt, it has raised a machine to the rank of a human being. The inescapable consequence would be to demand that the machine be entitled to the *whole* set of rights until now reserved to mankind.

Finally and consequently, having hinted that Sophia could interact autonomously and on an equal footing with human beings to the point of being considered a political interlocutor has reinforced the perception that a machine should have the upper hand in dictating decisions and policies.

This is so true that David Hanson—the owner of the company that manufactured Sophia—thinks that granting rights to robots is just a matter of 'when', not of 'if'.

> Hanson also believes that robot rights – the key premise on which Become Human hinges – are likely to be granted when robots begin to share conscious thought with humans. 'It requires not only physical capabilities, but a sense of desire for autonomy, as well as a curiosity and awareness of one's state,' he explains. 'My expectation is that it won't be until the mid-2040s or late 2050s that there will be a general worldwide recognition of android rights.'[25]

It is unclear which authority and hard scientific facts these claims are issued. Be that as it may, they confirm whether robots should have *rights* is a matter to be discussed mainly under continuing confusion between science fiction, business interests, and law.

Do (should) robots—and AI—have rights?

As elucidated in Chapter 2, the literary invention of cyberspace has had a significant (and negative) influence on legal analysis and legislators' choices. Nevertheless, it is nothing compared to the dire consequences of basing political and regulatory decisions about robotics and Artificial Intelligence on science fiction such as the three—nay, the four—Asimov's laws of robotics and other fictional creations.

Daneel Olivaw, the android who goes from being 'just' an investigator in *Cave of Steel* to becoming the almost immortal demi-god who decides the fate of mankind and the Bard, the 'mistreated' computer that 'knew then that computers would always grow wiser and more powerful until someday—someday—someday—...[26]' are the nightmare—or unconfessed desire—that populates the dreams of scientists, politicians, and jurists. They embody the archetype of *Frankenstein's Syndrome*,[27] the fear that a man-made 'creature' might rebel against his creator, a central element not only in Mary Shelley's novel, Karel Čapek's *Der goylem*, and other similar literary works. They are as recurrent as they are misunderstood in countless debates in sociology, philosophy, politics, and law.

'Andrew', the admittedly less threatening character of Asimov's *Bicentennial Man*, is at the heart of another side of the multifaced debate involving the relationship between men and machines, namely the possibility of setting a clear distinction between a human being and an artificial mechanism. The intersection between flesh, silicon chip, and artificial body is a recurring theme in Western literature and artistic production. However, the Japanese cyberpunk sci-fi genre explored at large and thoroughly alternate realities where robots, computers, and humans often co-existed without visible differences.

Over a 50 years' time span, many authors complemented Asimov's ideas and anticipated topics nowadays considered at the edge of the matter. In the mid-seventies, Nagai Go and Yoshida Tetsuo's mangas show the multifaced reality. In the first of the two Nagai's creations (*Great Mazinger*), Kabuto Kenzō, the super robot creator, hides behind his human appearance his true cyborg nature. In the second, *Kotetsu Jeeg*, Shiba Senjiro creates a super robot manned by his son conveniently turned into a cyborg. Before being killed by his enemies, he uploads 'himself' into a computer from where he continues his/its fight. Yoshida's *Neo-Human Casshern* is about Azuma Tetsuya, a young man who, retaining his human consciousness, willingly turns himself into an android to fight an army of rogue robots. 1990 Shirow Masamune's *Ghost in the Shell* somehow merges the two strains. On the one hand, the characters are full cyborgs with a human brain (like Kusanagi Motoko), or partially 'enhanced' humans. On the other hand, the Ghost in the Shell is a government-managed AI that acquires an independent will. Are Kabuto, Shiba, Azuma, and Kusanagi still 'alive'? Are they still human? Do they still have, have they ever had, or will they have 'rights'?

It would be easy to dismiss these questions by pointing out that they are just fantasy and that, as such, there is no point in addressing them in ethical, political, and legal terms. That would be—*is* actually—a sensible decision.

When studying anthropology, psychology, or sociology, it is legitimate—indeed, fundamental—to draw from literature and art. These epiphenomena of the human soul tell much more about the individual and society than quantitative studies could. On the contrary, it is impossible to do the same regarding the law. Regulating relationships between human beings and affecting personal freedom are activities that require extreme focus on reality. This is why artistic inventions dedicated to robots and AI should not enter the legal debate, just as the other literary fiction—cyberspace—should not have been used to the same end.

However, the inability, at every level, to understand the technological complexity of these phenomena, the unscrupulous marketing strategies of the technology industry, and the longstanding, not-so-suppressed, everlasting lust to play God and obtain the power to create and command life have caused different outcomes.

As it has been said *supra*, the push towards the design of anthropomorphic machines, the studies on the possibility of constructing human-like reasoning processes, and those on the use of large amounts of data from sensors and other sources to extend the operational capabilities of the software inductively have radically changed the scenario. The entertainment and technology industries have further stimulated this change in attitude. Their products—films, television series, and smart devices of all kinds—have blurred the difference between reality and fantasy. Despite the appearance of interactivity—hence, claimed Artificial Intelligence—many of the achievements of research and commercial products based on so-called AI are far from being considered genuinely autonomous, intelligent or both. Nevertheless, scholars—mainly of sociology, public policy, and law—and intellectuals ventured into territories of which, in reality, many of them can say no more than *hic sunt leones*.

A contradictory regulatory approach

Although robotics and Artificial Intelligence are two disciplines that have many points of contact, they remain pretty distinct both on a theoretical level and on an applicative level. Nonetheless, the regulatory approach tends to consider them substantially overlapping. This confuses the scenario and makes it challenging to identify the real political and legal problems to be faced and possibly resolved. This remark applies, in particular, to an essential question: do we need to regulate these technologies with particular pieces of legislation?

Rights and duties are human creations. The former are granted, partially, to other less evolved living beings such as animals. However, only humans are subjected to the latter. If a human infringes a duty, he will be sanctioned. For a human being to be sanctioned, he must know (or culpably ignore) what he is doing, and he must be able to understand the reason for the punishment. Obviously, this topic is extraordinarily more complex, but for now, it is sufficient to summarise it in this way. Therefore, giving, as it has been proposed, a robot or software a legal status similar to a natural person requires ascertaining whether these objects are, first and foremost, alive. Then it is necessary to understand if they are aware of existing and endowed with an intelligence that allows self-determination.

Depending on the answers to these questions, it will be possible to decide whether to attribute rights and duties to machines, only rights (as in the case of animals), or—as is apparent—none of this. Therefore, it is necessary to ascertain whether the predictions of futurologists and spin doctors from the technology industry about 'alternative form of life', 'uncontrollable AI', and other similar truisms are based or not upon solid scientific theories, unscrupulous marketing stunts, or pure delusion.

Sales departments of animatronic factories and software houses can use all the marketing techniques they want. This, however, does not change the fact that—to date—machines (or software) that fall under this definition of 'living being' or 'natural person' do not exist. Therefore, since the law does not care about *impossibilia*, if today there are no other forms of life evolved at the same level as mankind, it is useless to think of their possible rights.

This statement is usually countered by claiming that today, machines are not alive, but tomorrow they could be, so it is legitimate to ask how to regulate them in advance. The main flaw of this argument is epistemological. It is a remnant of 18th century positivism, according to which progress, thanks to science, can only go forward. Therefore, no mystery can stay unresolved, no goal can be out of reach, and no knot untangled. However, contrary to this still shared opinion, knowledge's evolution is not an arrow pointing straight upwards. Instead, a progress graph would be made up of broken stretches, curves that go backwards, but above all, of insurmountable limits and asymptotes.

True, many boundaries considered impossible to overcome have been crossed. It is also true that certain limits exist within the theory of which they are part, so changing the premises can change the conclusions. For instance, the Ptolemaic doctrine has been outdated, but it is still sufficient to find the due course in the limited scope of navigating with stars. This, however, does not authorise the generalisation of the statement according to which everything that is not yet possible today will undoubtedly be possible tomorrow. Cassius Clay's iconic quote *impossible is nothing* is an excellent one-line for marketing campaigns or self-motivation books, but it works poorly with logic and philosophy.

The counterargument challenging this positivist approach solves the problem of methodology. It shows that it would not be correct to ground public policies and pieces of legislation on a logical fallacy based on blind faith in the future. However, it does not address the merit of the matter: is it possible or not, to date, to argue that in the future, it will be possible to build a form of life other than the animal?

To follow this question, it would be necessary first to define 'life'. The task is not that simple because there is no absolute definition of this concept. *Are Virus Alive?* asks Luis Villareal on *Scientific American*.[28] The answer is far from being obvious—or definitive.

Before the advent of information technologies, it was a common assumption that intelligence (not to be confused with cleverness shown by animals and even insects) was an attribute of being conscious of existing. Different theoretical models have overcome this assumption, albeit in different ways. The functionalist approach adopted by weak AI scholars separated the two. Thus, a machine can *function* intelligently—solving problems efficiently or naturally interacting with humans—*without being intelligent* and *alive*. Integrated Information Theory proposes a conceptual framework in which 'computer systems with traditional hardware architectures would not share our experiences, even if they were to replicate our cognitive functions or simulate our brains in ultra-fine detail'.[29] Moreover, even if it is limited to psychiatric pathologies such as dementia, it is an unquestionable fact that there are living human beings with reduced capability.

The opposite, i.e. intelligent but lifeless entities, would not be possible. In fact, in the best-case scenario, we would interact with objects that *mimic*, not *own*, cognitive functions. For this reason, such devices can even detect that they are working. That does not make them alive and therefore entitled to have rights.

Moreover, even if it were possible to give life to an AI, it would already be forbidden.

It is not legally allowed to clone a human being, even if the technology is widely available. Therefore, if the principle is that life cannot be artificially created, it makes little difference if the ban is on genetic engineering, data science, or any other branch of human knowledge.

Regulating the Ghost *and* the Shell?

Put in these terms, the nature of the question changes profoundly. From a legal point of view, we should ask ourselves not whether to regulate a form of life other than human or animal but whether to issue laws regarding objects that operate, at various levels of autonomy, as if they *were* human beings. If this reasoning is correct, talking about 'living machines' or 'sentient AIs' becomes irrelevant because the only thing to adjust is how they are designed, manufactured, and operated. Public policy choices, at least in the EU, have followed a different path, strongly influenced by the cultural context based on science fiction previously described at length.

EU Parliament to endorse Asimov's Three Laws of Robotics

The European Parliament went so far as to propose Asimov's fictional 'laws' to be 'regarded as being directed at the designers, producers and operators of robots, including robots assigned with built-in autonomy and self-learning, since those laws cannot be converted into machine code'.[30]

Asimov's Laws are a brilliant literary invention but, from a legal standpoint, are flawed by the wrong assumption challenged in the previous paragraph: that robots are sentient beings with an autonomous will—persons, in other words.

To understand where the misinterpretation lies, just have a look at Asimov's Laws:

A robot may not injure a human being or, through inaction, allow a human being to come to harm.

A robot must obey the orders given it by human beings except where such orders would conflict with the First Law.

A robot must protect its own existence as long as such protection does not conflict with the First or Second Laws.[31]

The mistake is all in the (non) subject to Asimov's Laws: a robot. A robot is not alive and does not own free will. Therefore, it cannot harm people more than a hammer or any other piece of machinery wrongly designed, manufactured, and used. Actually, its builders, those who designed the hardware and the software, should carry the legal burden of their choices. Therefore, Asimov's Laws should be amended like the following:

The robot's designer and software programmer should ensure the machine does not harm people with an action or an omission.

The robot's designer and software programmer should make it so that the machine executes the commands imparted by a user, except when these commands conflict with the first law.

The robot's designer and software programmer should ensure the machine does not break, except if the break prevention conflicts with the first or the second law.

Stated in this way, the Three Laws of Robotics lose all their appeal. In the new version, they express nothing more than principles that are already widely known and incorporated into the safety regulations and procedures governing the construction of industrial machines. Of course, such mistakes are not Asimov's fault. The scientist did not want to write a piece of legislation. He just needed a literary invention to be used in the tales of his extraordinary universe.

Regulating the 'how' instead of the 'what'

Similar coherence issues affect the European Commission's upcoming regulation on Artificial Intelligence.[32]

The draft is based on two mistaken assumptions: the first is that Artificial Intelligence exists similarly to human intelligence. The second is that only Artificial Intelligence is potentially dangerous, while the rest of 'traditional' software is not.

As it is apparent, this proposal is more inspired by science fiction than the analysis of how the software industry has affected people's lives.

143

The commission, for instance, proposes to ban 'AI systems' from being used to send subliminal messages to manipulate the behaviour of individuals and minority people, causing them harm. Indeed, one should deduce that subliminal manipulation that does not harm people should be lawful. That paradoxical conclusion would open the door to 'nudging'—a public policy method heavily used by executives during the peak of the COVID-19 pandemic.[33]

With the support of AI, nudging can increase its effectiveness in circumventing parliamentary oversight on governmental affairs and weakening the rule of law. It is a motive of distress that the government wanting to use subliminal AI for the country's greater good will not be stopped by this regulation.

Similarly, EU Commission proposes to ban the use of AI to create social scoring and automated reliability assessment tools affecting people. However, social scoring—creditworthiness, tax loyalty, and business reliability—is already happening, without the need for 'Artificial Intelligence'. Also in this case, the critics just directed at the ban on subliminal AI only are valid. If social scoring is unacceptable, it should be banned regardless of how it is deployed.

A further conceptual error in the regulation proposal is that it is possible to tell AI from what is not. Article 3(I) of the draft states that software belongs to the category 'Artificial Intelligence' if it is developed using 'one or more of the techniques and approaches listed in Annex I and can, for a given set of human-defined objectives, generate outputs such as content, predictions, recommendations, or decisions influencing the environments they interact with'. Methods listed in Annex I are:

(a) Machine learning approaches, including supervised, unsupervised and reinforcement learning, using a wide variety of methods including deep learning;
(b) Logic- and knowledge-based approaches, including knowledge representation, inductive (logic) programming, knowledge bases, inference and deductive engines, (symbolic) reasoning and expert systems;
(c) Statistical approaches, Bayesian estimation, search and optimisation methods.

This meagre list of non-technical definitions seems more suitable for a commercial presentation than a legislative text. It does not account for the complexity of the information technology market and the other connected industrial sectors. It makes it challenging to establish a clear difference between what falls into one category or the other. Especially if shady business practices deliberately choose to make things less transparent.

Imposing unfathomable transparency on the algorithm

Arguably, however, the biggest delusion in the attempts to regulate the use of AI became apparent when also algorithms fell under the scrutiny of legislators and legal scholars.

Algorithms are at the core of AI research and applications. They are the intricate network of procedural connections that, once implemented in a computer programme fed with a massive quantity of data, are trained to operate with a high level of autonomy.

Faced with the terrifying power of these mysterious entities, capable of analysing the data concerning us, and—so goes the *vulgata*—deciding in our place what destiny is reserved for us, the reaction of governments, parliaments, and intellectuals has been to invoke the transparency of the algorithm.

The EU General Data Protection Regulation adopted in 2016 prohibits taking decisions affecting individual's rights using only automated tools. It also establishes the data subjects' right to be informed of the logic—that is, which algorithms—used in the processing. A similar provision is advocated for the upcoming AI regulation.

This goal is simply unattainable. Most people outside expert circles struggle with simple high-school mathematics, such as calculating the integral of partial derivative. There is no way they can understand algorithms behind, for instance, *Generative Pre-trained Transformer* (GPT)—a natural language processing system—even in its first, outdated version dating back to 2018. Not to mention the skills needed to understand how algorithms are implemented in computer software, the cost of the tools necessary to perform these tasks, and the time required.

Even experts summoned by the Panel for the Future of Science and Technology of the European Parliament had to concede that having access to algorithms and their technical documentation does not guarantee that an average person may understand them.[34] The proposal includes multiple solutions to address algorithmic governance, such as '1. Awareness raising: education, watchdogs, and whistleblowers. 2. Accountability in public sector use of algorithmic decision-making. 3. Regulatory oversight and Legal liability. 4. Global coordination for algorithmic governance'.[35]

The EU's standard regulatory approach essentially inspires these proposals. For example, the liability issue of information society service providers is dealt with in the same terms. The European Commission has signed a cooperation agreement with the large digital platforms. The Digital Service Act empowers trusted flaggers to report illegal content and set providers' obligations. Independent authorities assume additional supervisory and control powers, and consumers have more rights to be informed. However, very likely, when it comes to regulating algorithms, these hints will stay where they are now: on paper.

In highly technical subjects, the more we intend to regulate the deeper and structural parts of the world, the more this goal becomes unattainable. By following this path, one day, somebody could even delude himself into being able to legislate on how atoms, electrons, and quarks should work.

In the best-case scenario, a direct consequence of this desire for hyper-regulation is the substantial loss of the role of parliaments and, therefore, of citizens, in favour of a Platonic-type state governed by philosophers, i.e. scientists. In the worst case, we would fall back into a hardcore Stalinist-like rule, where the powers-that-be claim for them the power to rule nature. Again, the pandemic has provided concrete examples of both scenarios. The controversy between White House Chief Medical Advisors Anthony Fauci and then American President Donald Trump has occupied the media's headlines worldwide. However, in every nation, political power had to give way to bearers of knowledge impossible to acquire in a short time or rule against the hard evidence.

Explainable Artificial Intelligence (XAI) is a form of AI that promises to solve the problem of algorithmic transparency. In theory it should give back people (politicians and lawmakers, actually) the steering wheel of the decisional process. XAI was designed to overcome the black box approach, which—according to the researchers—would not have allowed to know the reasons behind a particular conclusion drive by an AI. An XAI, on the other hand, is based on principles of transparency, interpretability, and explainability. It should allow experts to understand better why specific results were produced and not others. In this way, the obstacle that, more than others, generates distrust of AI should be overcome: the fact that, as we hear obsessively repeating, no one can explain how it works. That, however, is not entirely correct.

Understanding how an AI has reached a particular conclusion is 'only' challenging and, therefore, possible for a limited number of suitably competent people.

> The international scientific community of machine learning has labelled as black-box models all those proposals containing a complex mathematical function (like support-vector machine and neuronal networks) and all those needing a deep understanding of the distance function and the representation space (like k-nearest neighbors), which are very hard to explain and to be understood by experts in practical applications.[36]

In reality, however, this problem does not only concern AI but, in general, all those frontier researches that try to overcome the known limits of a given discipline. Specific theoretical constructions are so complex that they are understandable only to a limited number of adequately gifted people from an intellectual point of view. Consequently, it makes little sense to

146

impose something to be 'made understandable' by someone unable to do so. From this point of view, science is not democratic, and the political ideals of transparency, access, and sharing of knowledge collide with the limits of individuals.

By transferring this reasoning to the level of public policies, instead of invoking a right to trivialise (not only) AI, one should push for the duty to broaden personal knowledge. This is not to transform all citizens into sorcerers' apprentices but to allow them to understand the correct attribution of responsibility for their choices.

The debate on the transparency of algorithms is, in fact, another demonstration of the shift of decision-making responsibility from human beings to inanimate or even immaterial objects. It is conceptually unthinkable that a non-specialist could understand the technicalities of a given problem. Moreover, the same specialist in one sector may not necessarily be able to understand what happens in other fields. The point, therefore, is not 'algorithmic transparency' but the accountability of the decision-making process.

In other words, there is a substantial difference between 'impossibility of knowing' and 'extreme difficulty of understanding'. In the first case, technologies based on such an assumption would have to be banned. In the second, the problem falls within the scope just described: the smaller the number of people who possess specific knowledge, the less citizens and decision-makers can consciously exercise their rights and duties.

On paper, therefore, XAI is very promising. In reality, it only serves to make life easier for experts who should be able to struggle less in understanding the results produced by the algorithms. Consequently, if XAI only serves to facilitate expert understanding, it would only expand the number of researchers involved. With XAI (if and when it works), the former will better understand their experiments' results. However, citizens and politicians will continue to depend on the opinions of scientists with no real possibility of understanding the basis of public policy and judicial decisions.

AI vs 'ordinary' software safety discrimination

AI is considered high risk when tasked with managing the safety of consumer products. However, the same concern is not applied, for instance, to electro-medical and diagnostic pieces of equipment running non-AI software licensed 'as is' (i.e. without any guarantee of proper and safe operation) or with limited liability bearing from the manufacturer. That leads to another conceptual weakness of the proposal: establishing a liability that depends on the instrument used and not on the damage it generates.

Suppose it is decided that only computer programmes based on 'Artificial Intelligence' are subject to the limitations of the regulation. This would imply leaving a free hand to all other software developed with different

147

methods and no less dangerous in their outcomes. That conclusion is clearly contradictory and untenable.

What (should) matter is to grant legal protection from the abuses committed by exploiting any technology, regardless of how it works. Consequently, it would make more sense to address the legal liability of data scientists, software designers, and developers. In other words, what should be of interest to the norm is what damages are (or can be) caused by software, not how the software is designed or implemented. The latter should count, if anything, to quantify the entity of the sanction or penalty according to the manufacturer's faults or deliberate intent to cause harm.

Contrary to what happened to life scientists, software developers, analysts, and 'computer hackers'—as well as corporations that hire them—have enjoyed a de facto state of impunity. In theory, all the principles of civil and criminal laws apply to those who work in this sector. If a computer programme has (or creates) a problem, whoever made it has to fix it and compensate for damages. However, this happens very rarely. Software is not sold like any other product but is licensed 'as is' also when employed in critical environments. Some manufacturers try to lighten its liability in license agreements by stating that the computer programme should not be used in life-endangering domains.

Since the dawn of the information revolution, technological marketing has convinced users that defects and malfunctions are entirely typical or even essential features. *It's not a Bug, It's a Feature*[37] is a well-known refrain of a song sung for decades by 'artists' ranging from solo performers (individual programmers) to big bands and symphonic orchestras (multinational software houses and platforms).

The same happens with the training of machine-learning models when it is done using publicly available data and information (texts, photos, metadata) without any particular concern under the 'better ask for forgiveness than permission' doctrine. Occasionally, when companies are found to have collected and used data without authorisation, claims are made in the name of copyright, privacy, racial bias, or other 'fundamental rights'. The focus, however, is on chastising the unscrupulous use of data, not the *choice* to manipulate it.

The ease and substantial impunity of this race towards creating an alleged artificial form of life are even more alarming when compared to the burdens placed by the law on collecting, analysing, and sharing data in the life science sector.

'Blame the algorithm': the new mantra of irresponsibility

The liability issue is central to regulating AI—or, better, its use—even if, in reality, it should not. Once established that AI is 'simply' software that processes information and controls devices at various levels of autonomy, all the provisions dictating safety requirements are enforceable without the need for specific regulations. It could be complex and costly to ascertain liability in a court case, but in terms of substantive law, the recipient of the legal action would be easily identifiable. As the last section has just highlighted, the current legal framework should only be complemented by addressing once and for all the issue of liability in software development and the use of data (not necessarily personal, indeed).

The personification of AI and the tendency to legally recognise its personhood make it difficult to adopt such a solution. Indulging in attributing person-like status to this technology induces a not-so-subtle change in the legal liability paradigms. Obligations shift to 'algorithms' instead of staying on those who designed, implemented, and used them. This shift would lead to impunity for those actually responsible for damage and the impossibility of obtaining compensation or applying sanctions. The contradictions of this approach become apparent when analysing the debate on autonomous vehicles and weapons and the promised miracles of 'predictive justice'.

Cars and Weapons

Two are the problems most frequently discussed in dealing with autonomous vehicles. The identification of the criteria based on which a car should select the most efficient behaviour to avoid an accident when the choice would, in any case, lead to consequences (even lethal) for human lives; and who should bear the responsibility for the consequences of choice.

These problems appear without a solution. On the one hand, a court should scrutinise the 'independent behaviour' of the AI to possibly 'sanction' it, but as just said, this would not make sense. On the other hand, designers and builders could argue that they cannot be involved in an act committed by an autonomous and independent 'subject'. This stall is as evident as it is revealing flawed assumptions.

A vehicle manufacturer's first and fundamental duty is to ensure the safety of those who buy, drive, and travel inside. Only recently has vehicle design been oriented towards reducing the damage caused to pedestrians and passers-by. Even if they have reached very high levels of efficiency, passive and active safety systems cannot guarantee 100% of preventing the cause of damage. Their success rate will improve over time, but accidents caused by unpredictable events or malfunction of these systems will always happen. Just as it is unrealistic to expect current safety systems to work at all times and in all conditions, it is equally unrealistic to expect a self-driving vehicle to do the same.

By giving up the sci-fi illusion of infallible AI, the trade-off in its practical use should be based on how many more lives could be spared by using it while being aware that there will always be the possibility of casualties.

Adopting this perspective, the matter is stripped of any ethical implication and returns to a classic issue of product liability, insurance, and actuarial mathematics. It is up to the manufacturer to comply with vehicle safety regulations, just as he is responsible for installing other safety systems and whether or not to adopt a specific technology according to a risk/reward assessment.

A similar argument can be made about autonomous weapons.

Weapons are built with a single purpose: to kill the opponent most efficiently. This implies maximising the enemy casualty ratio and minimising losses in terms of men and resources.

War is not supposed to be fought with an 'anything goes' attitude. International conventions prohibit using certain lethal weapons such as chemical, bacteriological, and nuclear ordnances, anti-personnel landmines, expansive or fragmenting bullets, and poisons. Moreover, the civil population should not be a target for military actions, and when 'collateral damages' happen, it is a matter for the military court. That is, at least, theory because the reality of conflicts tells a different story. Notwithstanding, there are criteria, right or wrong as they may be, establishing which weapons can be used and which cannot. Framed in this context, it is apparent that, like autonomous driving, the issue of autonomous weapons warfare is legal, not ethical.

Notwithstanding that such weapons have not yet been built, vast literature goes a long way to analyse the ethical problems associated with the use of non-existent objects. It goes without saying that science fiction literature and cinema are often placed as the basis of these thoughts.

The debate about the ethical acceptability of target dehumanisation through AI-operated weapons is exemplary.

> The last major ethical argument about LAWS is whether they might be inherently problematic because they dehumanise their targets. All human life is precious and has intrinsic value, so having machines select and engage targets arguably violates fundamental human dignity–people have the right to be killed by someone who made the choice to kill them. Since machines are not moral actors, automating the process of killing through LAWS is also by definition unethical.[38]

What, as in this case, is presented as an ethical problem involves, instead, a topic having nothing ado with AI: the dehumanisation of the adversary as a combat necessity.

Although killing one's fellow is common to many species in the animal kingdom, this instinct is not immediately operational in man. Killing is an act that brings severe consequences to a person's psyche, so much so that even in combat, it is not so easy to take the life of an enemy who is still seen as a person before being a foe. This has led to training systems that overcome this taboo. One indoctrination method is the dehumanisation of the opponent. This can happen through a process of demonisation, whereby the enemy is associated with values contrary to those practised by self-perceived 'righteous forces' or aberrant behaviour such as slaying women and children. Another way to achieve this is to create distance between the two fighters by inserting technological 'layers' between them. Killing with bare hands or a knife is a shocking experience, but the emotional impact of this act decreases as the distance increases. Firing an assault rifle at an advancing group of soldiers, maybe through a night-vision goggle or a digital visor on the helmet, means hitting a moving figure similar to an inkblot. He is still recognisable as a human being, but pulling the trigger is less heavy than using a knife. This is even truer if, miles away, a howitzer fire the shot. The disconnection with the enemy is maximised in carpet-bombing or missile launches.

At this point, even if some ethicists will vigorously disagree, it does not make much difference to press the release button of a bomb or to let a drone select and kill the target. Collateral damages may happen in both cases. What matters is if the act is performed under the law of war's criteria and if the weapons have been designed to meet such criteria.

So far, the question of the alleged legal subjectivity of organised pieces of computer code has been analysed in terms of possible liability shift from the human being to an intangible object. There is, however, another aspect to consider: attributing legal responsibility to a subject presupposes granting him a right and, consequently, a power. In the case of autonomous vehicles and weapons—but also in the case of surgeries without human supervision—this power consists in deciding whether a person should live or die. In the case of predictive justice, if someone has to lose his freedom.

Prosecutors and courts

Predictive justice is an umbrella word to indicate information technologies and neuroscience in managing police investigations and making civil and criminal decisions.

The use of automated tools to perform technical analysis is a fact. Courts must evaluate the scientificity and reliability of the method and results, after which the evidence acquires total value for the decision. 'DNA wars' fought in the US courtrooms in the 1990s, which ended with the definition of criteria for the validity of genetic evidence, are an example of what happens when data in input are selected wrongly.

In other areas, too, from the analysis of complex financial statements to the enormous amounts of internet traffic data, it is practically mandatory to use automated tools that help investigators find and correlate relevant information. For example, the US Sarbanes-Oxley Act even requires verifying the

151

correct functioning of the software used to produce financial data. Also, it is unthinkable that the intersection of metadata generated by devices connected to the internet to establish the network of relationships between subjects suspected of being involved in criminal actions can take place without automated analysis tools, even if not necessarily 'intelligent'. Just as in court cases in which a massive amount of documents must be analysed, the use of software to identify and extract relevant information is a necessity.

Even if there is human intervention at the end of the process, the automated analysis provides the fundamental elements of the case. Provided one can afford expensive technical consultants, contesting the data and its interpretation is always possible. The issue, therefore, is not 'whether' to automate evidence analysis but to understand the defendant's concrete possibilities to challenge the prosecutor's assessments coming from automated investigations.

A step further is to delegate the search for evidence, its evaluation, the definition of the accusation, and the case's decision entirely to AI. This is what, at least in part and in theory, is happening with 'AI-powered' computer platforms.

Profiling and predictive policing software, so it is claimed, 'can make sense out of "Big Data" collected from every kind of source, from public records to—again—camera feeds, from social networks to behavioural data'.[39] The crime-monitoring platform would then label an event as a possible criminal or anti-social behaviour and prompt the operator to investigate further. In 2022, Chinese researchers claimed to have developed

> The world's first Artificial Intelligence (AI) capable of analysing case files and charging people with crimes. The Orwellian device can already identify 'dissent' against the State and suggest sentences for supposed criminals, removing people from the prosecution process and human oversight. The program can file a charge based on a written case description with 97% accuracy, states the Chinese Academy of Science team who developed the system, but many see this as a device that can be potentially used for nefarious purposes.[40]

Assigning the power to file charges and rule to an autonomous system, provided that it could happen, is even worse than giving it the power to decide who should live or die in a conflict. This means hiding partisan political choices behind the presumed 'objectivity' of the sentence guaranteed by the 'infallible' and 'impartial' AI.

There is, however, another aspect of so-called predictive justice that its proponents have not considered, which is that they themselves can be victims of it.

The rules of the game are that the law is applied impartially. At law faculties, we all have been fed with Montesquieu's judge as *bouche de la*

Loi doctrine or with Kelsen's pure theory of law. The judge should not—or should not explicitly—manifest convictions about the case until he is confronted with all the evidence. Furthermore, his personal beliefs should not contribute to the final decision.

Deciding what is illegal or not presupposes a social, and therefore political, theory of law and rights. The responsibility for issuing and applying the rules that implement these theories lies and remains with the parliaments, executive powers, and courts.[41] Pretending that software can do all these activities more efficiently and without human supervision, no matter how sophisticated it could be, is the very negation of the idea of law.

This is another example, perhaps not immediately perceptible but no less critical, of what the consequences of attributing personhood to software may be.

The reality of the trials tells a different story, and judicial decisions often reveal the writer's ideas and orientations.

This knowledge is traditionally reserved for the litigators of every single court. Over time, by trial and error and word of mouth, each one builds a reasonably precise idea of a specific magistrate's orientation regarding a particular question of law or how elastic he can be, for example, in assessing the admissibility of evidence.

Searches in the ruling databases have been oriented to look for the principle of law necessary to set up a defence. However, it is no secret that litigators also base their decisions on personal, psychological, and character elements—as well as on the professional quality—of the judge who has to handle the case.

When a new magistrate sits on the bench, this knowledge is lost, and the process of collecting information starts all over again. This is why fairly common practice is to ask for information from some colleague who works in the court from which the new judge comes.

Enters 'predictive justice'.

Predictive justice's supporters focus on the possibility of identifying the principles of law applied by the court to specific cases. However, courts are made up of people, and the application of the principles of law is, in reality, at least partially conditioned by personal elements that have nothing to do with the pure and simple legal provision.

Just as natural language processing systems allow (with what reliability, it is a horse of different colour) to extract legal principles from rulings, in the same way, they can be used to identify the biases of individual magistrates and, therefore, lead to an individual profiling of those biases that influence their decisions.

From the perspective of a judge, the result of this automated, 'intelligent' profiling could be devastating because it would reveal not only his personal prejudices but also the actual professional skills. In those legal systems, such as the Italian one, where a magistrate can be, over the years, a public prosecutor, a civil judge, and then a criminal judge and then a magistrate who deals with bankruptcies or family law, it is unthinkable that a single person can achieve adequate competence in all individual areas of work. Furthermore, even if this were possible, it would necessarily only happen after a period of adaptation to new legal issues. That is, after a series of errors and misunderstandings that result in questionable verdicts.

As long as rulings were mute because they were written on paper and could only be read if they were available, this Pulcinella secret—an open secret—remained well hidden. Now that NLP systems promise to give voice to individual decisions and extract the meaning of what they say, it will be challenging to continue to believe a fiction—the neutrality of the judge—to which it is, nonetheless, necessary to pretend to give credit. This hypothesis is far from fanciful, so much so that someone has already posed the problem. For example, in the name of protection of personal data, a French law passed in 2022 makes it a criminal offense the use of data revealing magistrates' identity to 'evaluating, analysing, comparing or predicting their actual or presumed professional practices'.[42]

This is where the digital rights narrative shows its essential limit.

The right to be judged according to the law and not according to the individual convictions of a magistrate is a pillar of Western civilisation. When these convictions were hidden behind the wall of the formality of the trial and the impossibility of reading between the lines of the rulings written on paper, the right to an impartial judge was, instead, a matter of faith.

If, on the other hand, technology makes it possible to expose bias, prejudices, and errors of those who decide on people's freedom and life, this technology should be used at the highest level because it represents an extraordinary exercise in democracy.

By contrast, invoking privacy or the protection of personal data to prevent a judge from being subjected to public scrutiny is to distort the deep meaning of the right to control one's information. It means transforming the process into an empty rite celebrated by hooded subjects whose eyes and souls remains hidden. In a 180-degree turn, privacy, commonly considered the queen of digital rights, turns into an oppressive tyrant.

Words and ideas

Between July and September 2022, two AI-based text-to-image application have been released to the public. One is Dall-e 2,[43] a proprietary online platform, and the other is Stable Diffusion,[44] an open source project, also available as a stand-alone application for local processing.

Both, in their online version, ask to prompt a description of the expected output and press a button. The version of Stable Diffusion that runs locally on Linux, on the other hand, requires a little more effort in terms of installation, configuration, and hardware resources—a suitable video card and

Linux operating system are needed. All commands are given through the command line.

Both AI produces interesting results, not so much for the images as for the impact on individual rights.

The former are monotonous and lifeless. They will likely improve over time and replace graphic artists, designers, and, maybe, photographers in routine tasks. There is no need of 'artist-like quality' in all the cases where an image is 'just' a companion for a text, a brochure, or an online post. What matters is that the graphic representation is good enough. Therefore, by one side, only 'true' artist can stay in the market, while other valiant professionals risks of being thrown out of business. To some extent, the increasing of the image numbers and availability might even contribute to raise the bar of human-made arts. This phenomenon is already happening in photography. The massive amount of pictures taken daily with smart-phone has produced brilliant results, pushing photographers to do better if wanting to stand out. It is not relevant, to this end, if the vast majority of smartphone-taken pictures are of poor quality or astonishing photos have been taken by sheer luck or unintendedly. As a matter of fact, the more the pictures, the more the probability of very good results.

Moreover, for long time, stock content providers already lowered the price of images, videos, and sound.

The point is that, in general, every technical achievement implies a change of work and working conditions—steam engine killed horse-powered coach transport, driver had to learn how to steer a car. As always happens with the downward diffusion of new technologies, jobs disappear to be replaced by new professionals (the 'prompt designers'?). Business as usual, but with one caveat.

The following images are the Dall-e 2 (the former) and Stable Diffusion's stand-alone version (the latter) outputs of the same prompt: 'An oil painting in the style of Magritte of an Italian lawyer in foreground standing in court, with a judge in foreground facing a witness'.

Stable Diffusion performed better than Dall-e 2 providing a nearly-decent imitation of Magritte style. Other prompts might reverse the verdict on plat-forms' performances. However, quality and performance might matter in the contractual relation between the platform and the customer. They do not rise particular concerns.

By contrast, the possibility of getting money or exposure by mimick-ing somebody else style and applying it to produce an image from scratch deserves a deeper look. Such a feature is already available in professional retouching applications. They carefully avoid mentioning a specific artist, hinting instead at the genre; however, it is not hard to guess in whose style the software feature is working.

Videogames industry has done a similar thing for decades by mapping the biometry of athletes to make their digital clones perform the signature

155

Figure 5.1 Imitation of René Magritte's style made with Dall-e executing the author's prompt

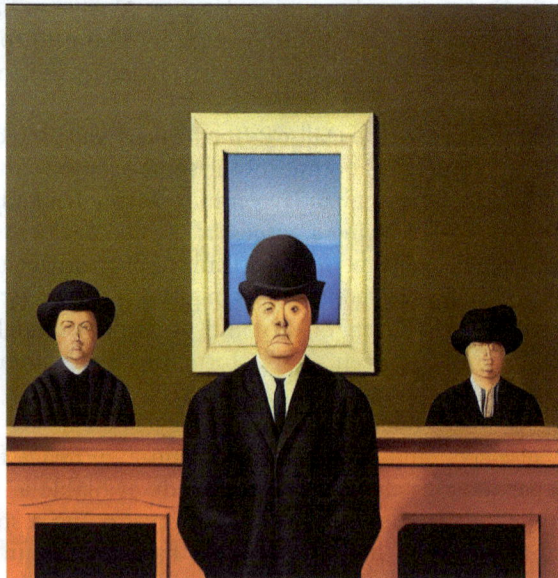

Figure 5.2 Imitation of René Magritte's style made with Stable Diffusion executing the author's prompt

moves of their human counterparts. Athletes get paid to license the bulk of data that, taken as a whole, make them unique. These data, having economic value, fall under the legal regime of intellectual and industrial property. If the very same point is valid when it comes to artistic expression, training an AI to paint in somebody else's style should require a 'raw data license'. Moreover, it might infringe, for instance, artist's dignity or demote the economic value of his works if the output is contrary to the 'original' artist views or if imitations of his work flood the market.

Only time—and courts—will tell the full story but, on the other hand, the impact of these kind of AI on individual rights deserves some more attention.

A prompt like 'soft pencil sketch headshot portrait of a standing up, outraged Italian lawyer dressed with lawyer's robe in foreground giving his closing argument in tribunal weawing his hands, towering judges dressed in judge's robe, seated on the bench and in blurred background' triggered in Dall-e 2 a preemptive warning about an infringement of the terms and condition and the possible account blocking.

The goal was to obtain an image representing the heat of a criminal hearing from the perspective of a particularly passionate lawyer. However, the platform misinterpreted the word 'headshot', which in the photography lingo means 'portrait of a person's head' with something related to killing somebody by shooting him in the head. An empirical evidence of this explanation was that by resubmitting the prompt without this word made the software work flawlessly.

Like Dall-e 2, the online version of Stable Diffusion also applies limitations to the use of prompts and even the model itself. By contrast, the open source version that runs locally has no limitations. The user is free to use any description, no matter how controversial.

As it is apparent, in this case the problem is not the AI, but the automatic parsing of the prompts to block 'forbidden' words on a binary, yes/no basis. The 'headshot prompt' was entirely legitimate and not connected to any improper imagery. Moreover, it would have remained legitimate also if 'headshot' actually meant headshot. A pathologist or a crime reporter might have had interest in having an illustration for a paper or an article, and they would have ended up with an automatic warning, then a denial of service, and finally a strike. This 'behaviour' has striking similarities with social networking platforms' moderation style that raised harsh criticism for its rigidity. It makes it wonder if AI-powered decisions are more frequent that they should. Still, this is not the most serious issue.

The terms and conditions that forbid by default the use of a word list, prohibit, in reality, the use of the concepts to which the words refer. Concepts, however, express ideas. If an idea cannot be expressed, it cannot be thought of. And if it cannot be thought of, it ceases to exist. Switch 'headshot' with 'freedom' and you get the point.

A similar problem aroused at the beginning of automated grammar check[45] and dictionary features in word processing. By taking control of what words are in the vocabulary, how and if they should be written, those who control the software control the ideas. At the time it was more a dystopian claim of a few activists. Now it is becoming true.

What is interesting, though, that words-banning terms and conditions look like they are mainly concerned about 'not hurting' people's feelings and, probably, avoiding possible legal actions. In other words, they adopt a moral stand and use the law to enforce it, even at the cost of sacrificing a fundamental right like free speech.

Of course, these platforms are private companies. They are free to make their services available at whatever conditions they like. However, if there is a sole provider—or if there will be a limited number of them—the business needs and ethical stands will overcome the legal rights as it already has happened in the case of social networking and cryptography.

Even the choice to provide AI-based services through platforms is not neutral for the respect for fundamental rights. The pre-emptive analysis of the prompt implies that controversial text might also be stored, analysed, and reported (as happens with client-side scanning described in Chapter 4). That might lead to an unjust criminalisation of mere thoughts, that is forbidden by every Western jurisdiction (and allowed, by contrast, in Nazi Germany and Stalinist Russia).

The use of remote computing is indeed practically unavoidable, given the hardware (in particular, graphic cards) required to run an AI-based application. What a data centre infrastructure does in minutes would take hours, if not days, using a home computer. It does not mean, however, that *all* applications should be available this way. Having an open source computer programme available locally, such as Stable Diffusion, offers at least a minimal possibility of expressing one's thoughts with a reasonable expectation of freedom.

The relation between AI and language is also relevant in terms of technological geopolitics. AI models are primarily trained in English. There are, of course, some built in other languages, but English is certainly prevalent. Since building and training an AI model requires significant investments, it would not make much sense to invest resources to reinvent the wheel and build AIs that understand Italian, French, or Hindi. From a strictly economic point of view, this is the case. However, the concentration of theoretical and applied research on a single language increases its political importance. Those who do not speak it cannot access specific research or use certain applications. Moreover, those who control that language may decide they do not want to teach it to those who do not belong to the same area of geopolitical influence. This is another step towards the weaponisation of knowledge, a topic that would require a book in itself to be thoroughly explored.

Exorcising the Ghost in Shell

Autonomous vehicles and weapons, predictive justice, and geopolitical relations are extreme cases involving the life and death of people. Consequently, legislative choices should be taken with extreme care and following a broad public debate, that is not happening. Even fundamental rights are endangered by the poor understanding of AI, whose case is exemplary in various ways.

The regulatory debate developed without real attention (or without genuine interest) to the technical aspects. AI marketing and the unscrupulous use of the word have spread the perception that there is, or will soon exist, an artificial life form that will have to coexist with human beings. This has extended to AI the clichés repeatedly recalled in the pages of this book.

Moreover, the mirage of dealing with such powerful technology has amplified the annoyance with regulations, perceived as quibbles uncoupled from reality. Unsurprisingly, this has resulted in a bureaucratic technocracy based on nudging and resorting to ethics-based rather than law-based decision-making processes. A call for ethics, however, is a perilous choice because it represents a regulatory shortcut. As Chapter 2 highlighted, the construction of a right starts with a widespread claim of a company's constituencies. Each bears its own world vision, asking that a specific social event—divorce, abortion, and access to education or health care—be recognised as a right. The normative rule arises from the contrast of opposing views. By contrast, the abuse of the recourse to ethics caused by the false claim that there are no rules to regulate the applications of AI, or that AI is impossible to keep at bay has reversed the process of forming a legal right. Groups of experts express their personal views on 'roboethics', governments and parliaments appoint 'scientific committees', and what are essentially minority positions—or in any case not widely understood and shared[46]— become the basis for legislating.

This way of proceeding increasingly cuts the umbilical cord that should bind citizens, parliament, and government. With the excuse and complicity of ethics, it transforms the law from a means of protecting people into an instrument for the imposition of power released from any control. In the name of AI rights, the rule of law becomes rule by law. Ethics has a strong appeal and is a convenient shortcut for a politician or a legal expert. It makes is unnecessary to rely on hard facts, legal frameworks, or figures because the goal is 'to do the right thing'. However, when moving from the personal domain to entering the public, political stage, it is unavoidable to ask if a democratic State should be entitled to *define public* ethics and make it compulsory for the citizen. We already have plenty of examples, at every latitude, of what happens when ethics blends with power. None of them is remotely acceptable in a democratic society.

Using the law to regulate Artificial Intelligence is undoubtedly much more boring. It deprives decision-makers of the visionary allure of those that anticipate the future, thus earning a place in history. Furthermore, it forces jurists to analyse the enormous number of statutes and regulations to understand which ones can be used and what, instead, requires new laws. Yet, even without wishing to carry out too deep a legal core drilling, many rules are already immediately applicable to robotics and AI.

The product liability regulations and related technical standards already contain provisions applicable to mechanical components of systems that operate with software. European legislative proposals take this aspect into account but do not fully develop it.

Quickly reminding what has already been highlighted in the previous pages about the creation of artificial life, this is not possible, and even if it were, it would already be forbidden, in analogy to what has been established for biotechnological and genetic research. There is no need to furtherly legislate the issue.

Central to the development and operation of an AI-based product is the availability of vast data to train the models. On the one hand, this raises the question of the right of those who build such software to use content available on the Internet instead of financing the construction of their dataset. The first forms of protection that come to mind are those of copyright and of personal data. However, much data and metadata available directly or sold by large information brokers are not 'creative' and not 'personal'. Still, they have considerable economic value. One example is the amount of information on attacks collected by cybersecurity service providers via their centralised platforms. Individually, this data generated by their customers' systems is worthless. Collectively, however, they become fundamental to allow, for example, the training of threat prevention models. Data, as such, have economic value. That has been known for decades. As a result, they can be subject to legal claims in the event of unauthorised use and contractual negotiation. These principles also apply to AI datasets. If a company needs tools to develop its products, it either builds them or buys them. The fact that many data are directly accessible online does not imply that they can be exploited for commercial purposes without paying a sum to those who generated them. In other words, data grabbing is an extra-contractual offence. At the same time, if—as in the case of cybersecurity or translation and grammar correction or health services—a company needs the data generated by customers to improve its services, this can be subject to contractual regulation also in terms of pricing.

In real life, few, if any, people claim the right to be compensated for the use that a company has made of their (even non-personal) data. Moreover, the prevailing rule of the trade is the well-known 'better to ask for forgiveness than for permission'. However, it does not change the essential point. The problem is not the absence of rules but the possibility of applying them effectively. Therefore, instead of chasing unlikely specific rules for AI, it would be necessary to create an infrastructure to quickly and cheaply manage these legal claims and guarantee effective compliance with the ruling. As the practitioners or International Law know, this is not an issue privy with AI only.

What is missing, and this is what should be regulated, is to abandon the legal fiction that software is the subject of copyright and fully acknowledging it as an industrial product. This would make it possible to apply established accountability criteria for application design and development. The legal regime of product liability is far from perfect. In any case, it clearly states that any product must follow safety and security standards. For AI, therefore, a law is not needed but the definition of standards setting the technically acceptable risk threshold. A side effect, but not of secondary importance, of this approach is that if a software—*any* software—does not meet the standards, it cannot be made available to the public. More than any ethical imperative, giving clear legal responsibility and effective sanctions is the way to hope for AI-based products that are reasonably safe.

These are just some examples of how a certainly less fascinating but equally certainly more concrete approach makes it possible to identify the critical elements for the regulation of AI. These are the only relevant problems, nor the proposed solutions are necessarily correct. What matters is to demonstrate that, even in the case of AI, there is no need to stray from reality to enforce or design effective statutes and regulations.

As Occam's *entia*, also legal rights *non sunt multipicanda praeter necessitatem*.

Notes

1 *Convention for the Protection of Human Rights and Dignity of the Human Being with regard to the Application of Biology and Medicine* 4 April 1997 https://www.coe.int/en/web/bioethics/oviedo-convention visited 22 August 2022.
2 Gottschalk, Simon. 'The Infantilisation of Western culture'. *The Conversation* 1 August 2018, https://theconversation.com/the-infantilization-of-western-culture -99556 visited 22 August 2022
3 Ronkowits, Kennet. 2016. *ELIZA: a very basic Rogerian psychotherapist chatbot* https://web.njit.edu/~ronkowit/eliza.html visited 22 August 2022.
4 Bain Campbell, Mary. 2010. 'Artificial Men: Alchemy, Transubstantiation, and the Homunculus.' *Republics of Letters: A Journal for the Study of Knowledge, Politics, and the Arts* Vol.1, no. 2p.7. http://rofl.stanford.edu/node/61, visited 16 August 2022.
5 Highley, Sarah. 1997. 'Alien Intellect and the Roboticization of the Scientist'. *Camera Obscura* Volume 14, Issue 1–2 (40–41):129–160 p. 135. https://doi.org /10.1215/02705346-14-1-2_40-41-129 visited 16 August 2022.
6 Ball, Philip Mand Made: A History of Sinthetic Life. *Distillations* 15 April 2016. https://www.sciencehistory.org/distillations/man-made-a-history-of-synthetic -life visited 16 August 2022.

7 Tan, Hsieh-Yin et al. 'Human mini-brain models'. *Nature* 14 December 2020 https://www.nature.com/articles/s41551-020-00643-3 visited 26 August 2022.

8 Will Yard, Cassandra. 'Mouse embryos grown without eggs or sperm: why and what's next?'. *Nature* 25 August 2022 https://www.nature.com/articles/d41586 -022-02334-2 visited 26 August 2022.

9 Ball, Philip. 'Life as a chemical reaction'. *Chemistry World* 2 April 2018. https:// www.chemistryworld.com/opinion/the-scientists-who-create-life/3008853.arti- cle visited 17 August 2022.

10 Snyder, Carl. 'Bordering the mysteries of life and mind'. *McClure's Magazine* Vol. XVIII, March 1902 n. 5 p. 394 https://babel.hathitrust.org/cgi/pt?id=uc1 .b000254606&view=1up&seq=405&skin=2021&q1=Loeb visited 17 August 2022.

11 Ball, Philip *cit.*

12 Mayor 2018:13

13 Mayor 2018:103

14 Reisch, Gregor. 2017. *Technical Devices in Ancient Alexandria and their Equivalents in the Indian Cultural Area* p. 17 https://www.academia.edu /33891339/Technical_Devices_in_Ancient_Alexandria_and_their_Equivalents _in_the_Indian_Cultural_Area visited 16 August 2022.

15 Peters, Benjamin. 'Normalising Soviet Cybernetics'. Information & Culture, 2012, Vol. 47, No. 2 (2012), pp. 145–175. University of Texas Press. p. 149. https://www.jstor.org/stable/43737425 visited 20 August 2022.

16 Rosenthal and Iudin 1954: 23.

17 Guizzo, Erico. 'Hiroshi Hishiguro: the man who made a copy of himself'. *IEEE Spectrum* 22 April 2010 https://spectrum.ieee.org/hiroshi-ishiguro-the-man-who -made-a-copy-of-himself visited 16 August 2022

18 Mori, Masahiro. 1970. '不気味の谷', Energy, vol. 7, no. 4, pp. 33–35, 1970. English translation by Mac Dorman, Karl, Kageki, Norri. 'The Uncanny Valley'. *IEEE Spectrum* 12 June 2012 https://spectrum.ieee.org/the-uncanny-valley vis- ited 17 August 2022.

19 Mori, Masahiro *cit.*

20 Guizzo, Erico *cit.*

21 Vincent, James. 'Pretending to give a robot citizenship helps no one'. *The Verge* 30 October 2017 https://www.theverge.com/2017/10/30/16552006/robot-rights -citizenship-saudi-arabia-sophia visited 19 August 2022.

22 Estrada, Daniel. 'Sophia and her critics'. *Medium* 18 June 2018 https://medium .com/@eripsa/sophia-and-her-critics-5bd22d859b9c visited 20 August 2022.

23 Lawrence, Chris. 'Sophia and SingularityNET: Q&A'. *h+ Magazine*, 5 November 2017, https://hplusmagazine.com/2017/11/05/sophia-singularitynet-qa/ visited 20 August 2022.

24 Slack, Megan. *President Obama Speaks at the Miraikan Science Expo* 24 April 2014 https://obamawhitehouse.archives.gov/blog/2014/04/23/president-obama -speaks-miraikan-science-expo visited 20 August 2022.

25 Reynolds, Emily. 'The agony of Sophia, the world's first robot citizen condemned to a lifeless career in marketing'. *Wired* 1 June 2018 https://www.wired.co.uk /article/sophia-robot-citizen-womens-rights-detriot-become-human-hanson -robotics visited 20 August 2022.

26 Asimov 1956-1990:301

27 Syrdal, D.S., Nomura, T., Hirai, H., Dautenhahn, K.2011. Examining the Frankenstein Syndrome. In Mutlu, B., Bartneck, C., Ham, J., Evers, V., Kanda, T. (eds) *Social Robotics. ICSR 2011. Lecture Notes in Computer Science*, vol 7072. Springer, Berlin, Heidelberg. https://doi.org/10.1007/978-3-642-25504 -5_13

28 Villareal, Luis. 'Are Virus Alive?'. *Scientific American* 8 August 2008 https://www
.scientificamerican.com/article/are-viruses-alive-2004/ visited 22 August 2022.
29 Findlay, Graham et al. 'Dissociating Intelligence from Consciousness in Artificial
Systems – Implications of Integrated Information Theory' in *Papers of the 2019
Towards Conscious AI Systems Symposium* http://ceur-ws.org/Vol-2287/short8
.pdf visited 22 August 2022.
30 European Parliament resolution of 16 February 2017 with recommendations to
the Commission on Civil Law Rules on Robotics. *Civil Law Rules on Robotics*
16 February 2017 https://www.europarl.europa.eu/doceo/document/TA-8-2017
-0051_EN.html visited 16 August 2022.
31 Asimov 1956-1990:126
32 EU Commission COM/2021/206 final *Proposal for a Regulation of the
European Parliament and of the Council laying down harmonised rules on
Artificial Intelligence (Artificial Intelligence act) and amending certain union legislative acts* 24 Aprile 2021 https://eur-lex.europa.eu/legal-content/EN/TXT/?uri
=CELEX:52021PC0206
33 Monti,Wacks, 2021: 143.
34 Koene, Ansgar et al. *A governance framework for algorithmic accountability
and transparency* 12 June 2019 p. II https://op.europa.eu/en/publication-detail/-/
publication/8ed84cfe-8e62-11e9-9369-01aa75ed71a1/language-en visited 22
August 2022.
35 EU Parliament Panel for the Future of Science and Technology *A governance
framework for algorithmic accountability and transparency* 4 April 2019 https://
www.europarl.europa.eu/stoa/en/document/EPRS_STU(2019)624262 visited 26
August 2022.
36 Loyola-González, Octavio. 'Black-Box vs. White-Box: Understanding Their
Advantages and Weaknesses From a Practical Point of View'. *IEEE Access*,
vol. 7, 1 November 2019, pp. 154096-154113, p. 154096, doi: 10.1109/
ACCESS.2019.2949286 visited 26 August 2022.
37 Carr, Nicholas. "It's Not a Bug, It's a Feature.' Trite—or Just Right?' *Wired.com*
19 August 2019 https://www.wired.com/story/its-not-a-bug-its-a-feature/ visited
22 August 2022.
38 Horowitz, Michael. 2016. 'The Ethics & Morality of Robotic Warfare: Assessing
the Debate over Autonomous Weapons'. *Daedalus* Fall 2016 https://www
.amacad.org/publication/ethics-morality-robotic-warfare-assessing-debate-over
-autonomous-weapons visited 26 August 2022.
39 Monti – Wacks 2021: 141
40 Petersen, Michelle. 'China has created the world's first AI prosecutor'. *ZM
Science* 6 January 2022 https://www.zmescience.com/science/china-has-created
-the-worlds-first-ai-prosecutor/ visited 26 August 2022.
41 See Maestri, Enrico 'Intelligenza artificiale e ragionamento giudiziale: il diritto
all'infelicità giudiziale'. *Filodiritto* 17 June 2022 https://www.filodiritto.com/
intelligenza-artificiale-e-ragionamento-giudiziale-il-diritto-allinfelicita-giudiziale
visited 8 September 2022
42 Article 33 Loi 2019-222 'Les données d'identité des magistrats et des membres
du greffe ne peuvent faire l'objet d'une réutilisation ayant pour objet ou pour
effet d'évaluer, d'analyser, de comparer ou de prédire leurs pratiques profession-
nelles réelles ou supposées. La violation de cette interdiction est punie des peines
prévues aux articles 226-18,226-24 et 226-31 du code pénal, sans préjudice des
mesures et sanctions prévues par la loi n° 78-17 du 6 janvier 1978 relative à
l'informatique, aux fichiers et aux libertés.' https://www.legifrance.gouv.fr/jorf/
article_jo/JORFARTI000038261761 visited 9 September 2022.
43 https://openai.com/dall-e-2/ visited 8 September 2022.

44 https://stability.ai/blog/stable-diffusion-public-release visited 8 September 2022.
45 McGee, Tim, Ericsson, Patricia. 'The politics of the program: ms word as the invisible grammarian'. *Computers and Composition* 19 (2002) 453–470 https://citeseerx.ist.psu.edu/viewdoc/download?doi=10.1.1.469.3001&rep=rep1&type=pdf visited 8 September 2022.
46 Stock, Kathleen. 'Effective altruism is the new woke'. *UnHerd* 8 September 2022 https://unherd.com/2022/09/effective-altruism-is-the-new-woke/?tl_inbound=1&tl_groups%5B0%5D=18743&tl_period_type=3&mc_cid=41ef462441&mc_eid=e2e8b65bee visited 9 September 2022.

6

CONCLUSIONS

The painting that emerges from reading this book is in dark colours. It leaves little room for hope and does not allow us to be very optimistic about the future of law as an instrument for regulating social relations.

In the industrial and economic fields, information technologies have extended the interconnection of research, production, and marketing processes but have created a network with weak geopolitical links and a few, strong centre of gravity. In the public sector, they have made it possible to automate the functioning of civil services. However, they have not eliminated bureaucracy in those countries where an authentic high administration culture lacks. In the private sphere, they have contributed to feeding people a hyper-individualism presented as a promise of freedom, but concretely consisting in building golden cages to lock the hens laying golden eggs.

The absence, in industrialised societies, of a clear strategy for technological governance has left a free hand to Big Tech. They have imposed models based on the substantial absence of responsibility on the private control of technological evolution and, above all, on appropriating the power to define rights. Without the counterweights of state control and educated citizenship, Big Tech could operate freely. It increases the complexity of contemporary society to a level that makes it extremely difficult to balance the interests at stake.

Little, if any, awareness of lawmakers on science and technology issues has increased confusion. Political positions and regulatory proposals are victims of technological marketing strategies. Instead of applying established legal categories, they fall under the spell of science fiction, seeking to transform literary creations into legal norms. In the name of modernism at all costs, they seek to impose 'new rights' and, as in the case of Artificial Intelligence and robots, 'new subjects'.

Civil society also has its responsibilities for this state of affairs. Since the early 1990s, activists and intellectuals had a clear vision of the phenomenon. They warned about the distortions caused by constructing a society

DOI: 10.4324/9781003373636-6

where relationships are technologically mediated. However, these warnings were largely ignored.

In the beginning, the impact of technological intermediation was limited by the inconvenience and awkwardness of the tools. Computers were bulky, interfaces unattractive, and the experience was limited. The spread of laptops, smartphones, and wearable technologies such as augmented reality glasses has revolutionised the scenario. The greater availability and usability of the tools have increased their diffusion. Consequently, services such as platforms of any type have developed that take advantage of the vast base of potential customers. However, the increase in the number of people who have come into contact with information technologies has not been accompanied by an increase in awareness of individual rights.

The process of devaluation of rights was instrumental to build a Big Tech-centric world. It began with the fascination of being able to experience 'separate realities'. Initially, it was about individual behaviours or relatively limited groups which operated outside of purely commercial or speculative logic. Subsequently, Big Tech quickly understood the importance of this psychological need and created an entire dystopian system in which to cultivate a simple mental perception—virtual worlds—as true.

Seamlessly, inventions such as cyberspace have migrated from literature to the market and finally to the benches of parliaments and courts. However, in this passage, the law has changed its nature. It has been transformed into the affirmation of the principle that any individual claim is worthy of legal protection.

This paradoxical conviction has further reduced individual sensitivity to the need for the rules of coexistence to be shared and decided on the basis of democratic processes. It is no longer the law (understood as the result of a mediation between opposing social interests) that regulates people's behaviour. Its seat has been taken by ethics in the form, as said, of individual creed. Also, governments and supranational institutions have also forcefully used ethics as the centre of gravity of their political action. In the name of 'doing the right thing', as in the case of AI, principles are established by a small group of 'experts' to be used subsequently for issuing binding legal regulations. This trend is worrying because perhaps, even more than law, ethics is a highly delicate and potentially dangerous public policy tool.

Ethical regulation is the prerequisite for legal regulation. However, a democratic state has no 'state morality'. The law results from the mediation between opposing world views—ethics, in other words.

It is, therefore, intuitive to understand that for this reason, only competent scholars should have a say in the matter. However, ethics is not a science and there is not a serious possibility to understand how knowledgeable and capable a philosopher can be from a law-making perspective. In other areas, such as biomedicine, the relationship between ethics, law, and politics has found a complex and precarious balance, but still a balance. In the case of information technologies, however, it is sufficient to call oneself a 'roboethicist'—once again, a word belonging to Isaac Asimov's science fiction world—or 'digital ethics expert' to convey personal beliefs as generally shared principles to be translated into binding rules or used in their stead.

The legal issues posed by the impact of information technologies on each of us are manifold and concern about any area of our life. Never as in this moment, therefore, is a solid culture of rights and the rule of law indispensable to keep society together.

However, the capitalism of loneliness, based on the transformation of individual rights into marketable and freely available goods, has traced a different path for us, which, like that leading to hell, is paved with promises and delusions. Like those of 'digital rights'.

BIBLIOGRAPHY

Agamben, Giorgio, Attell Kevin (translator). 2005. *State of Exception*. Chicago: University of Chicago Press.

Alberts, Gerard, Oldenziel, Ruth. 2014. *Hacking Europe*. London (UK): Springer.

Alemanno, Alberto, Spina, Alessando. 2014. Nudging legally: On the checks and balances of behavioral regulation. *International Journal of Constitutional Law*, Volume 12, Issue 2, April 2014, Oxford (UK): New York University School of Law and Oxford University Press.

Altwicker, Tilmann. 2020. Non-universal arguments under the European convention on human rights. *European Journal of International Law*, Volume 31, Issue 1, February 2020, Oxford (UK): Oxford University Press.

Asimov, Isaac. 1951. *Foundation*. New York: Gnome Press.

Asimov, Isaac. 1953. *Social Science Fiction. Bretnor, Reginald Modern Science Fiction: Its Meaning and Its future*. New York: Coward-McCann.

Asimov, Isaac. 1956–1990. Someday. In *Robot Vision*. New York: Roc Books.

Asimov, Isaac. 1986–2022. *Foundation and Earth*. New York: Del Rey Books.

Baughan, Amanda et al. 2021. Someone is wrong on the Internet: Having hard conversations in online spaces. Proc. ACM Hum.-Comput. Interact. 5, CSCW1.

Biggar, Nigel. 2020. *What's Wrong With Rights*. Oxford: Oxford University Press.

Chiccarelli, Stefano, Monti, Andrea. 2011. *Spaghetti Hacker*. Pescara (IT-EU): Monti&Ambrosini Editori.

Cohen, Julie. 2007. Cyberspace as/and space. *Columbia Law Review*, Volume 107, Issue 1 (Jan., 2007). New York: Columbia Law Review Association Inc.

Donald, Alice, Gordon, Jane, Leach, Philip. 2012. *The UK and the European Court of Human Rights. Research Report 83*. London: Human Rights & Social Justice Research Institute.

Galgano, Francesco. 2010. *Le insidie del linguaggio giuridico: Saggio sulle metafore nel diritto*. Bologna (IT-EU): Il Mulino.

Gibson, William. 1984. *Neuromancer*. New York: Ace Books.

Hill, Doug. 2019. in Wiener, Norbert. *Cybernetics or Control and Communication in the Animal and the Machine, Reissue of the 1961 Second Edition*. Boston: MIT Press.

169

Hunter, Dan. 2003. Cyberspace as place and the tragedy of the digital anticommons. *California Law Review*, Volume 91, Issue 2, March 2003. Berkeley: California Law Review Inc.

Josephson, Matthew. 1934. *The Robber Barons*. New York: Harcourt, Brace and Company.

Kaye, Linda. 2021. Exploring the "socialness" of social media. *Computers in Human Behavior Reports* vol. 3. Amsterdam (NL-EU): Elsevier.

Langford, Malcolm. 2018. Critique of human rights. *Annual Review of Law and Social Science*, Volume 14, Issue 1, October 2018. https://doi.org/10.1146/ annurev- lawsocsci- 110316–113807

Lee, Carolin. 2015. *Do-It-Yourself Democracy: The Rise of the Public Engagement Industry*. Oxford (UK): Oxford University Press.

Leonhoard, Chunlin. 2017. Dangerous or benign legal fictions, cognitive biases, and consent in contract law. *St. John's Law Review*, Volume 91, Issue 2. New York: St. Johns School of Law.

Levy, Stephen. 1984. *Hackers: Heroes of the Computer Revolutions*. New York: Doubleday.

Levy, Stephen. 2001. *Crypto: How the Code Rebels Beat the Government—Saving Privacy in the Digital Age*. New York: Penguin Books.

Livraghi, Giancarlo. 1997. L'anima e il corpo. *Internet News*. Milan (IT-EU): Tecniche Nuove.

Ludlow, Peter. 1996. *High Noon on the Electronic Frontier: Conceptual Issues in Cyberspace*. Boston: MIT Press.

Lütfiye Cana, Nihat Kayab, 2016. Social networking sites addiction and the effect of attitude towards social network advertising. *Procedia - Social and Behavioral Sciences* volume 235. Amsterdam: Elsevier.

Mayor, Adrienne. 2018. *Gods and Robots: Myths, Machines, and Ancient Dreams of Technology*. Princeton: Priceton University Press.

Monti, Andrea, Wacks, Raymond. 2019. *Protecting Personal Information*. Oxford (UK): Hart Publishing.

Monti, Andrea, Wacks, Raymond. 2020. *COVID-19 and Public Policy in the Digital Age*. Abingdon (UK): Routledge.

Monti, Andrea, Wacks, Raymond. 2021. *National Technology in the New World Order*. Abingdon (UK): Routledge.

Mutua, Makau. 2008. 'Human rights and powerlessness: Pathologies of choice and substance'. *Buffalo Law Review*, Volume 56, 1027–34. Buffalo: University at Buffalo School of Law.

Olivito, Elisa. 2013. Le finzioni giuridiche nel diritto costituzionale, Napoli (IT-EU): Jovene.

O'Neill, Onora. 2005. The dark side of human rights. *International Affairs* (Royal Institute of International Affairs 1944–), Volume 81, Issue 2, 427–439. Oxford (UK): Oxford University Press.

Romano, Santi. 1918. *L'ordinamento giuridico*. Firenze (IT-EU): Sansoni.

Rosenthal, Mark, Iudin, Pavel (eds.). 1954. *Kratkil filosofskiĭ slovar'* 4th ed. Moscow (RU): Gospolitizdat.

Samson, Colin. 2020. *The Colonialism of Human Rights: Ongoing Hypocrisies of Western Liberalism*. Cambridge: Polity Press.

Schmid, Michael, Gutmann, Hans-Christian. 1999. *Dreiundzwanzig - 23 - Die Geschichte des Hackers Karl Koch*. München (DE-EU): DTV.

Stoll, Clifford. 1989. *The Cuckoo's Egg*. New York: Doubleday.

Theilen, Jens. 2021. The inflation of human rights: A deconstruction. *Leiden Journal of International Law*, Volume 34, Issue 4, 831–854.

Turner, Fred. 2008. *From Counterculture to Cyberculture: Stewart Brand, the Whole Earth Network, and the Rise of Digital Utopianism*. Chicago: Chicago University Press.

Vespaziani, Alberto. 2003. 'Per un'ermeneutica della metafora giuridica'. ISLL Papers. *The Online Collection of the Italian Society for Law and Literature* Vol. 2/2009. Bologna (IT-EU): Italian Society for Law and Literature.

Wacks, Raymond. 2015. *Law: A Very Short Introduction (Very Short Introductions)*. Oxford: Oxford University Press.

Wacks, Raymond. 2021. *The Rule of Law under Fire?*. Oxford: Hart Publishing.

Weber, Rolf. 2015. *Principles for Governing the Internet. A Comparative Analysis*. Paris (FR-EU): UNESCO Publishing.

Wiener, Norbert. 1948. *Cybernetics: Or Control and Communication in the Animal and the Machine*. New York: John Wiley & Sons.

Yang, Guobin. 2009. *The Power of the Internet in China: Citizen Activism Online*. New York: Columbia University Press.

Zimmermann, Philip. 1995. *PGP Source Code and Internals*. Boston: MIT Press.

INDEX

Page numbers in *italics* refer to figures.

For Product Safety Concerns and Information please contact our EU
representative GPSR@taylorandfrancis.com
Taylor & Francis Verlag GmbH, Kaufingerstraße 24, 80331 München, Germany